Entrepreneur® *M*ADE EASY *Series*

*A*CCOUNTING AND FINANCE FOR SMALL BUSINESS MADE EASY

Secrets You Wish Your CPA Had Told You

ROBERT LOW

EP
Entrepreneur.
Press

Editorial Director: Jere Calmes
Cover Design: Beth Hanson-Winter
Composition: CWL Publishing Enterprises, Inc., Madison, WI, www.cwlpub.com

This publication is designed to provide accurate and authoritative information in
regard to the subject matter covered. It is sold with the understanding that the
publisher is not engaged in rendering legal, accounting, or other professional services. If legal advice or other expert assistance is required, the services of a compe-
tent professional person should be sought.

> —From a Declaration of Principles jointly adopted by
> a Committee of the American Bar Association and
> a Committee of Publishers and Associations

ISBN 1-932531-17-3

Library of Congress Cataloging in Publication Data

Low, Robert J., 1957
  Accounting and finance for small business made easy: secrets you wish your
CPA had told you / by Robert J. Low
    p. cm.
  Includes bibliographic references.
  ISBN 1-932531-17-3
    a. Accounting. 2. Corporations—Accounting. 3. Managerial accounting.
    I. Title
HF5686.C7L6542 2004
658.15'11—dc22

                                                                200403233

Printed in Canada

09 08 07 06 05   10 9 8 7 6 5 4 3 2 1

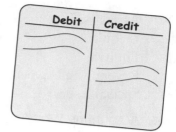

Contents

Preface   vii

How to Use This Book   xi

Part One. The Accounting Primer   1

1. **Understanding Financial Management**   3
   Financial Information Gap   5
   Controllership   7
   Financial Accounting as a Hindrance   10
   A Language Gap   12

2. **Accounting Professionals and Organizations**   15
   The Most Trusted Profession   15
   Types of Accounting   16
   Governing Bodies   19
   Accounting Certifications   21
   CPA Firms   22
   CPA Reports   25
   Negotiating CPA Services   29
   Industry Crisis   29
   A Word About GAAP   31

3. **Accounting 101**   36
   Financial Statements   37
   Double-Entry Accounting   41
   What Gets Recorded?   43

Assets   46
Liabilities   50
Equity   52
Revenue and Expenses   53
Special Issues   56

4. **Accounting Workflow**   **65**
The Accounting Flow   65
The General Ledger   66
Closings   72
Year-End Procedures   79
What Is Ahead   83

5. **Financial Reporting Pitfalls**   **87**
Balance Sheet Pitfalls   89
Valuation Pitfalls   90
Income Statement Pitfalls   95
Creative Accounting   100
Accounting Gimmickry   101
Summary   107

Part Two. Beyond Financial Accounting   **111**

6. **Controllership: Managing with the Numbers**   **113**
Controllership or Accounting   114
Beyond the Numbers   118

7. **Management Accounting**   **128**
Information Needs   129
Financial vs. Management Accounting   130
Traditional Cost Accounting   133
Analysis Pitfalls   137
Other Concepts   143
Influencing Behavior   147
Conclusion   147

Part Three. Managing Your Assets   **149**

8. **Inventory Management**   **151**
The Walk-Through   152
Analyzing Inventory Levels   153
Shrinkage   155

Successful System Elements   157
Inventory Control Techniques   158
Converting Excess Inventory   164
Tracking Inventory   165
Valuation   166
Summary   171

 9. **Cash Management and Liquidity**   **173**
Cash Flow vs. Profit   174
Maximizing Cash Flow   180
Crisis Management   184

10. **Credit and Collections**   **188**
The Check Isn't in the Mail   188
The Check Is in the Mail   192
Collections Made Easier   197

Part Four. Taking Control   **201**

11. **Planning and Forecasting**   **203**
Why Plan?   204
Planning Process Outputs   208
Mechanics of Projections   209
Long-Range Planning   213
Learning from the Planning Process   214
Planning or Control?   215
Business Plans   216
Conclusion   218

12. **Budgeting**   **223**
Planning and Control   224
People and Budgets   229
Customize Your Budget   233
Budget Dynamics   237

13. **Evaluating Projects**   **239**
Net Present Value   240
Opportunity Cost   248
Breakeven Analysis   250
Nonclassic Breakeven Analysis   252
Conclusion   252
Net Present Value Project Evaluation Worksheet—Instructions 254

Net Present Value Project Evaluation Worksheet   255
Breakeven Analysis Worksheet—Cost-per-Unit Basis   256
Breakeven Analysis Worksheet—Percentage-of-Sales Basis 257

14. Computers, Software, and the Internet   259
PC Accounting Software   260
Conversion   266
The Internet   267
Other Software   268
Conclusion   270

15. Internal Controls   272
Comparison to a Personal Checkbook   273
Basic Concepts   275
Delegating Authority   279
Maintaining Control   280
Computers and Controls   284
Audits   285
Conclusion   286
Internal Control Questionnaire for Cash Disbursements   286

16. Conclusion: A 10-Step Plan for Control   289
Getting Started Now   292
Final Words   297

Appendix: Glossary   299

Index   317

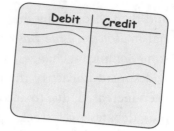

Preface

> If it's boring and dull and soon to be forgotten, continue to
> learn until you love double-entry bookkeeping. You should
> love the mathematics of business.
>
> —Ken Olsen[1]

THIS BOOK FIRST CAME OUT UNDER THE TITLE BOTTOM LINE BASICS in 1995. At the time, much of my consulting work was focused on companies in financial distress. Nearly all of these clients shared a lack of financial discipline and control. This in turn led to some of the symptoms of poor financial management, including strained cash flow, poor customer service, seat-of-the-pants operating decisions, and strained banking relations.

My goal in writing a book was to communicate that effective financial management in smaller businesses is critical for success and involves much more than just accounting. By focusing on the practical uses and benefits of accounting, planning, and control, rather than the mechanics, I also hoped to motivate nonfinancial managers to take a more active interest in financial management.

Nearly 10 years later, through a lengthy period of business expansion and then through another sustained downturn, I find that most of the material in *Bottom Line Basics* remains as relevant as ever. Yes, there have been some significant changes, most notably the impact of technology, including the widespread impact of the internet. The profile of accounting issues has also been increased, due to accounting scandals at Enron, WorldCom, and others, plus debates over stock option accounting, pooling, and earnings management. But the core issues of financial management remain remarkably unchanged.

Nonetheless, every chapter in this book has been updated. The chapter on computers was completely rewritten and the chapter on financial reporting pitfalls was updated with the most recent scandals and legislation. Examples and anecdotes were updated and sidebars have been introduced to provide some background on topics that might otherwise have been outside the scope of the book.

Gaining Financial Skill

In a study of leadership skills surveying several hundred top entrepreneurial CEOs in America, financial management was perceived as the most important of 34 skills for guiding their businesses through previous stages of development and achieving the next level of success. This was defined as acquiring and maintaining adequate capital, plus using the acquired funds wisely. The latter included anticipating cash needs, controlling spending, collecting receivables, and monitoring cash flow. The necessary skills for doing these tasks were seen as general accounting knowledge and the ability to apply it.[2]

I realize that, for most people, financial management is not the most interesting aspect of running a business. Most business owners and managers probably find it more stimulating to design a product than compute its cost, more enjoyable to close a sale than collect payment. But these financial tasks are critical.

The job of implementing the controls suggested in this book rests with nonfinancial managers as well as with their bookkeepers, accountants, controllers, or chief financial officers. Though there is no need for nonfinancial managers to become accountants to ensure financial control, a working knowledge of accounting and control helps them communicate with financial staff as well as direct and understand their work. This book is intended to provide that working knowledge, for both smaller business owners and managers of large corporations.

This book should also be helpful to financial professionals. While the mechanics of accounting will be familiar, there may be a need to look beyond the numbers and play a more proactive, operating role. This book illustrates how to apply financial skills not just to report the bottom line, but also to actually improve it.

When I first wrote this book, I believed it was the first to focus on the practical, management applications of financial accounting and control. I still believe this book occupies a unique niche. By presenting applied knowledge, rather than just mechanics, and providing specific tips on achieving financial control, I hope I have made this book both interesting and rewarding. Not all topics will be equally relevant to you, though, and I encourage you to focus on the sections you feel are most important and skim over the other material.

I also welcome your comments and suggestions (rlow@perronlow.com). Your feedback will help strengthen future editions and better communicate the techniques and benefits of effective financial management.

—Bob Low
January 2004

Acknowledgments

The content and organization of this book were shaped by the comments of Florence Graves, Bart McAndrews, Andy Dumaine, and Charles Markham. They reviewed my earliest outlines and chapters and provided much needed encouragement.

I would also like to thank Andy Bangs, Brad Howe, Fred Kofman, Mike Quattromani, Ed Simches, and Dave Tenney, who agreed to be interviewed for this book and referred me to additional sources.

Much of my perspective on accounting and management is owed to Dan Perron, Ron Lang, and Roy David, with whom I have teamed up at multiple companies over the last 20 years. Their example and insights have provided models for learning and applying my skills in finance and management.

I thank my editor, John Woods of CWL Publishing Enterprises and his staff, for their work in converting my draft into a finished manuscript.

Thanks, too, to the original editor of *Bottom Line Basics*, Linda Pinkham.

Finally, I would also like to thank Jere Calmes and the rest of the Entrepreneur Press staff for sharing my belief in this book and contributing their expertise to its preparation and marketing.

Notes

1. Quoted in *The Boston Globe*, August 1, 1993, p. 80.

2. John D. Eggers and Raymond W. Smilor, "Leadership Skills of Entrepreneurs: Resolving the Paradoxes and Enhancing the Practices of Entrepreneurial Growth." Study sponsored by the Center for Creative Leadership and the Ewing Marion Kauffman Foundation Center for Entrepreneurial Leadership. In Raymond W. Smilor and Donald Sexton, *Leadership and Entrepreneurship: Personal and Organizational Development in Entrepreneurial Ventures* (Westport, CT: Greenwood Press/Quorum Books, 1996), pp. 15-38.

How to Use This Book

Overview of this Book

THIS BOOK IS NOT AN ACCOUNTING TEXT OR A CONTROLLER'S DESK reference. Rather, it provides an overview of the critical issues concerning financial management and accounting in smaller companies. The goal is not to turn you into an accountant, but to illustrate the impact effective controllership can make on a company. Accounting has a reputation for being boring—and much of it is. This book minimizes the amount of technical information and includes what is needed for a working knowledge of controllership—which ultimately helps make you money.

Part One

This book is divided into four parts. Part One, The Accounting Primer, contains chapters that survey the current practice of accounting and controllership and the basics of accounting for nonaccountants. Part One concludes with a chapter that explains the benefits of going beyond financial accounting. Don't be overwhelmed by the details of accounting, but just strive to understand the basics presented in Chapters 3 and 4.

Part Two

Part Two, Beyond Financial Accounting, begins with a detailed job description for a modern controller. This job description provides the outline for the remainder of the book, including a chapter on one aspect of controllership—management accounting.

Part Three

Part Three, Managing Your Assets, concerns yet another aspect of controllership, asset management. Chapters in this section go into detail on two of the most critical areas for the majority of businesses—controlling inventory and increasing cash flow.

Part Four

Part Four, Taking Control, covers a number of topics related to effective controllership, including planning, budgeting, computer systems, and internal controls. The concluding chapter of this section contains a 10-step plan to help you get started right away with effective financial management.

Glossary

The book concludes with a useful glossary of terms used in accounting.

Overall, the chapters are organized in a logical sequence, but feel free to skip around to topics that are most relevant to you. Of course, not all sections will apply to you or interest you. For example, service businesses have no inventory to manage and retailers may not offer credit. You can skim or skip past any section that is not relevant or you can use some of the more detailed chapters as if they were part of a desk reference.

Examples of actual businesses are in gray-shaded boxes throughout the text. You will also find sample financial statements, forecasts, and more.

Several useful worksheets are included in the book:

▶ The Net Present Value Project Evaluation worksheet can be used to determine the value of a project.

▶ The Breakeven Analysis worksheets can help you calculate the amount of sales needed to break even on a project or business.

▶ The Internal Control Questionnaire for Cash Disbursements can help you decide whether your internal controls for cash are adequate.

Included in the chapters are formulas, tables, and illustrations, to help you understand the material and allow you to put it to work for your business.

Note

1. Quoted in *Manager's Book of Quotations*, Lewis D. Eigen and Jonathan P. Siegel, eds. (New York: American Management Association, 1989), p. 393.

Part One

The Accounting Primer

Chapter 1

Understanding Financial Management

Is it not as impossible in trade that a merchant should be as prosperous without being a thorough-pac'd accountant … as that a mariner should conduct a ship to all parts of the globe without a skill in navigation?
—Anonymous London Merchant, circa 1700

A STORY IS TOLD ABOUT A BALLOONIST WHO GETS LOST AND IS forced to make an emergency landing in an open field. The balloonist flags down a passerby and asks him, "Where am I?"

"You are in a balloon basket in the middle of a field" is the reply.

"You must be an accountant," says the balloonist. "The information you just gave me is perfectly accurate and of absolutely no use."

"And you," replies the passerby, "must be a CEO [chief executive officer]. You are operating a craft over which you have no control and want me to tell you where you are going."[1]

This story depicts the gap that can exist between nonfinancial managers and accountants. Accountants often focus on providing accurate numbers, which may not be relevant or timely. Many business owners and managers, though, steer their businesses using a seat-of-the pants style and could benefit from financial know-how and controls.

As a small business owner or manager, you will want strong communication and support between you and your financial staff. Effective accounting, planning, and control often mean the difference between success and failure for smaller companies. Yet, many smaller business owners, although skilled providers of a service or product, often operate with little background in financial management. This can contribute to:

Effective accounting, planning, and control often mean the difference between success and failure for smaller companies.

▶ Shortsighted management decisions

▶ Misallocation of resources

▶ Failure to anticipate crises

Whether you are the owner of a smaller business or a manager in a larger corporation or division, you can avoid these costly mistakes if your company has an accounting and finance department that plays a dynamic and diversified role in management support. To get there, nonfinancial managers need enough interest and background to work with their key finance and accounting people. Conversely, the financial managers must appreciate the aspects of accounting and controllership beyond simply processing transactions and producing financial statements. These include management accounting, planning, asset management, and internal controls, activities that support internal management and decision making.

The number and types of financial advisors and staff members you employ will vary depending on the needs of your business. Your accounting department may consist of only a bookkeeper, an accountant, or both. On the other hand, you may employ a chief financial officer (CFO) or controller, plus an entire support staff. You will likely rely on an outside certified public accountant for tax work and, perhaps, financial statement audits or more. While the next chapter goes into greater detail about the types of financial and accounting players, the main distinctions among the job titles you might encounter are as follows:

▶ **Bookkeepers and accountants** usually do the mechanical work of daily transactions and the compiling of financial statements.

- ▶ **Controllers** oversee accounting, but also have operating responsibilities, including interpreting financial information, controlling expenses and cash flow, planning, and implementing internal controls. See Chapter 6 for more information about the controller's role.

- ▶ **CFOs** usually supervise the controller, but also have responsibility for the financing, treasury, and administrative activities of a company.

- ▶ **CPA firms** are outside advisors who specialize in tax preparation and auditing.

No matter how small or large your business is, and no matter how many and what kind of financial advisors you employ, your leadership and direction of your accounting department are the important factors for having the information you need to become a hands-on manager.

This introductory chapter provides you with an overview of the financial management issues you need to be aware of to successfully operate your business. It discusses why it is critical for business owners and financial advisors to work well together and why, in practice, they don't.

Financial Information Gap

In many, if not most companies today, a wide gap exists between the needs of business owners and managers for financial information, systems, and control and what is being provided by their internal financial managers and CPAs. This gap creates a serious vulnerability, particularly for smaller businesses, which operate with less margin for error than large corporations.

While the risk may not be easily quantifiable, it seems hard to overstate. Several authors have blamed 60-80% of business failures on financial problems, including poor record-keeping and factors linked to cash flow.[2] On the positive side, a study has established the existence of a direct relationship between the financial and quantitative skill of entrepreneurs and the sales and bottom lines of their companies.[3]

The sources of financial management problems that can cause business crises are diverse. Consider some of the following examples:

- ▶ **An industrial heating and air conditioning system installer** was losing money. Essentially, three separate businesses were operating under one

Several authors have blamed 60-80% of business failures on financial problems, including poor record keeping and factors linked to cash flow.

roof: installation of systems, service contracts and maintenance, and sale of replacement parts. Management needed to know how each product line was performing to make decisions on pricing, staffing, or whether to divest the line entirely. Because sales, expense, and time sheet data had always been aggregated, rather than collected by business line, this information was unavailable and the company was eventually unsuccessful in designing a turnaround strategy.

▶ **A furniture manufacturer** with annual sales of $5 million was forced to write off $500,000 of receivables from customers unable or unwilling to pay. Lack of credit controls, applying payments randomly to invoices, and incomplete records all contributed to the problem. The company was forced to file for bankruptcy.

▶ **A moving company**, modestly profitable but with flat sales, failed to aggressively collect past due accounts. The company experienced write-offs that threatened to wipe out the accrued profit and suffered a surprise cash squeeze. Operations were hastily slashed to conserve cash and, because the company was an S corporation, where profits are taxable to the stockholders, the owner ended up without the cash to pay a $50,000 personal income tax obligation.

▶ **A jewelry manufacturer** suffered with a manual order entry system that was redundant and paper-laden. Seven separate forms were used to track orders, beginning with the receipt of the order, to issuing a production order, to shipping, and finally to invoicing. Five people set up individualized files, procedures, and double checks as the paper worked its way through the office and plant. In addition to the costs of redundancy, the process was costly in terms of lost orders, poor customer service, and an inability to track historical information for management.

Sometimes these types of management problems can lead to one of the most critical problems a business can face—running out of cash. Joe Namath once said he never lost a football game; he just ran out of time on a few occasions. Similarly, entrepreneurs often blame their demise on simply not having enough cash. Unfortunately, this is usually just a symptom. The problem may be failing to anticipate a crisis, waiting too long to take action, or taking the wrong action.

No matter how good a company's employees, products, or services, strong financial management is a critical ingredient for success.

Turnaround expert C. Charles Bahr had this to say:

Although the famous 'bottom line' is our agreed upon measuring stick, financial difficulties are usually the result of other ignored warning signs rather than the cause of them.

But in troubled businesses, we observe the top executive has marginal numbers skills and won't admit it. He lacks personal grasp of the numbers and their meaning in his own business. He may claim that his understanding of the numbers is 'good enough' when in fact it is not good enough. This leaves him at the mercy of the skills and diligence of others. It is [like an airplane pilot with] iced-up windows and disabled instruments. It is remotely possible to 'talk down' a blinded pilot, but the expected outcome, shall we say, is likely to be sub-optimal.

Numbers are just a means of communication, projection, and planning. In troubled companies, we see a lot of numbers, but they are too complex, too simple, mismatched to the requirements or just ignored. And they are nearly always late. Indeed, I don't believe you have to be a financial wizard to run a company today. ... I just want a CEO to understand basic addition and subtraction and to do it.[4]

Controllership

Unexciting and underestimated, the controller's role is more important than you may think. Avoiding and steering through problems like those mentioned above is the joint task of manager and controller. If a business owner or CEO is a company's navigator, the controller provides the dashboard or instrument panel. Yet, time after time, companies drift because these two key players fail to address vital financial and control issues. Why? From the perspective of a business owner, two related reasons are apparent.

Unexciting and underestimated, the controller's role is more important than you may think.

▶ First, smaller businesses usually owe their initial success and growth to entrepreneurs' skill in producing a product, delivering a service, or selling. However, these entrepreneurs usually do not have commensurate experience, skill, or interest in financial management and administration. Though finance is, arguably, the most common route to the top in large companies, few smaller business owners have such backgrounds. They find financial management tedious and are happy to leave the details to their accountants and concentrate on sales, production, or product development.

▶ Second, and more important, business owners can underestimate the scope and potential contribution of sound financial management. Financial management is often thought of in a very narrow sense, perhaps not much more than basic bookkeeping. Little is demanded of the accounting department beyond paying and collecting bills, producing regular financial statements, and filing tax returns.

Just as most businesspeople today have no trouble distinguishing between sales and marketing, it is beneficial to understand that controllership is distinct from accounting.

This narrow perception of the controller's responsibilities falls well short of the mark. Just as most businesspeople today have no trouble distinguishing between sales and marketing, it is beneficial to understand that controllership is distinct from accounting. True, controllership encompasses basic accounting, but it also includes:

▶ Management accounting

▶ Cash planning and management

▶ Credit and collections

▶ Inventory management and control

▶ Planning and budgeting

▶ Expense reduction

▶ Internal controls

▶ Information systems

In a smaller company, if limited resources preclude having two top financial managers, a controller may also handle financing and treasury functions, which in larger organizations would be reserved for the chief financial officer (CFO). Controllers also frequently handle a variety of administrative functions, such as payroll, and may also be responsible for tax work.

In addition to underestimating the scope of the controller's job, business owners and CEOs also underestimate the job's potential impact. Accounting is often viewed as a necessary evil, an overhead function, whose costs should be minimized. It may even be seen as constricting if paperwork or other procedures interfere with managers' day-to-day freedom of action. As a result, rather than investing in information systems, controls, or planning, companies run in more informal, even haphazard, styles.

Nonetheless, even when business owners seem to devote too little time and resources to the controllership function, they are usually aware a gap exists. Many business owners admit to not fully understanding the finance function and are uneasy at not having a better understanding or handle on it. But this vague feeling of concern generally does not provide enough impetus for the owners to dive fully into financial reporting and control.

What business owners and CEOs often do have, though, is a strong instinct for the type of critical or sometimes "soft" information they need to stay on top of operations. Such information could include bookings-to-shipments ratios, the number of customer complaints, employee headcount, or sales by square foot. Each business is different, each business owner zeroes in on different indicators, and little of it is routinely picked up by traditional accounting systems. Where the controller fails to provide this feedback through systematic means, the business owner is forced to collect it in a hit-or-miss manner, in a stream of special reports, or fails to get the information at all.

Controller's Side of the Gap

On the other side of the gap, many accountants lack the training, desire, or perspective to get involved in management issues. As a result, the shortcomings in financial management do not get remedied from the controller's end either.

To begin with, most companies work with two very different sets of accountants. Working on the outside is a company's CPA firm. Though CPA firms have expanded the breadth of their services, their focus is on tax work and auditing or reviewing financial statements. Day-to-day issues are beyond the normal scope of a CPA's work. This is true even in very small companies, where a CPA may be called upon to actually compile the financial statements, perhaps sitting down with the bills and checkbook at the end of a month.

Working internally, side by side with management, are controllers, accountants, and bookkeepers.

Working internally, side by side with management, are controllers, accountants, and bookkeepers. The experience and training of these people can vary widely, making it important to properly match the skills to the job. Expecting people trained only in bookkeeping or basic accounting to assume full controllership duties is unfair.

Even a well-trained controller may not have significant general manage-

9

ment expertise. Differentiating between accurate and useful information and anticipating needs rather than reporting after the fact are skills not easily taught.

Personality also plays a role. The stereotype of all accountants as unimaginative, rather humorless souls who spend their day poring over figures is unflattering. Nonetheless, people who are comfortable working with figures may not be as comfortable working with people. A controller needs to work actively with managers. A controller who is shy and unassertive will be ineffective.

Similarly, a controller who prefers to work with figures and stays rooted to the accounting offices cannot establish needed contact with other departments. If you do not seek out the controller, you may discover that he or she is very happy to be left alone. Instead of building a strong working relationship, you and your controller work in separate spheres, coming together only to discuss monthly financial statements and routine issues in collections, invoicing, and payments.

A controller needs to work actively with managers. A controller who is shy and unassertive will be ineffective.

Just as business owners get wrapped up in day-to-day crises, daily processing and the monthly accounting cycle can bottle up a controller. When times get hectic, the controller may fail to sit in on management meetings and may give emphasis to getting invoices out, processing payroll, and issuing statements. Important tasks that provide needed checks and balances can get pushed aside and time is not taken to analyze information. Reconciliations fall behind and collection calls aren't made.

In short, you will need to have a controller or accountant who has the ability to anticipate needs as well as provide financial information, who is aggressive and willing to meet with you and your managers, and who has the skills and background that best fit your business's needs.

Financial Accounting as a Hindrance

Financial accounting, the accounting used to prepare standard financial statements, should form just a cornerstone of the controller's job. Unfortunately, it often dominates, squeezing out the other, vital aspects of controllership, such as planning, asset management, and internal controls. In subtle ways, financial accounting also influences how nonfinancial work is performed by creating pressure for profits—as opposed to cash flow—or imposing a rigid reporting calendar. As much as any factor, the dominance of financial accounting interferes with effective communication with and support for management.

An interesting note is that, before the 20th century, management accounting—not financial—accounting prevailed. The focus was on collecting information relating to internal operations and their effectiveness. Managers knew if they could do certain operations effectively, they would be successful over the long haul. The need to measure profit, particularly over defined periods, was far less important.

That emphasis changed with the need to raise financing and to report results to outside investors. The demand for objective standards that outsiders could use to evaluate and compare companies led to the rise of financial reporting and generally accepted accounting principles (GAAP).

The needs of internal managers for information on the efficiency of their organizations did not disappear. But those needs were eclipsed by the demand for financial statements complying with GAAP. It's ironic that GAAP statements, designed to serve the information needs of investors, not management, dominate the work of internal accountants.

Nevertheless, financial accounting is an impressive discipline. While financial accounting has some crucial weaknesses, which are discussed in Chapter 5, the ability to summarize the financial performance of even the largest corporations on a few, short reports is noteworthy. In general, investors are well served by financial reporting standards and the institutions that support them. But the reporting, which is highly aggregated and prepared well after the fact, is of much more limited use to internal management, whose decision making depends on current, detailed, often nonfinancial information.

So why are GAAP statements frequently the only statements produced by a company? First, most accountants are given little impetus to push beyond financial accounting. Financial and tax reporting are required; management accounting, budgets, and detailed cash flows are not. A conscious decision is needed to push beyond the required accounting into those other aspects of controllership, such as management reporting, not to mention planning and asset management. Second, the training of most accountants is in financial accounting. Management accounting, at best, ranks a distant second in an accountant's education, together with taxes. Other controller skills may not be taught at all. Finally, CPAs, on whom small companies rely

The demand for objective standards that outsiders could use to evaluate and compare companies led to the rise of financial reporting and generally accepted accounting principles (GAAP).

heavily, are specialists in taxation and compliance with GAAP, not controllership. A certified financial statement assures investors that transactions have been recorded in accordance with GAAP. It says little, if anything, about efficiency or the quality of management. So, what satisfies a CPA may not help you directly with the operational decisions of your business.

Of all the aspects of the controller's job, financial accounting is probably the least interesting to business owners and their top managers. Financial accounting is the most technical aspect—this is where debits and credits are spoken. While business owners are interested in seeing the final numbers, those numbers are historical and aggregated and so have little direct impact on running the business. If GAAP reporting dominates a controller's activity, is it any wonder a business owner or CEO takes little interest?

A Language Gap

The mention of debits and credits is a reminder of the language barrier that can exist between business owners and accountants. Beyond just knowing whether a debit goes on the left or the right side of the ledger page (the left) and when a credit balance is a good thing, accounting can introduce terms and concepts that are alien to business owners.

For example, business owners intuitively understand cash flow; accountants talk in terms of profit. Owners want to know what something is worth; accountants talk of cost and they value assets based at what was paid for them (historic cost) less depreciation. Business owners spend money on R&D and advertising to get long-term benefits; accountants assign no future value to these expenditures. The list goes on. Dual definitions may be unavoidable, since they serve different but necessary purposes, but it helps communication when both business owners and accountants can translate back and forth.

The difference in language also highlights a difference in focus. When reviewing a set of financial statements, you may have noticed that accountants always seem to present the balance sheet first, while you instinctively flip to the income statement. Note that the balance sheet comes first in audited statements and annual reports. This observation demonstrates how accountants often focus on the more static "snapshot" the balance sheet provides and less on the more dynamic "flow" of the income statement.

When asking for input on operating issues, an owner may think to himself or herself, "Don't think like an accountant." The implication is that accountants tend to be unimaginative, their thinking narrowed by perceived rules and guided by the numbers. Put another way, although putting a financial dimension on problems is important, not everything a company does can be translated into numbers.

Bridging the Gap

For you and your controller to work together, your dialogue must move beyond financial reporting. You both must understand the dynamic role accounting and controllership can play in your company and dedicate the time and resources needed to realize it.

A controller is in a position to know more about a company's operation than anyone except the president or owner. This doesn't mean that he or she will know more about sales than the sales manager or more about product development than an engineer. But being in a position to see the transactions from all departments and work with managers throughout the company, the controller is exposed, in great detail, to the entire operation. As a result, your controller has an opportunity to contribute insights and information and improve the quality of overall management. He or she should not focus just on the bookkeeping aspects of the controller's job.

At the same time, the controller is usually the specialist in reducing company costs, managing assets, implementing systems, performing financial analysis, and planning for future goals. These skills contribute directly to your company's profitability, so you need to put your controller's skills to work.

From an owner's or manager's perspective, you have no need to become an accountant. However, a basic knowledge of accounting is needed to properly interpret financial statements. And, while no business can be "run by the numbers," an instinctive feeling for what the figures mean and which numbers are relevant is valuable.

The bottom line is knowing how to make a controller accountable. To do this means understanding not only accounting, but key financial operating issues such as the following:

▶ Why do profitable businesses run out of cash and what can be done to prevent that?

▶ How should accounting information be used to set prices or make pro-

When asking for input on operating issues, an owner may think to himself or herself, "Don't think like an accountant."

13

duction or buying decisions?

▶ How can cash be wrung out of receivables and inventory?

▶ How do you know that everything shipped is invoiced or that nothing is paid for twice?

Armed with a basic knowledge of the controller's role and responsibilities, you can be part of a true dialogue on financial management. More importantly, you can truly take control of your company's "balloon" and steer it in the proper direction.

This introductory chapter has generally highlighted some of the problems businesses face. Many solutions and preventive measures can be implemented, starting in your accounting department.

The rest of Part I provides you with background material to help you understand the fundamentals of basic accounting, beginning with a more detailed description of the accounting industry. If you already possess a good background in accounting, you may want to jump ahead to Chapter 5, for a discussion of how traditional financial accounting fails to provide all of the information necessary to successfully manage your business. Chapter 6 describes the modern controller's function and leads into the remainder of the book.

Notes

1. Lee Berton and Jonathan B. Schiff, eds., *The Wall Street Journal on Accounting* (Homewood, IL: Dow Jones-Irwin, 1990), p. iv.

2. Shelly Branch, "Go with the Flow—or Else," *Black Enterprise*, November 1991, p. 77.

3. John D. Eggers and Raymond W. Smilor, "Leadership Skills of Entrepreneurs: Resolving the Paradoxes and Enhancing the Practices of Entrepreneurial Growth." Study sponsored by the Center for Creative Leadership and the Ewing Marion Kauffman Foundation Center for Entrepreneurial Leadership, p. 22. Reprinted in *Leadership and Entrepreneurship: Personal and Organizational Development in Entrepreneurial Ventures*, Raymond W. Smilor and Donald L. Sexton, eds. (Westport, CT: Greenwood Publishing, 1966).

4. C. Charles Bahr, "Sick Companies Don't Have to Die," speech given in Houston, Texas, 14 June 1988, printed in *Vital Speeches of the Day*, 1 September 1988, p. 687.

Chapter 2

Accounting Professionals and Organizations

> When you have mastered numbers, you will in fact no longer be reading numbers, any more than you read words when reading books. You will be reading meanings.
>
> —Harold S. Geneen, former CEO of IT&T[1]

The Most Trusted Profession

THE ACCOUNTING PROFESSION ENJOYS AN EXALTED, BUT SOMEwhat misunderstood status in the business world. While accountants are considered the most trusted professional group in America,[2] large numbers of executives and small business owners are unclear on what accountants do and how to purchase accounting services. And, while accounting is often called the language of business, few nonfinancial managers are fluent in it.

Most smaller business owners place a lot of faith in their internal and outside accountants. This is at least partly due to the stellar reputation CPAs and top financial managers have for maintaining confidentiality.

15

Not only do managers need to trust the people who handle their financial affairs, they may also use them as confidants. A few CPAs even feel like religious confessors for clients, frequently hearing not only about business affairs, but also of family and marital problems.

But underneath this faith is a lack of understanding about what accountants do. In a survey of 632 executives, 40% were confused about the scope and purpose of an audit.[3] Another survey of very small business owners—fewer than 20 employees—found that the majority failed to recognize the difference among CPA, accountant, and bookkeeper.[4]

This last study, by Emmett D. Edwards, concluded that small business owners frequently fail to differentiate among the skill levels of professionals offering accounting services and are ineffective in defining the services to be provided. Not only can you end up overpaying, but you may get incompetent help. According to Edwards:

> *Popular misconceptions about competency in accounting and failure to realize the impact accounting and financial management areas have on success often lead owners of very small businesses to hire less-than-competent external providers.*
>
> *Failure by owners of very small businesses to recognize the impact of accounting and finance activities on their business and, as a result, to master even the most rudimentary concepts of accounting applications almost certainly is a contributing factor to the high incidence of failure among that group.*[5]

Accounting practices are largely self-regulated, guided by several key institutions. To clear up any misconceptions you may have, this chapter discusses the different types of accounting methods in use, the kinds of services available, and the players—both industry organizations and the kinds of accountants associated with each.

Types of Accounting

The first step in becoming an educated customer of accounting services is understanding that there are several different types of accounting. The four main branches of accounting are financial, tax, management, and nonprofit accounting. Accountants specialize in different areas, so you will want to hire accordingly.

For example, CPAs are experts in tax work and authorized to certify financial statements. However, CPAs may lack operating experience and, depending on what review services they provide to a company, may be prohibited from preparing internal reporting. In addition to distinct branches of accounting, there are two main methods for recognizing expenses and revenues—accrual accounting and cash method accounting.

Financial Accounting

Financial accounting is used by for-profit businesses to prepare financial statements and is probably the most familiar type of reporting. All public companies are required to issue regular financial statements that conform to GAAP; most private companies do so voluntarily. Pick up a textbook on accounting or take an introductory class and it will almost certainly be about financial accounting. This topic is covered in more detail in the next two chapters.

Financial accounting is used by for-profit businesses to prepare financial statements and is probably the most familiar type of reporting.

The standard reports of financial accounting are an income statement, a balance sheet, and a statement of cash flows. Companies usually prepare these reports on an accrual basis. This means revenue is recorded when it is earned and expenses are recorded when resources are used or obligations incurred, which is not necessarily when cash is exchanged. For example, a sale shipped on account would usually be counted as revenue, even though the payment might come in several weeks later.

While accrual accounting is nearly always required to comply with GAAP, it is possible to prepare other types of financial statements on a cash basis. Cash-based accounting is what most individuals use to keep their own records and compute personal income for tax purposes. Smaller professional service firms and businesses with no inventory and few long-term assets also might use cash-based reporting.

Cash-based accounting is as simple as a checkbook register. Cash in from customers is income and cash out to vendors is expense. This is adequate in simple situations, but accrual accounting is usually needed to get a true picture of profits as businesses get more complex.

For example, if you are a retailer and make a $600 cash or credit card sale, recording the sale that day is all right. However, if you sell a year-long service contract or subscription for $600, recording the entire sale right away is misleading. You get a more accurate picture of what your business actually earned with an accrual system that recognizes $50 of revenue per month over the course of the year.

As is discussed later in Chapter 9, however, profit is not the same as cash flow, and accrual-based statements do not eliminate the need for tracking cash flow.

Tax Accounting

Tax accounting has its own set of rules, laid down by the Internal Revenue Service (IRS). Figuratively speaking, businesses may keep two sets of books for operating and tax purposes. There are two main reasons for this.

First, the timing of some expenses and revenues differs under GAAP and tax laws. Here are some examples:

▶ Capital lease payments—These are deducted for tax purposes in most cases, but for GAAP are treated as if they were installment payments on long-term debt, with a portion allocated to interest expense and a portion to principal.

▶ Unrealized losses on marketable securities—GAAP requires recognizing the expense, but the securities must be sold to take a loss on your taxes.

▶ Reserves for anticipated inventory write-offs and markdowns—these are expenses under GAAP, but no tax write-off is allowed unless you actually dispose of the inventory.

No matter who performs your company's internal accounting or what conventions are used, consult a tax specialist on how to minimize your tax payments.

Second, a company may want to show as little taxable income as possible, while issuing public statements with healthy profits. For some items, like depreciation, a company can choose different accounting methods for tax and book purposes. By using accelerated depreciation for tax purposes, while spreading the costs more slowly for book purposes, a company can reduce taxable income while limiting the hit to net income.

No matter who performs your company's internal accounting or what conventions are used, consult a tax specialist on how to minimize your tax payments. A little advanced planning can save you a significant amount in taxes. Also, an expert can help make sure you take advantage of available tax credits, avoid double taxation on funds removed from the business, and prevent extra costs from rules such as the alternative minimum tax.

Management Accounting

Financial and tax accounting satisfy the needs of outsiders. While the information can be useful internally, it is highly aggregated and usually prepared well after the end of the period it reports on. Management accounting—also called *cost accounting*, especially in manufacturing businesses—is a separate discipline that addresses management's need for current, detailed, internal operating information, which might include unit costs of production, sales by store, or profitability of individual projects. Chapter 7 covers management accounting in more detail.

Nonprofit Accounting

Nonprofit organizations, such as governments, colleges and universities, and some hospitals, have different accounting standards. In some cases, the distinctions are slight. If a hospital that operated for profit were suddenly changed to be nonprofit, but still got all its revenue from sales, the only accounting changes might be to recognize that there are no shareholders and that success is not measured by profit. Instead of net income, the bottom line would be "excess of revenues over expenses." The shareholders' equity section of the balance sheet might simply be called "equity."[6]

Nonprofit organizations, such as governments, colleges and universities, and some hospitals, have different accounting standards.

At organizations such as universities and hospitals, funds are received from nonsales sources such as donations and grants. Much of this is earmarked for special purposes. If donors give money specifically for a school's endowment or a specific program, for example, it cannot be used for general operating purposes. The funds are segregated and the accounting system must track the revenues and expenses for each fund separately.

Accounting for state and local government often gets extremely difficult to understand. One problem is that they carry fund accounting to an extreme. Funding comes from multiple revenue sources, such as bonds, taxes, and fees. Many of these, such as gas taxes and highway tolls, get earmarked for specific purposes. In addition, some agencies use encumbrance accounting, which tracks contractual obligations as well as actual expenditures.

Governing Bodies

Two primary bodies set for-profit accounting standards. The Securities and Exchange Commission (SEC) was established by Congress in the 1930s and holds the authority for setting accounting standards for the financial statements of publicly traded companies. For the most part, the SEC has delegated this responsibility to the accounting profession. However, the SEC has released more than 200 opinions in its Accounting Series Releases and occasionally exerts its power by disagreeing with positions taken by the accounting profession.

Before 1973, committees of the American Institute of Certified Public Accountants (AICPA, www.aicpa.org) developed accounting principles. The Committee on Accounting Procedure was active from 1938 to 1959 and the Accounting Principles Board (APB) from 1959 to 1973.

The Financial Accounting Standards Board (FASB, www.fasb.org), formed in 1973, is an independent organization with full-time members having a wide range of backgrounds in industry, academia, and public practice. The FASB has issued more than 100 standards and continues to be the primary standard-setting accounting body.

The IRS has a strong influence on financial accounting practice, even though tax and financial accounting have different objectives and principles.

In the wake of numerous accounting scandals in 2002, legislation was passed creating the Public Company Accounting Oversight Board (PCAOB, www.pcaobus.org). The board's duties include registration of public accounting firms, establishing audit and quality control standards, and enforcing compliance of securities laws and professional standards.

The IRS has a strong influence on financial accounting practice, even though tax and financial accounting have different objectives and principles. IRS regulations are not GAAP and, technically, good financial accounting practice should be independent of tax accounting. In practice, though, to minimize taxes and avoid the need to keep duplicate records, managers often adopt the accepted accounting practice that results in the lowest taxable income.

The Cost Accounting Standards Board (CASB, www.whitehouse.gov/omb/procurement/casb.html) is authorized by Congress to establish cost accounting standards for contractors negotiating federal defense contracts over $100,000. Like IRS regulations, CASB standards influence financial accounting practice where the FASB has not established a principle.

Although the AICPA no longer establishes GAAP, this organization of accountants is still the largest, with more than 300,000 members, and the most influential. In addition to certifying accountants, the AICPA is an influential advisor to the FASB. The AICPA is the leading force in establishing and maintaining a professional code of ethics and in continuing education. The AICPA is also the leader in developing auditing standards, issued through one of its committees.

A major organization for accounting professionals in industry rather than public practice is the Institute of Management Accounting (IMA, www.imanet.org), formerly the National Association of Accountants. The IMA has approximately 70,000 members and sponsors the certified management accountant (CMA) program. More than 10,000 certificates have been issued; those who pass the exam become members of the Institute of Certified Management Accountants (ICMA). Also, together with Financial Management Association International (FMA, www.fma.org), a 5,000-member organization, the IMA jointly sponsors a designation, certified in financial management (CFM). The CFM was first offered in 1996.

The National Society of Accountants (NSA, www.nsacct.org) has 12,000 members and provides support for 30,000 independent practitioners of accounting, tax, audit, and financial planning. The National Association of Enrolled Agents (NAEA, www.naea.org) has 10,000 members who are licensed, independent tax professionals. The American Accounting Association (AAA, www.aaahq.org) is primarily for accountants in academic work.

Accounting Certifications

The certified public accountant (CPA) is the best-known and most popular professional accounting designation. Certification requirements are fairly stringent, but vary slightly from state to state. A four-part exam is administered nationwide by the AICPA, presently covering four parts:

- ▶ Business law and professional responsibilities
- ▶ Auditing
- ▶ Accounting and reporting—taxation, managerial, governmental, and nonprofit
- ▶ Financial accounting and reporting for business enterprises

All four parts must be passed; however, this can be done over several sittings. In addition to the test, accountants must work a specified time in public accounting. Sometimes, general accounting experience can be substituted for part of the time required. To maintain certification, continuing education is necessary.

In contrast with the CPA exam, the CMA and CFM exams contain sections on economics, finance, decision analysis, management reporting, and behavioral issues. The CMA exam also includes a section on financial accounting and reporting, while the CFM covers corporate financial management. Candidates must also be members of the IMA, have two years of management accounting or financial management experience, and meet continuing education requirements. The examinations are becoming more popular and the IMA aggressively promotes them in corporate and academic arenas.

Enrolled agents (EAs) are certified by the federal government and, like CPAs, are allowed to represent taxpayers in front of the Internal Revenue Service. The EA designation can be earned by passing a two-day examination administered by the IRS that covers taxation of individuals, corporations, and partnerships plus procedures and ethics. Candidates must also pass a background check conducted by the IRS. Alternatively, an individual may qualify based on a minimum of five years' employment with the IRS. EAs are also required to meet continuing professional education requirements.

CPA Firms

In addition to offering a full range of accounting services, the Big Four, as well as most larger CPA firms, have also branched out to provide a wide range of consulting services.

CPAs work in both public and private practice. Public accounting firms range from one-person shops to the omnipresent "Big Four," so named because of the gap in size between them and their nearest competitors. In a 2004 survey, all Big Four firms enjoyed U.S. billings of over $3.7 billion, more than six times the revenue of the next ranked tax and audit firm. The Big Four firms are:

▶ PricewaterhouseCoopers

▶ Deloitte & Touche

▶ Ernst & Young

▶ KPMG

The Big Four are all international firms, with a presence in most major U.S. cities. In addition to offering a full range of accounting services, the Big Four, as well as most larger CPA firms, have also branched out to provide a wide range of consulting services. However, because auditors are required to maintain independence and objectivity, their ability to provide nonaudit services to their clients is sharply limited. Many firms had already spun off their consulting practices before the accounting scandals of 2002 at Enron and other companies brought the potential for conflicts of interest under scrutiny. New laws were enacted (see sidebar) to define services auditors of public companies are prohibited from providing. These include:

▶ Bookkeeping and other services related to preparing client accounting records

▶ Accounting system design and implementation

▶ Appraisal and valuation services

▶ Management or human resource functions

▶ Investment banking, broker, or dealer services

Choosing a CPA

If you compare large and small CPA firms, you will find that their professional credentials are pretty much the same. Your decision is more likely to be driven by investor requirements, cost, service, and personality factors. A Big Four firm makes sense for companies with aspirations of going public—or being acquired by a public company—or where required by investors. The larger firms also offer a broader scope of services. However, they tend to cost more and you may find yourself dealing with different staff members each year.

There are plenty of full-service firms besides the Big Four. The next tier of firms, including RSM McGladrey, BDO Seidman, and Grant Thornton, also boast a nationwide and international presence. Major regional firms, such as Moss Adams on the West Coast and Clifton Gunderson based in Peoria, Illinois, have billings over $100 million per year. Many local CPA firms boast of revenues exceeding $20 million.

Small CPA firms may provide more long-standing and personal service. But if you need fairly specialized expertise, the chances are less good that a small firm will have it. In addition, some CPA licenses don't allow work on public companies. The same is true for nonprofits, for which CPAs need special training and certification.

If you need fairly specialized expertise, the chances are less good that a small firm will have it.

A survey of 1997 *Inc.* 500 companies showed the diversity of choices made by smaller companies. In some ways, the selections mirrored the national rankings of CPA firms. Each of the then Big Five CPA firms (including Arthur Andersen) represented at least 25 *Inc.* 500 firms, compared with seven for the next largest firm. Among companies planning to go public within three years, 72 out of 122 went with one of the Big Five. Overall,

Sarbanes-Oxley Made Easy

The Sarbanes-Oxley act was passed in 2002 in response to accounting excesses at Enron, WorldCom, and other firms (see addendum to Chapter 5). It applies almost exclusively to public companies. These are its key provisions:

▶ The act prohibits auditors from performing specified services for audit clients, including bookkeeping or preparation of financial statements, financial information systems design and implementation, appraisal or valuation services, internal audits, management functions or human resources, or broker or dealer.

▶ The audit firm cannot have employed the CEO, controller, and CFO during the one-year period preceding an audit. Audit partners must rotate off the audit every five years.

▶ Audit committee members must be independent, which includes not receiving any fees other than for service on the board of directors.

▶ The annual report requires a management assessment of internal controls; also, CFOs and CEOs must certify financial statements.

▶ Companies are barred from making personal loans to officers and directors

Why should private companies care, other than general interest, for how Congress chose to deal with accounting scandals? For one, they may want to consider voluntarily complying with some of the act's key provisions as a best practice. This might include limiting the services they hire their CPA firms to provide or ensuring independence of directors or CFO candidates. Another possibility, though, is that if a company anticipates being acquired by a public company, the act's provision may come immediately into play. Loans to officers would need to be repaid and there could be considerable added effort in either the due diligence process or after closing to document internal controls.

Finally, there are two provisions that apply to all enterprises, including nonprofits. These make it illegal to punish whistleblowers or to destroy litigation-related documents.

though, 72% of the *Inc.* 500 companies went with small firms or individual accountants. Three companies used no outside firm at all.[7]

Not All Accountants Are CPAs

This last statistic highlights that, while CPAs are the only professionals who can certify financial statements, they are not the only ones who can prepare tax returns or contract accounting services. This is both good and bad news. Using a tax preparation service or a bookkeeping service to compile but not audit financial statements may be an opportunity to save money.

Distinguishing how qualified a practitioner is may be difficult. Most professionals in the accounting field have no certification and few states regulate who can call themselves "accountants." However, lack of certification does not mean accounting professionals are unqualified. Conversely, some states allow only CPAs to call themselves "accountants," which seems particularly unfair to certified professionals, including CMAs and enrolled agents.

Moreover, using a certified professional such as a CPA or CMA does not guarantee a correct match-up for a company's needs. A CPA, for example, is a somewhat narrow designation: the designation demonstrates skill in tax, audit, and theory, but says nothing about management skills or cost accounting. A CPA is also likely to be overkill for a bookkeeping job. An accountant with significant industry experience may not be a CPA, but could have valuable experience dealing with operating issues. But, even if an accountant holds a CMA, his or her experience may be limited to a few companies and he or she is probably not current on tax issues.

Most professionals in the accounting field have no certification and few states regulate who can call themselves "accountants."

Minimizing the amount spent on accounting is often tempting. But the contractor doing basic accounting work for a low fee may not be the right person to give financial advice or ensure proper controls. A bookkeeping service does different work and promises a different level of expertise than a part-time controller. Accountants who are moonlighting or doing temporary work can have a wide range of experience. Failing to sort out the qualifications can lead to inadequate reporting and controls.

CPA Reports

CPA firms can provide several types of financial statement preparation and examination services—such as audits, reviews, or compilations—depending on your business needs. Review the following descriptions of services to determine the differences among the services and which ones you may need. Included at the end of this chapter are samples of both qualified and unqualified audit opinions and a review opinion.

Audits

Auditing consists of examinations of a company's financial statements and internal controls. An audit by a CPA is required of all public companies—companies whose ownership shares are publicly traded—and the audit opinion is an important part of the financial statements. The audit opinion includes a description of the scope of the audit, an opinion on whether the financial statements were prepared in accordance with GAAP, and any qualifying remarks.

If you manage a private company, do you need an audit? Although audits may be perceived as suitable only for large corporations, some compelling arguments can be made for smaller company audits. Some of the reasons for which you may want an audit are listed below.

▶ If your company has or anticipates having outside investors or a loan from a bank, you will almost certainly need to obtain an independent opinion.

▶ Audited financials may facilitate your dealings with vendors and customers.

▶ If your company is considering going public or being acquired, you will want a history of audited statements.

▶ The CPA's assessment may provide you with peace of mind about the soundness of your accounting systems and procedures, plus an opportunity to get an objective viewpoint of your management practices.

On the other hand, if you have no internal requirement for an audit, you may want to avoid the expense. Expect to pay at least $10,000 for a company with sales of $500,000-$1,000,000, increasing up to $50,000 and higher for a $20-million company.

Actual costs will vary depending on the following:

▶ The type of CPA firm used—the Big Four are usually more expensive than local companies

▶ The amount of work performed internally

▶ Whether the CPA also does the company's tax work

▶ The extent of testing required.

An independent CPA examination may take one of two forms: an audit or a review opinion. The audit requires testing internal procedures, reviewing certain transactions, and verifying account balances. (Specific procedures are discussed in more detail in Chapter 4.) After the audit, the CPA issues a formal report on the company's financial statements that states the following:

▶ Whether the statements conform to GAAP,

▶ Whether accounting principles have been consistently applied from year to year,

▶ Whether disclosure is adequate (assumed so, unless otherwise stated), and

▶ An expression of an opinion or the reasons why an opinion cannot be given.

In addition, a description of the scope of the audit is included. A sample of a typical unqualified audit opinion is located at the end of this chapter. Even though each CPA firm adopts its own language, the three-paragraph format shown is fairly standard.

If the auditor fails to express an opinion or issues a qualified opinion or (rarely) an adverse opinion, serious problems exist and can be a major setback to a company. These are some reasons why an auditor may not issue a favorable opinion:

If the auditor fails to express an opinion or issues a qualified opinion or (rarely) an adverse opinion, serious problems exist and can be a major setback to a company.

▶ There may be uncertainty over whether the company is financially stable; in other words, survival over the next year may be in doubt;

▶ Accounting has not conformed to GAAP;

▶ Sufficient data cannot be gathered or tested; or

▶ Statements may be subject to resolution of a significant uncertainty, such as a major lawsuit.

The formats of qualified and adverse opinions differ from the normal three-paragraph format, making them easy to spot. A sample qualified audit opinion is located at the end of this chapter, so that you can compare the qualified and unqualified opinions.

Adverse opinions are issued only if the departures from GAAP are so severe that the financial statements as a whole are unreliable. A disclaimer of opinion might be made if an auditor is unable to collect enough data to form an opinion.

What an Audit Is Not

Audits do not guarantee that financial statements are accurate. Rather, the scope of the audit is to determine whether material differences exist. The definition of "material" will differ from company to company. A discrepancy of $100,000 will be material to a small company but probably immaterial to the statements of a billion-dollar corporation. The auditor exercises considerable professional judgment in deciding what is material for a particular audit. In addition, because the main purpose of the audit is to protect outside investors, greater emphasis is usually put on possible overstatements of income or net worth than understatements.

If you suspect fraud, alert your CPA. Detecting fraud requires a different set of procedures than for a normal audit.

In addition, an audit or review is not intended to detect fraud. Uncovering fraud may be a by-product of the audit, but auditors do not specifically search for fraud. If you suspect fraud, alert your CPA. Detecting fraud requires a different set of procedures than for a normal audit.

To get a specialist in fraud investigation, call on a forensic accountant—someone who seeks out evidence of cheating or theft, whether by insiders or outsiders. According to *CFO Magazine*, "The forensic accountant is to a regular accountant what the pathologist is to the family doctor."[8] Forensic accounting is a rapidly growing field. The Association of Certified Fraud Examiners—founded in 1986 and the sponsor of a four-part, 10-hour certification exam—has more than 25,000 members.

Reviews: An Alternative to Audits

A less rigorous and less expensive alternative to a full-blown audit is a review. A review is similar to an audit in that it involves steps in examining the accounting system, transactions, and balances. However, the purpose is only to determine whether major deviations from GAAP exist and the scope of information examined is much smaller. Where a problem is suspected, the auditor may decide to expand tests to the same level as an audit.

As with an audit, the CPA expresses an opinion, but the opinion states that the auditor is "not aware of any material modifications that should be made" to conform to GAAP.[9] Contrast this with the much more positive assertions made in the audit letter. (A sample review opinion is included at the end of this chapter.)

The cost of a typical review is about half that of an audit. Since being endorsed by the AICPA in 1979, reviews have grown in acceptance. Check if your bank or investors will accept a review before opting out of an audit. If they will, the review is a cost-effective alternative.

For very small businesses, a *compilation* is a third alternative that is available. For a compilation, a CPA simply assembles the company's data into a statement, but gives no opinion or assurance about the statements.

Negotiating CPA Services

No matter what services are chosen, be sure to get an engagement letter that spells out the scope of any audit or tax work. Get a breakdown of the proposed fee and see if you can save money by shifting some of the work in-house. A capable controller, or even a temporary worker, can usually prepare many of the audit schedules at a lower cost than the CPA firm. You may also find you can do without some of the proposed services or can substitute less expensive audit personnel for high-priced partners and seniors.

Don't be afraid to negotiate price. CPAs will often offer lower rates to lure customers. However, don't jump from CPA to CPA without a compelling reason, as not only does this disrupt a potentially rewarding long-term relationship, but investors also frown upon it. Finally, be aware that, while a CPA will usually assist you if an IRS audit occurs, you are still responsible for any return you sign, whether or not a CPA prepared it. You cannot escape penalties and interest just by using a CPA.

Don't be afraid to negotiate price. CPAs will often offer lower rates to lure customers.

Industry Crisis

In recent years, the CPA profession has faced a series of crises related to liability cases brought by investors and government regulators. Largely as a result of the savings and loan (S&L) scandals of the late 1980s, lawsuits faced by accounting firms reached 4,000 in 1992, double the number from 1985. During that period, Price Waterhouse was hit with a $387 million judgment for its role as auditor in a bank acquisition.[10] Ernst & Young agreed to a $400 million settlement against charges that it inadequately audited four S&Ls.[11] The nation's seventh-largest CPA firm, Laventhol & Horwath, filed for bankruptcy in 1991 due to litigation.

The CPA industry fought hard for legislation to limit litigation and appeared to win a major victory with the Private Securities Litigation Reform Act of 1995, which raised the standards for lawsuits and reduced the likelihood of frivolous claims. In fact, shareholder lawsuits dropped from 231 in 1994 to 110 in 1996.[12] However, claims rose back to 258 in 1998 and then shattered all previous records with 483 lawsuits in 2001.[13] This all came before the accounting scandal at Enron that caused the collapse of Arthur Andersen and further scandals that surfaced at WorldCom, Tyco, and numerous other companies.

In 1991, the Big Six accounting firms spent an estimated 9% of their auditing fees on related legal costs.[14] In 2001, it was estimated that what was then the Big Five spent 15% on litigation-related costs.[15] These financial pressures have produced changes in the industry, including additional legislation to limit liability, increased regulation, and higher fees. Most CPA firms shifted their legal form from partnerships to limited liability partnerships or corporations (LLPs and LLCs) to gain limits on legal liability. CPA firms have also become more selective about whom they choose as clients, walking away from those who pose excessive risk. These trends are likely to continue in the wake of the accounting scandals that started surfacing in 2001-2002.

Most lawsuits stem from the auditing function and the CPAs' certification of statements. Where work has been sloppy, auditors can certainly be held liable. However, fraud is beyond the scope of a standard audit. This point is not always well understood, which itself can help lead to lawsuits. In 1997, Statement of Auditing Standard No. 82 (SAS 82) was issued, which clarified, but did not broaden, auditors' responsibility to detect fraud. The standard states that the auditors' objective is to express an opinion on whether the client's financial statements fairly present its financial position. Responsibility for detecting fraud relates to detection of any material misstatements and not to seeking fraudulent activities themselves.

If a CPA firm discovers fraud that has a material impact, the auditors should discuss the problem with management and report the problem to the audit committee. While many people feel CPAs should blow the whistle on clients, auditors often prefer to walk away quietly from these accounts. If that happens to a publicly traded firm, the client must file a report with the SEC explaining why the auditors resigned. However, the details are typically played down.[16]

A Word About GAAP

Selecting the right accounting services requires understanding the role of financial and tax reporting. This book repeatedly stresses how this required reporting is only part of financial management. Most experienced bookkeepers and accountants can do the mechanics and your CPA can provide insurance that they are done properly.

Accounting skill does not imply financial management and operating savvy. Audited financials do not guarantee proper controls or provide detailed information. Sound financial management also demands attention to costs, planning, controls, and asset management. Whether hiring internal or external financial people, look for those with experience beyond basic accounting.

Accounting skill does not imply financial management and operating savvy.

The importance of financial accounting is not to be diminished. It is fascinating how the myriad activities of any business can be captured by accounting transactions, then be summarized in financial statements comprehensible by readers inside and outside a company. Like a picture, financial statements are worth at least a thousand words.

But GAAP reporting is primarily intended to meet the needs of investors and other outsiders. While the statements are still valuable to management, they provide an overview rather than a detailed picture. And, in protecting the interests of investors, trade-offs in GAAP make the statements more objective but less informative. The next three chapters examine issues of financial accounting.

Notes

1. Alvin Moscow, with Harold Geneen, *Managing* (New York: Doubleday, 1984), p. 185.
2. Emmett D. Edwards, Jr., "What Financial Problems?" *Management Accounting*, August 1992, p. 54.
3. Gary Siegel, "Public Accounting Report," 1993 survey of 632 executives by DePaul University.
4. Edwards, p. 56.
5. Ibid., p. 57.

6. Robert N. Anthony and Regina E. Herzlinger, *Management Control in Nonprofit Organizations* (Homewood, IL: Richard D. Irwin, Inc., 1980), p. 134.

7. Ilan Mochari, "To Big Five or Not to Big Five," *Inc. Magazine*, October 1998. Reprinted at www.inc.com/magazine/19981015/1092.html.

8. S.L. Mintz, "The Fraud Detectives," *CFO Magazine*, April 1993, p. 29.

9. Martin C. Miller, *Miller's Comprehensive GAAP Guide* (New York: Harcourt Brace Jovanovich, 1986), p. 40.

10. The judgment was later thrown out and a new trial ordered.

11. Julia Homer, "How Did We Get Here?" *CFO Magazine,* October 2002, p. 42.

12. Richard H. Gamble, "The Perils of Shareholder Lawsuits," *Business Finance*, September 2001, www.businessfinancemag.com/magazine/archives/article.html?articleID=13787.

13. PricewaterhouseCoopers, *2001 Securities Litigation Study*, p. 1, www.10b5.com/2001SecuritiesLitigationStudy.pdf.

14. Tom Ehrenfeld and Gerald A. Polansky, Chairman of the AICPA, quoted in "Survival of the Fittest," *CFO Magazine*, August 1992, p. 7.

15. Mark LaPlace, testimony before the Ohio state senate, June 13, 2001. Printed in Ohio Alliance for Civil Justice, www.alliancecourtwatch.com/efforts/sb120/LaplaceTestimony.asp.

16. Thomas McCarroll, "Who's Counting?" *Time*, 13 April 1992, p. 49.

Exhibit 2-1. Unqualified Audit Opinion—Sample

Unqualified audit opinions typically have the following sections:

- ▶ An introductory paragraph identifying management's responsibility for the financial statements, giving a brief description of what an audit is, and stating that any opinion is based upon the audit work;
- ▶ A scope paragraph describing the work performed during the audit;
- ▶ An opinion paragraph asserting that the statements are in accordance with GAAP; and
- ▶ The auditor's signature and the date of the report.

Exhibit 2-2. Report of Independent Auditors

Stockholders and Board of Directors:

We have examined the balance sheet of XYZ Corporation as of December 31, 2003 and 2002, and the related statements of income, stockholders' equity, and cash flows for the years then ended. These financial statements are the responsibility of the Company's management. Our responsibility is to express an opinion on these financial statements based on our audit.

We conducted our audits in accordance with generally accepted auditing standards. Those standards require that we plan and perform the audits to obtain reasonable assurance about whether the financial statements are free of material misstatement. An audit includes examining, on a test basis, evidence supporting the amounts and disclosures in the financial statements. An audit also includes assessing the accounting principles used and significant estimates made by management, as well as evaluating the overall financial statement presentation. We believe that our audits provide a reasonable basis for our opinion.

In our opinion, the financial statements referred to above present fairly, in all material respects, the financial position of XYZ Corporation at December 31, 2003 and 2002, and the results of its operations and its cash flows for the years then ended in conformity with generally accepted accounting principles.

[Date] [Signature]

Exhibit 2-3. Qualified Audit Opinion—Sample

Qualified audit opinions typically have the following sections:

- ▶ An introductory paragraph as shown in the unqualified opinion;
- ▶ A scope paragraph as shown in the unqualified opinion, unless the qualification results from the scope being limited. In that case, the words "except as explained in following paragraph" are added to the start of the paragraph;
- ▶ An explanatory paragraph describing the reasons for the qualified opinion and the potential impact of the qualification on the financial statements;
- ▶ An opinion paragraph similar to the unqualified opinion, but containing the phrase "except for" or "subject to" and referring to the explanatory paragraph; and
- ▶ The auditor's signature and the date of the report.

Exhibit 2-4. Report of Independent Auditors

Stockholders and Board of Directors:

We have examined the balance sheet of XYZ Corporation as of December 31, 2003 and 2002, and the related statements of income, stockholders' equity, and cash flows for the years then ended. These financial statements are the responsibility of the Company's management. Our responsibility is to express an opinion on these financial statements based on our audit.

We conducted our audits in accordance with generally accepted auditing standards. Those standards require that we plan and perform the audits to obtain reasonable assurance about whether the financial statements are free of material misstatement. An audit includes examining, on a test basis, evidence supporting the amounts and disclosures in the financial statements. An audit also includes assessing the accounting principles used and significant estimates made by management, as well as evaluating the overall financial statement presentation. We believe that our audits provide a reasonable basis for our opinion.

As more fully described in Note A to the financial statements, the Company is involved in continuing litigation relating to patent infringements. The amount of damages, if any, resulting from this litigation cannot be determined at this time.

In our opinion, subject to the effects, if any, of such adjustments as might have been required had the outcome of the uncertainty discussed in the preceding paragraph been known, the financial statements referred to above present fairly, in all material respects, the financial position of XYZ Corporation as of December 31, 2003 and 2002, and the results of its operations and its cash flows for the years then ended in conformity with generally accepted accounting principles.

[Date] [Signature]

Exhibit 2-5. Review Opinion—Sample

A review opinion has the same sections as an audit opinion. The wording is modified to reflect the lesser scope and the auditor is does not express an opinion as to whether the statements conform with GAAP. Rather, the opinion states whether the auditor is aware of any material modifications that are needed.

Report of Independent Auditors

Stockholders and Board of Directors:

We have reviewed the balance sheet of XYZ Corporation as of December 31, 2003 and 2002, and the related statements of income, stockholders' equity, and cash flows in accordance with standards established by the American Institute of Certified Public Accountants.

A review consists principally of inquiries of company personnel and analytical procedures applied to financial data. It is substantially less in scope than an examination in accordance with generally accepted auditing standards, the objective of which is the expression of an opinion regarding the financial statements taken as a whole. Accordingly, we do not express such an opinion.

Based on our review, we are not aware of any material modifications that should be made to the accompanying financial statements in order for them to be in conformity with generally accepted accounting principles.

[Date] [Signature]

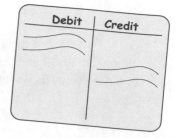

Chapter 3

Accounting 101

Few have heard of Fra Luca Pacioli, the inventor of double-entry book-keeping; but he has probably had more influence on human life than has Dante or Michelangelo.

—Herbert J. Muller[1]

I DON'T WANT TO BE AN ACCOUNTANT." THIS IS THE REFRAIN of most business owners when trying to choose an accounting software package, read financial statements, or keep financial records. While there is certainly no need to learn to write journal entries or pore over FASB pronouncements, a basic understanding of financial accounting can help you wade through the bombardment of financial information you get from internal and external sources.

Admittedly, accounting is not the most fascinating subject to study. However, it is assumed that readers of financial statements are knowledgeable about accounting principles; the financials provide little guidance for the unsophisticated user. Therefore, a basic knowledge of accounting is needed to properly interpret statements. The ability to interpret financial statements is a skill with a wide range of applications, from analyzing internal statements to gleaning competitive information from the statements of rivals, to reading annual reports for personal investing.

More importantly, since many companies devote a disproportionate amount of financial management resources to GAAP accounting, knowledge of this field will help you sort out unneeded activity. And when terms and statistics such as "gross margin," "book value," and various ratios are bandied about by accountants and investors, you will understand how relevant each measure actually is.

If the bad news about accounting is that it is, indeed, boring, the good news is that the basics are nearly all you really need to know. Once you have learned the underpinnings, the rest of accounting is mostly just clarification, interpretation, and application of these rules. In addition, most smaller businesses deal with only a small variety of transactions, so most transactions are repetitive and many accounting rules are not applicable.

The nuts and bolts of accounting are covered in this one basic chapter, which explains debits and credits, types of financial statements, and the underlying principles of financial accounting. Dry as accounting may be, learning basic accounting principles is worth the effort.

If the bad news about accounting is that it is, indeed, boring, the good news is that the basics are nearly all you really need to know.

Financial Statements

Financial accounting is simply the recording of transactions and events that can be objectively measured in monetary terms. Transactions of a nonfinancial nature and events with an unmeasurable future impact are not recorded.

Accounting results are generally summarized in a few standard formats— the balance sheet, the income statement, and the statement of cash flows. Statements may include footnotes and a management discussion to clarify or add to the information presented. Samples of these statements are included at the end of this chapter.

The Balance Sheet

The balance sheet presents the financial position of a company at a single point in time. Since the balance sheet is a snapshot as of the end of the accounting period, it may or may not be representative of the entire period. A change in the timing of events immediately before or after the end of the period, such as a large loan payment, the sale of securities, or collecting a major account receivable, can significantly alter a company's balance sheet.

Numbers on the balance sheet are listed in two columns. By convention, the assets of a company are presented first. Depending on the presentation format, this will be either on the left side of the page (with liabilities listed on the right), at the top of the page (with liabilities listed afterward), or on the first page of a two-page layout. Assets are defined as resources of the business, items that provide future economic benefit. These include cash; accounts receivable; inventory; and property, plant, and equipment. An expense is an expired resource.

Listed after the assets are the liabilities and owner's equity. Whereas assets are the available resources of a company, liabilities and owner's equity are the sources of assets. These include earnings, equity invested, borrowing, and payables. Liabilities are the future obligations of the company, such as accounts payable, taxes due, and debt. Owner's equity includes the capital contributed by the company's owners, plus the cumulative earnings, less any dividends paid.

Typically, assets and liabilities are listed from the most liquid to the least. They are further grouped as:

▶ **Current**—assets expected to be converted to cash, and liabilities due, within one year; and

▶ **Noncurrent**—assets expected to be in service, and liabilities due, beyond one year.

The Income Statement

While the balance sheet is a snapshot of a company, the income statement presents the performance of a company over a distinct period of time. Net income or loss, which is shown on an income statement, equals the net change in assets versus liabilities during a period, or the increase or decrease in a company's value.

A convention underlying financial statements is that a one-year period is used to measure performance. The 12 months chosen by a company for its fiscal year do not have to conform to the calendar year. Car companies, for example, set their fiscal calendar so that year-end coincides with the end of a model year. Retailers typically choose a January 31 year-end, which enables their peak sales season to be captured in one period and is probably more convenient for taking year-end inventories. Many companies simply start their fis-

Whereas assets are the available resources of a company, liabilities and owner's equity are the sources of assets.

cal year with the date they were founded. In addition to annual statements, most companies also prepare interim monthly or quarterly reports to provide more timely information.

By convention, the income statement—also called a *profit and loss statement* or P&L—starts with revenues or income and then lists expenses. Companies that produce or sell products list the cost of sales as the first expense category, including the purchase of goods and any manufacturing expenses. Revenue less the cost of sales equals gross profit, which is often shown as a subtotal on the income statement.

Operating expenses related to sales, marketing, research and development, and administration follow. A subtotal at this point is called *operating income* or *earnings before interest and taxes* (EBIT). Many financial analysts like to insert yet another subtotal, called EBITDA, an acronym for *earnings before interest, taxes, depreciation, and amortization.* By calculating operating income that doesn't include depreciation and amortization, expenses that don't involve a current outflow of cash as discussed below, these analysts feel they get a better picture of the cash flow from ongoing operations.

By convention, the income statement—also called a profit and loss statement *or P&L—starts with revenues or income and then lists expenses.*

Interest, taxes, and any other items that are ongoing, but not part of the main operations of a company, are listed next. Although part of continuing operations, these are considered nonoperating income and expenses. For most companies, these are the last categories. In the unusual circumstance that a company discontinues an operation, has a one-time or extraordinary event, or changes an accounting principle, any gain or loss appears below all other items on the statement. *Net income* is the total of the expenses and revenues.

Public companies must also publish *earnings per share* (EPS). This calculation can get complex, particularly when a company has issued convertible securities, such as options and warrants; however, EPS is basically calculated by dividing net income by the number of shares of common stock outstanding. If a company pays dividends, these are shown last. Dividends and other distributions to shareholders are not considered expenses and therefore not included in calculating net income.

The Statement of Cash Flows

The third basic financial report is the statement of cash flows, which provides a fuller picture of a company's sources and uses of cash and equivalents. In recognition of the importance of cash to companies, this report has evolved from the statement of sources and the uses of funds report, which reported on either a cash or working capital basis.

Many activities of a company generate or use cash without affecting net income. Examples include raising debt financing, issuing new stock, or acquiring fixed assets. Since it is cash, not net income, that is critical to a company's survival, and investors need to know the ability of a company to finance operations, additional information beyond the income statement is needed. The statement of cash flows attempts to meet that need by reconciling between net income recorded on an accrual basis and actual cash flow.

Required Reporting

The Securities and Exchange Commission (SEC) requires public companies to publish annual financial statements that include these three reports—balance sheet, income statement, and statement of cash flows. The statements must be audited by certified public accountants. Public companies must also file quarterly, unaudited statements. These are familiar to anyone who owns common stocks and receives annual and quarterly reports.

Private companies are not subject to the SEC requirements, but often choose to adhere to the practice of preparing annual and interim statements. Outside lenders and investors may require this practice as well. Unlike public companies, privately held businesses may be able to save on cost and effort by opting for less formal reporting formats. Rather than an audit, they may elect to have their CPAs do a review, which is less extensive, as discussed in Chapter 2.

Full disclosure of all relevant financial information is an essential role of financial statements and vital to analysis of a company's position.

Footnotes

Footnotes are an essential part of financial statements. These contain a description of the company's accounting policy, provide added detail behind various financial statement lines, and disclose information on things such as future lease obligations and stock option grants not required to be recorded on the balance sheet or income statement. Examples are contained in the sample financial statements at the end of this chapter.

Full disclosure of all relevant financial information is an essential role of financial statements and vital to analysis of a company's position. Because the footnotes contain information not available in the numbers on the balance sheet and the income statement, they should be read just as closely as the numbers themselves.

Double-Entry Accounting

Did you ever look at balance sheets and wonder why the assets and liabilities always came out exactly equal? Did you wonder what amount had been plugged to force everything to balance? Of course, there are no plug numbers. What is really responsible is the simple elegance of double-entry bookkeeping.

Basically, every transaction that changes a company's assets, obligations, or equity has a simultaneous and equal impact on other accounts. An increase in cash has to come from somewhere, just as a payable to a vendor must arise from the receipt of some goods or services.

Double-entry bookkeeping is the process of determining which two or more accounts were affected when a transaction has occurred and recording the results.

Double-entry bookkeeping is the process of determining which two or more accounts were affected when a transaction has occurred and recording the results.

A Simple Example

Suppose your cash on hand increases from $100 to $200. You will make an entry to increase the balance on your records by $100. However, you cannot stop there; in accounting, no event is ever isolated. The $100 had to come from some source.

One possibility is that another asset was reduced, which might occur if you collected an outstanding customer invoice. Another possibility is that you incurred an increase in obligations or liabilities, as would be the case if you borrowed the $100. If you acquired the $100 through a sale of stock, you would show an increase in owner's equity.

Possibly all or part of the $100 was profit. Perhaps it was interest earned on a savings account or a royalty payment. You would make an entry to your income statement increasing revenue by $100. Your balance sheet is kept balanced because net income is a component of owner's equity.

The increase in cash may be from a combination of changes in more than one account, which may increase the complexity of your bookkeeping entry, but the basic concept is the same. Say the $100 cash came from the sale of equipment that cost you $60. You would still record the $100 increase in cash. Then you would have to show a decrease of $60 in an asset (equipment). The remaining $40 would be recorded as an increase in profit.

All accounting entries work on this basic symmetry. Walk through a few simple transactions and you will quickly see this point. Buy inventory on credit and an asset (inventory) increases, as does a liability (accounts payable). Pay the bill and both cash and accounts payable are reduced. Ship the inventory to a customer as a warranty replacement and inventory is reduced, as is net income.

Debits and Credits

As mentioned earlier, the balance sheet has two sides, with assets listed on the left and liabilities and owner's equity on the right. The accounts on each side total to the same figure and, through the symmetry of double-entry book-keeping, stay in balance at all times. (See the sample balance sheet at the end of the chapter.)

By convention, balances that appear on the left side of the balance sheet are referred to as *debits* and those on the right as *credits*. The terms are rather arbitrary and can seem misleading if you expect all debits to be bad and all credits to be good.

Since assets are listed on the left side of the balance sheet, their normal balance is a debit balance. This means that increases to asset accounts are debits and decreases are credits.[2] Similarly, since liabilities and equity are listed on the right side of the balance sheet, the normal balance is a credit balance. So, for liabilities and equity, increases are credits and decreases are debits. Since net income is part of equity, revenue is a credit entry and expenses are debits.

A debit to one account must be offset by a credit elsewhere, either a decrease to another asset or an increase in liabilities or owner's equity. In the example above, if the $100 came from a collection from a customer's outstanding invoice, your entry would be a debit of $100 to your cash (checking) account and a credit of $100 to accounts receivable, as is illustrated in the samples below. The first example shows what is called a *T-account*, a common tool that helps in visualizing the bookkeeping process. The second sample shows the entry in a *journal entry* form, a common way of writing out entries.

Using T- Accounts

Checking Account		Accounts Receivable	
Debit	Credit	Debit	Credit
$100			$100

Using Journal Entry

Account #	Account Name	Entry Description	Debit	Credit
1100	Checking Acct	To record payment	$100	
1200	Accts Receivable	Received on Acct		$100

If debits and credits seem hard to keep straight, do not worry. They are simply the accountant's ways of referring to left and right. And even many accounting students survived their classes only by using the rule that "debits are toward the door"—a rule that works in about 50% of classrooms. As long as you understand that double-entry bookkeeping always affects at least two accounts—one as a debit and the other as a credit—you will be able to comprehend your financial statements and the general bookkeeping and accounting that goes into them.

If debits and credits seem hard to keep straight, do not worry. They are simply the accountant's ways of referring to left and right.

What Gets Recorded?

Now that you have a better understanding of the basic mechanics of bookkeeping and financial statement preparation, the next question to ask is "At what point is a transaction recorded and how is the amount determined?" Six broad principles underlie how accounting entries are recorded.

Historical cost. Assets and liabilities are initially recorded at their acquisition cost—as opposed to market value, replacement cost, or other possibilities. In most cases, they will remain valued at historic cost until the company disposes of them.

Revenue realization. Revenue is not recognized until performance of services is virtually complete and measurable compensation (cash or receivable) has been received. In most cases, revenue is recognized at the point of sale, when product is shipped, or a service is completed.

Matching. Expenses should be recognized in the same accounting period as the revenues associated with them. Expenses not directly connected with revenues are recognized in the period they occur.

Consistency. The accounting principles used by a company should be consistent over time. Consistency helps ensure that useful period-to-period comparisons can be made.

Full disclosure. Financial statements must include sufficient information for a prudent, knowledgeable reader to make informed judgments. The information can be in the form of the account balances or included in footnotes and parenthetical notations.

Objectivity. The information should be based on fact. Some discretionary judgment is inevitable, but the basis of the judgment should be verifiable by outside parties.

In addition, these principles are modified and may vary according to the following three accounting conventions.

Materiality. When a particular disclosure is material, it must be reported only if it is likely to affect a decision of a reader. Where this line is drawn varies from company to company and requires a judgment: what may be material to a business decision may not be material to an outsider evaluating a company. During an audit, materiality is a key factor in deciding the scope of testing done by the outside auditor.

Industry practices. Companies in certain industries that have unusual processes or procedures are allowed to make departures from convention. One example is the inventories of meat packers, which, because of the impracticality of tracking the costs of individual pieces back to the cost of the animal, are valued based on market prices, not historic costs.

Conservatism. When more than one accounting method is possible, the one least likely to overstate assets or income should be chosen. This rule is meant to be a guide to difficult decisions where more than one accounting treatment is possible. Conservatism does not mean income should be deliberately understated.

The six principles and three accounting conventions described above encompass the methodology your bookkeeper or accountant applies when taking care of your books. Throughout this book, you will discover over and over how these practices can affect your management decisions.

From Principles to Practice

Although knowing the underlying principles of accounting is a good basic step toward understanding your financials, you will need to translate that knowledge into knowing how these principles are applied. Before applying these principles, a few other general comments are needed.

First, you must assume that a company is a going concern. Many valuations make sense only when an enterprise will be in business for the foreseeable future. If assumed otherwise, assets might need to be valued at liquidation prices and concepts that take a long-term outlook, such as depreciation, would be illogical.

Second, financial accounting deals only with transactions that can be clearly measured in monetary terms. Implementation of a quality improvement program, the resignation of a key employee, or a change in the economy are all events that affect a company's fortunes, but they are not recorded because their impact cannot be assessed.

Occasionally, events such as the filing of a major lawsuit or loss of a significant contract arise that could significantly have an impact on a company's value, but the outcome is not yet known or the effect is unclear. Though these are not accounting events, they are not ignored. Rather, these types of events are disclosed in footnotes to the financial statements, so that, even if the events cannot be quantified, readers have sufficient facts to make informed evaluations.

Another general rule is that a transaction must be essentially complete, or reasonably ensured of completion, before being recorded. For most routine transactions, some exchange of money, goods, or services must take place before accounting recognizes an event. When a customer places an order, it is not recorded as a sale, but when the goods are shipped, it generally is; hiring an employee does not create an expense, but any actual time that employee works and earns wages does.

Finally, as discussed earlier, GAAP accounting is accrual-based. Cash or other assets do not have to change hands for a transaction to be complete. Conversely, a transaction is not necessarily complete just because cash has been received or paid. Revenue, for example, is generally recognized when goods or services have been delivered, which may or may not be when cash is received. Accrual entries are also needed to properly match expenses to the revenues with which they are identified.

Individuals, professional firms, and small companies that don't require audited statements can use cash accounting.

Individuals, professional firms, and small companies that don't require audited statements can use cash accounting. Cash accounting is simpler and is generally used for tax accounting if inventory is insignificant. But GAAP accounting is accrual-based and, as can be seen from the issues discussed below, differs substantially from cash reporting.

45

The following sections of this chapter discuss how the six principles and the factors that modify them are applied in practice to various parts of your financial statements. Take a look at the sample financial statements at the end of this chapter to familiarize yourself with the different parts.

Assets

Assets, the first component on the balance sheet, are defined as resources having a future value to a business. Assets can present a variety of different issues when you try to quantify them. However, several conventions make asset valuation a reasonably standardized and consistent process.

The next several pages will show you how assets are recognized and valued. You will also understand how reserves, write-downs, depreciation, and amortization are used in this process.

Asset Recognition

Since accounting attempts to match expenses to the period they benefit, when an expenditure occurs you must decide whether it applies to the current accounting period or has a future value. If the expenditure applies to the current accounting period, it is expensed, reducing income in the current period. If the expenditure has future benefit, though, it is recorded as an asset and expensed in future periods as it is consumed. In short, an asset is basically something that carries a future economic value.

Compare the following transactions to see how future economic value is determined:

▶ Payment of monthly rent is normally expensed. If it is being prepaid, however, it is recorded as an asset and then expensed in the month to which it applies.

▶ Merchandise bought for resale is added to inventory and expensed when sold.

▶ Machinery is capitalized (recorded as an asset) and, through depreciation, expensed over its useful life.

▶ Most wages are expensed in the same period they are earned. However, any labor that went into producing inventory would also be added to the value of inventory and expensed when the goods are sold.

As with any transaction, the value of an asset must be quantifiable in monetary terms and its acquisition must be essentially complete. Assets can be intangible, such as patents and trademarks. However, GAAP requires that expenditures for R&D and advertising, whose future benefit is hard to determine objectively, be expensed.

Asset Valuation

When an asset is purchased, it is valued at whatever was paid for it—its historic cost. For example, if you buy a new computer from a dealer for $3,000, either with cash or on credit, it is valued for $3,000. Any incidental costs of completing the acquisition or installation of the computer, such as shipping, handling, and sales taxes, are added to the base cost. Measuring value according to cost is objective and logical, since an asset's value should be what you are willing to pay for it.

Notice what would happen if a discrepancy arose between the historic cost and what you consider the computer's true value and you tried to update how the computer was valued on your books. If one side of the entry is to change the value of the computer, for the entry to balance, a gain or loss would have to be booked. This type of income from an unrealized gain is not permitted under GAAP.

Buying something at a bargain price or, conversely, overpaying also does not produce accounting income or losses. Suppose a week after the transaction above you buy an identical computer from a discount mail order company for $2,500 and record it as an asset. Even though the two computers are identical, one will be valued at $3,000 and the other at $2,500. While this may seem like an anomaly, setting the two values equal is not a better solution. You would have to decide whether the $2,500 machine was a bargain or the other system overpriced before you could set the value.

What if your company is a reseller of computers and you can prove that customers are eager to buy these same machines at $3,500? Can they be valued at $3,500? No matter what you may think they are worth, no accounting transaction has occurred until they are actually sold, so the computers are still valued at their historic cost.

With a few exceptions, historic cost holds as long as the asset is held. Even though assets fluctuate in value due to obsolescence, scarcity, or inflation, their accounting value is fixed. Fluctuations from historic cost are not a problem for current assets, since they turn over fairly rapidly. However, some assets can remain on a company's books for years with no change in valuation. For example, many companies carry land on their ledgers at prices they paid decades earlier, regardless of the current market value.

The use of historic cost arises from the desire for objective valuations and for profits to be realized only from completed transactions, not just holding onto assets. Another key reason for using this approach is because it satisfies the conservatism convention. The use of historic costs, rather than measures such as market values, is less likely to allow companies to overstate asset values or net income.

The use of historic cost arises from the desire for objective valuations and for profits to be realized only from completed transactions, not just holding onto assets.

Reserves and Write-Downs

Conversely, because of conservatism, if the value of fixed assets or inventory drops below historic cost, GAAP requires that you write down the value of the assets.[3] This rule, recording certain assets at the lower of cost or market, introduces a certain lack of symmetry. But the rule prevents asset values and, therefore, profits from being inflated. If the value of assets that you previously wrote down rise, you write them up, but no higher than their historic cost.

Similarly, you can expect that, over time, the full value of certain assets will not be fully realized. Some receivables may prove uncollectible and inventory may spoil or become obsolete. To account for these potential losses, GAAP requires that you establish reserves, so that the total asset value more closely approximates the expected realizable value.

You can calculate reserves by identifying specific uncollectible accounts or obsolete items. More frequently, you will make an estimate based on history or other judgment. You may reserve for just a portion of an asset's value and not necessarily have to physically dispose of an asset in order to write off its value.

The reserve calculation is often a sticky issue in preparing financial statements. Inventory and receivables can account for most of a company's assets, so reserves can create a large hit to net income. In addition, reserves are often required even when no specific assets may be identified as overvalued.

Depreciation and Amortization

Assets are assumed to have a future value and the accountant's objective is to defer recording any expenses or expired costs until the periods when the value is realized.

For assets such as buildings and equipment, which are used over a number of years, this is accomplished by calculating depreciation. Depreciation is a method of accounting that allows recognition of part of an asset's cost as an expense during each year of its useful life.

Of the several acceptable methods for calculating depreciation, the simplest is taking an equal amount every year for the asset's useful life, called the *straight-line* method. You may also use one of the *accelerated depreciation* methods, which book a higher expense in the earliest years an asset is held. Theoretically, accelerated depreciation has some appeal. As can be seen with new cars, the greatest drop in value comes in the first year or two of use. However, it is usually tax considerations, not theory, and the desire that write-offs be taken as soon as possible that drive choice of an accelerated method.

After you choose a depreciation method, the entry you make each accounting period simultaneously records an expense and reduces the asset's value with an entry to an account called *accumulated depreciation*. If your company buys a car for $20,000 and you choose to depreciate it over five years using the straight-line method, the entry each year will be $4,000 for depreciation expense and $4,000 for accumulated depreciation. At the end of five years, even though the car may remain in service, no further depreciation is taken.

Accumulated depreciation is a balance sheet account and the entry serves to reduce the company's assets. However, it does so, not by reducing the recorded value of the car, which remains at the historic cost of $20,000, but by creating what is called a *contra account*, which serves as an offset. Both the historic cost and the accumulated depreciation appear on the balance sheet—generally listed next to each other. So, together the $20,000 historic cost and the ($4,000) accumulated depreciation add up to a net book value of $16,000.

Amortization is similar to depreciation, but is applied to intangible assets such as patents. Unlike depreciation, amortization must be done using the straight-line method and no contra account is used. Rather, the asset account is reduced directly.

Inventory

In the previous example of the computer system, what if your company assembled the computer, rather than simply purchased the finished product? In this case, the cost of acquiring the computer would include all the materials used

Of the several acceptable methods for calculating depreciation, the simplest is taking an equal amount every year for the asset's useful life, called the straight-line method.

plus any labor. In addition, you would allocate to the cost of the computer a portion of any overhead expenses used in the assembly process.

Valuing inventory—whether for GAAP reporting, internal cost accounting, or taxes—is one of the most complex accounting topics. Chapter 8 addresses this subject in more depth. In general, GAAP reporting is mostly concerned with the valuing of inventory in total, rather than the unit cost of each item. In addition, GAAP requires that the entire cost of manufacturing be allocated to the inventory produced in a period and the expense recognized in the period the items are actually sold. This treatment is consistent with the matching principle.

Valuing inventory—whether for GAAP reporting, internal cost accounting, or taxes—is one of the most complex accounting topics.

Liabilities

Liabilities, another component of the balance sheet, are the future obligations of a company. (Refer to the sample balance sheet at the end of this chapter.) Unlike assets, which are generally valued at historic cost, the values of liabilities are based on the future payout expected. In addition, where gains on assets must generally be realized to be booked, liabilities can be recorded when expectations change and the amount of change can be reasonably measured.

This method of accounting for liabilities satisfies both the matching principle, ensuring that expenses are recorded when incurred rather than when paid, and, notably, the conservatism convention. The more aggressive approach to booking liabilities, relative to assets that are carried at historic cost or below, once again serves to prevent income from being overstated. More importantly, this helps protect investors from being blindsided by unreported or unexpected corporate obligations.

Estimating liabilities is not always a straightforward process. If, in the computer example, you bought the first computer on 30 days' credit, you would clearly have a liability, a trade payable, for $3,000. The transaction is complete at the time you receive the computer and the price and payment due date are clear.

Note that the computer has to be received before a liability is recorded. Though placing an order to buy the system may obligate a company to accept the computer, the transaction is not complete. Neither the buyer nor the seller has transferred any money or goods. However, if a future obligation or potential obligation not recorded as a liability is considered material, it may be required to be disclosed in a footnote.

A tricky and controversial issue is raised if the computer is leased rather than purchased. In general, rental agreements, whether for office space or equipment, are also considered unexecuted contracts and no obligation is recognized until payment is due. However, many leases are akin to installment purchases and the lease is essentially a financing vehicle. In these cases, GAAP accounting requires that the lease be treated as if there were two separate transactions: borrowing money, which creates a liability, and then using the proceeds to buy an asset. GAAP uses a complicated, four-point test for distinguishing between rentals and capital leases. (See the discussion of off-balance-sheet financing in Chapter 5.)

If your company sells the computer, again, no liability is booked when a customer places an order. However, if the customer puts down a deposit, a transaction has occurred. Because delivery has not been completed, the cash received cannot be treated as revenue. Instead, the deposit is treated as a liability, because you are now obligated to complete the transaction or return the money. Other types of prepayments made to you, such as for theater subscriptions, annual service contracts, and advance rent paid on property, are also liabilities. As services are actually delivered, the liability is reduced and revenue is recognized.

Selling the computer may create obligations to perform warranty work or accept returns. There is no way of telling if a particular machine will ever fail or exactly how much a repair may cost. However, if a reasonable estimate—normally based on history—can be made of what total future expenses will be, you must record it. Usually this is computed as a percentage of sales. An entry is made to both warranty expense and a liability account for warranty work payable. As the work is actually performed, the liability account is reduced. This accounting helps match the warranty expense to the sale that gave rise to it and fully discloses an expected, if undetermined, future expenditure.

What if a company is being sued, is threatened with a product recall, or has signed loan guarantees of another entity? These events also are potential future obligations, but whether they ever need to be paid is uncertain, contingent on future events. In general, these are not recorded as liabilities unless the future expense is deemed probable—which is not defined in GAAP, but in practice is likely close to 90%[4]—and the amount can be fairly estimated. If the potential obligation is material, a footnote disclosure may still be required.

Equity

The final component of the balance sheet is owner's equity. Equity is the sum of funds invested in the company by shareholders or partners, plus cumulative earnings, less any dividends that have been declared. Owner's equity equals the difference between a company's assets and liabilities. As such, net equity is also referred to as a company's *net worth* or *book value*. (See the balance sheet example in the sample financial statements at the end of this chapter.)

Equity is the sum of funds invested in the company by shareholders or partners, plus cumulative earnings, less any dividends that have been declared.

When new shares of stock are sold, equity increases. By convention, the actual entry is usually split into two pieces. The par value of the shares issued—the stated value of the stock—is booked to an account for either common or preferred stock. The par value is a minimal amount, such as $0.01, and has no relation to the market value of the shares. Any excess, which is usually the bulk of the proceeds, is recorded in another equity account, such as paid-in capital, reflecting the amount of capital paid in excess of the par value. This split is done even though the concept of par value has become nearly meaningless.

Accumulated income or losses make up retained earnings. Mechanically, entries are not normally made directly to the retained earnings account. Instead, they flow through the income statement. At year-end, when income statement accounts are reset to zero to start the new year, the difference between the revenue and expense accounts, which is net income, is closed out to the retained earnings account.

Earnings are often redistributed to owners through dividends. Cash dividends are not considered an expense, since they do not help generate revenue. Rather, dividends are a distribution of earnings and are recorded as a reduction of retained earnings.

A company sometimes chooses to issue stock dividends or declare stock splits. Though the number of shares outstanding increases, no cash is actually paid out and total equity is unchanged. However, accounting rules may require some shuffling between equity accounts.

Similarly, a company may buy back some of its stock with the intent to retire it or redistribute it, perhaps as part of an employee stock purchase plan. Without going through the mechanics, these entries also are not considered expenses and, other than the cash actually paid, only involve transfers between equity accounts.

Revenue and Expenses

So far, the discussion has centered on the balance sheet accounts, which provide the snapshot view of a company's financial assets, obligations, and capital. As mentioned earlier, the income statement summarizes the flow of activity during a fiscal period and shows revenue and expenses.

As seen above, decisions about entries to balance sheet accounts are inextricably linked to entries having an impact on the income statement. Most of the remaining issues in recognizing revenue and expenses have to do with questions of timing. At what point is a sale complete and what period's sales do expenses support?

Revenue

Basically, for revenue to be realized, delivery of goods or services has to be substantially complete and some measurable compensation has to be received. For most transactions, this comes at the point of sale when one of the following happens:

▶ Product is shipped.

▶ Service is complete.

▶ Sale of a security is executed.

For revenue to be realized, delivery of goods or services has to be substantially complete and some measurable compensation has to be received.

Simply having an order in hand is not sufficient. In addition, if a customer is entitled and is likely to return a product, such as when goods are sold on consignment, the sale should not be recognized.

One exception is when a company works on a long-term venture, such as a construction project, spanning several accounting periods. If progress and total costs for the project can be reasonably determined, a company can recognize revenue and expenses on a percentage-of-completion basis.

These calculations are independent of when cash is actually received. For example, a 25% up-front payment is not counted as revenue unless a proportionate amount of the total project expense has been incurred. In addition, if the last 20% of the project takes 80% of the cost, that portion of the project is also allocated 80% of the revenue.

Though rules for recognizing revenue may seem straightforward, accounting for revenue can get very involved and is highly scrutinized by auditors and investors. Slight changes in contract wording can alter when a sale can be booked, future obligations may require deferring revenue, and bundling several products or services into one deal may require significant work to justify how much revenue goes to each element. For more information, please see the sidebar on revenue recognition. Chapter 5 also includes some examples of companies that have abused revenue recognition principles.

Revenue Recognition

Revenue recognition is extremely complicated. Because of the likely scrutiny from auditors, investors, and potential acquirers, it is important to be aware of the issues and adhere strictly to the rules. It's also possible that a slight rewording of a sales contract can make a big difference in when revenue can be recognized. Be aware of these elements of revenue recognition:

▶ Can the customer cancel the sale, return product, or withhold payments? If so, the sale may not be complete until any contingencies are met.

▶ Is there a future deliverable, such as a software vendor promising a future upgrade or implementation services? Again, all or part of the sale may be deferred.

▶ Is there a future service obligation? Subscriptions, service contracts, and insurance policies might be paid for a year in advance. Revenue should be recognized in equal pieces over the life of the contract.

▶ If a donor makes a pledge to a nonprofit, is it in writing and is it irrevocable?

▶ Was the product shipped prior to the period cut-off? If terms are FOB destination, was it actually received? If a contract was involved, did both parties sign in time?

▶ Was the customer given some free future services or the option to buy additional products at a steep discount? If so, the fair value of these add-ons might need to be carved out of the purchase price and revenue recognition deferred.

▶ If the customer leases product, does the contract qualify as a capital lease or must it be accounted for as a rental?

▶ If a product is new so no track record exists to establish that it meets contract specifications, recognition may need to be deferred until the customer formally accepts the product or makes payment, even if all work is complete.

Expenses

Expenditures—any purchase or spending—generally are classified as either:

▶ Period expenses, recognized in the period they are incurred, or

▶ Costs with a future benefit, or assets.

In most cases, the distinction between expenses and assets is fairly straight-forward. Most expenditures for ongoing operating costs are period expenses. These would include wages, rent, supplies, travel, interest, and taxes. Purchases of physical items with a useful life exceeding one year and the payment of a refundable deposit would both be assets.

Expenditures that go toward intangibles can be harder to classify. Consider sales and marketing expenditures, including advertising. A strong argument can be made that these carry a significant future benefit. However, because of the difficulty in sorting out the present and future benefits and matching specific efforts to product sold, GAAP requires you to expense them in the period they are incurred.

General and administrative expenses are also period expenses, since they cannot be closely associated with product sold. But how about research and development expense? Unsuccessful R&D has little future value, but R&D that results in significant new products and patents enhances a company's value. Because of the uncertainty of the future value, these, too, are period expenses. However, as discussed earlier in the section about amortization, purchased patents are capitalized—treated as assets.

On the other hand, 100% of manufacturing expenses are added to the value of inventory and are expensed only when product is sold. Labor on projects started in one year, but not completed until the next, is also not expensed until the revenue is realized. In addition, expenditures made in constructing fixed assets, such as making leasehold improvements or building test equipment, are capitalized.

When relatively small dollar amounts are involved, the technical accounting rules can give way to expediency. For example, most companies establish dollar limits for capitalizing tangible assets. Rather than track every desk, phone, and chair that is bought, a company will decide to expense items costing less than a reasonable threshold, perhaps $500 or $1,000. In fact, with PCs becoming commodities, companies increasingly choose thresholds high enough so that most PCs are expensed. Also, companies receive many invoices, such as utility bills, that span more than one accounting period. Instead of breaking the costs out by period, the entire invoice is usually expensed in the current period. The amounts involved are not usually material and, because a bill is received every month, any discrepancies balance out over time.

Special Issues

So far, the discussion has covered how financial accounting principles are applied to everyday business transactions. However, not all business transactions are routine. Two such issues—errors and consolidations—are discussed below.

Errors

Sometimes errors occur in preparing financial statements and are not discovered until after a period has been closed. An invoice may be overlooked, the bad debt reserve may turn out to be too low, damages might be assessed on an old lawsuit that had not been accrued for, or some figures may simply have been added up wrong. Should you go back and correct financial statements from prior periods or take your lumps in the current period?

In general, GAAP calls for correcting errors in the period they are discovered. Companies rarely restate prior years' statements. You should do the same with monthly statements. Once a month is closed, don't reopen it, especially once statements have been distributed to investors or other outsiders. If amounts related to prior periods are considered material, they are disclosed in the footnotes.

Consolidated Statements

Many companies, large and small, operate several separate legal organizations under common ownership and control. When one company owns more than 50% of another, the parent company will generally prepare a consolidated set of financial statements.

Separate financial statements of each subsidiary are still important, but the consolidated statement is needed to properly present the performance of the entire entity.

In general, a consolidated statement is simply the sum of the separate statements. However, the impact of any transactions between or among the commonly owned companies must be eliminated.

For example, if one subsidiary sells to another, it records the sale on its books. From the corporate viewpoint, though, the item only transferred from one pocket to another and no revenue or profit was really created. Therefore, the intercompany sale gets offset as part of the consolidation process, so only sales to independent entities are included in the consolidated sales number. This prevents a company from inflating revenue by generating sales transactions between companies it controls.

Similar adjustments are made for any intercompany receivables, payables, and profit.

Even where a parent company owns less than 100%, a subsidiary's results are fully consolidated. However, the portion of profit and net worth belonging to minority owners, allocated as a percentage of stock they hold, is listed separately.

More Art than Science

More advanced accounting deals with how to handle the complications—seemingly endless—that can arise in business transactions. The theory, though, remains fairly consistent throughout. An understanding of the basic principles of accounting presented here not only covers most transactions seen in a smaller business, but also provides the essence for understanding even advanced topics.

Double-entry bookkeeping has a certain elegance and GAAP standards help ensure consistency across companies. Nonetheless, accounting remains more art than science.

This chapter has discussed the theories and practices your accountant follows. The next chapter deals with the basic recording of the day-to-day information about your business.

More advanced accounting deals with how to handle the complications—seemingly endless—that can arise in business transactions.

Interpreting Financial Statements

This exhibit shows sample financial statements for a fictitious company. Here are some tips on what to look for when reading these statements:

▶ The first observation is that net income has jumped 78% or just over $1 million. Gross margin increased from 34.6% to 37.3%, so that even though sales rose 9%, gross profit jumped $2.5 million or 17.2%.

▶ Operating expenses stayed roughly the same percentage of sales, confirming that improved cost of sales margins were the main profit driver.

- Though net income was $2.45 million, cash increased only $1.85 million. One concern is that inventory rose more than $1 million and turns (cost of sales divided by inventory) decreased from 3.6 to 3.3. This raises questions about both the level of inventory and the validity of the lower cost of sales figure. For example, if some excess inventory exists, added write-offs would increase cost of sales.
- Accounts receivable rose $400,000, creating a use of cash. However, as a percent of sales, receivables stayed flat at 10.9%, indicating no new management issues.
- The company entered into a significant capital lease arrangement, evident by the jump in Land and Buildings (an asset) and Capital Lease liabilities. More information is available in footnote 4.
- The effective tax rate dropped from 41.5% to 36.2%. Accrued taxes dropped $280,000 or 34%. Footnote 6 provides additional information on taxes, but does not fully explain the reason for the declines.
- Other accrued expenses increased more than the rate of sales, a good sign that the company is not shaving accruals to show higher income.
- Common stock and paid-in capital are unchanged, indicating no new equity was raised during the year.

Balance Sheet XYZ Corporation Year Ended December 31		
Assets	**2004**	**2003**
Current Assets		
Cash and equivalents	$6,908,026	$8,756,427
Marketable securities	2,525,309	0
Accounts receivable	4,992,962	4,586,079
Inventories	8,602,173	7,583,095
Prepaid Expenses	901,968	634,380
Total Current Assets	23,930,438	21,559,981
Property, Plant, and Equipment		
Leased land and buildings	7,153,896	4,367,591
Leasehold improvements	3,105,954	3,098,496
Machinery and equipment	10,093,714	9,402,344
Construction in progress	83,698	110,453

(Continued on next page)

Balance Sheet
XYZ Corporation
Year Ended December 31 (continued)

Assets	2004	2003
Subtotal Property, Plant, and Equipt.	20,437,262	16,978,884
Less: Accumulated Depreciation	(11,869,714)	(10,614,599)
Total Property, Plant, and Equipt.	8,567,548	6,364,285
Deferred Charges		
Income Taxes	861,997	919,378
Other	189,929	21,152
Total Deferred Charges	1,051,926	940,530
Total Assets	**33,852,682**	**29,188,896**

Liabilities and Equity	2004	2003
Current Liabilities		
Accounts Payable	1,007,034	938,972
Accrued Wages and Benefits	1,181,373	1,016,614
Accrued Taxes	542,311	821,149
Accrued Dealer Incentive	1,050,000	760,422
Accrued Warranty Expenses	485,170	444,790
Other Accrued Expenses	763,891	609,488
Current Portion of Long-Term		
Debt	666,118	843,098
Total Current Liabilities	5,695,897	5,434,533
Capital Lease Obligation	4,743,801	2,499,200
Long-Term Debt, Net of Current		
Portion	630,000	945,000
Shareholders' Equity		
Common Stock	13,553,890	13,553,890
Additional Paid-in Capital	1,604,184	1,604,184
Retained Earnings	13,048,115	10,595,039
Less: Treasury Stock	(5,423,105)	(5,443,250)
Total Shareholders' Equity	22,783,084	20,309,863
Total Liabilities and Equity	**33,852,782**	**29,188,596**

Income Statement XYZ Corporation Year Ended December 31		
	2004	**2003**
Net Sales	$45,812,436	$42,156,980
Cost of Sales	28,712,589	27,565,874
Gross Margin	17,099,847	14,591,106
Other Operating Expenses		
Sales and Marketing	5,897,421	5,401,723
Research and Development	684,597	542,136
General and Administrative	6,452,141	6,021,458
Allowance for Doubtful Accounts	84,000	66,000
Total Other Operating Expenses	13,118,159	12,031,317
Other Income (Expenses)		
Interest	(175,842)	(178,650)
Gain on Disposal of Assets	46,054	25,401
Lost on Discontinued Operations	0	(50,000)
Total Other Income (Expenses)	(129,788)	(203,249)
Income Before Taxes	3,851,900	2,356,540
Income Taxes	1,395,624	978,524
Net Income	2,456,276	1,378,016
Earnings per Share	$1.13	$0.65

Statement of Cash Flows
XYZ Corporation
Year Ended December 31, 2004

Operating Activities	
Net Income	$2,456,276
Adjustments to reconcile net income to net cash provided by operating activities	
Depreciation and Amortization	1,697,966
Deferred Income Taxes	57,381
Provision for Doubtful Accounts	84,000
Gain on Disposal of Assets	(46,054)
Changes in Operating Assets and Liabilities	(406,867)
Receivables	(1,019,094)
Inventories	(465,163)
Prepaid Expenses and Other Assets	68,062
Accounts Payable	193,302
Accrued Expenses and Other Payables	2,619,809
Investing Activities	
Property and equipment purchases	(1,044,904)
Proceeds from sale of assets	39,729
Investment in marketable securities	(2,429,351)
Net cash provided (used) in investing activities	(3,434,526)
Financing Activities	
Principal payments on capital leases	(823,684)
Principal payments on long-term debt	(210,000)
Net cash provided (used) in financing activities	(1,033,684)
Increase (Decrease) in Cash and Equivalents	(1,848,401)
Cash and Equivalents at Beginning of Year	8,756,427
Cash and Equivalents at End of Year	6,908,026

Financial Statements—Sample Notes
Notes to Financial Statements
XYZ Corporation
December 31, 2004

1. Significant Accounting Policies

Recognition of Revenue: Revenue is recognized at the time a customer order is shipped.

Cash Equivalents: The Company considers all highly liquid investments with a maturity of three months or less when purchased to be cash equivalents.

Marketable Securities: The investment in marketable securities is recorded at cost, which approximates fair market value.

Inventories: Inventories are stated at the lower of cost or market using the first in, first out (FIFO) method.

Property, Plant, and Equipment: Property, Plant, and Equipment are stated at cost. Depreciation and amortization are computed using the straight-line method over the estimated useful lives of the assets. Lease amortization is included in depreciation expense.

Federal Income Taxes: The Company provides for deferred income taxes applicable to timing differences in the recognition of certain items of income and expense for tax and financial statement purposes.

2. Inventories

Inventories at December 31, 2004 consisted of the following:

Finished goods	$4,012,570
Work in process	1,245,855
Raw materials	3,343,748

3. Debt Arrangements

Long-term debt consists of a note from First State Bank. The note bears interest at a rate of 90% of prime rate, which resulted in a rate of 3.60% at December 31, 2004. All property, plant, and equipment are pledged as collateral under the terms of the loan agreement.

4. Leases

The Company has a capital lease for land and building from Realty Associates. The lease expires June 30, 2012, and the company has an option to purchase the property at fair market value as determined by appraisal or renew the lease for an additional 10-year period.

Future minimum lease payments under the capital lease and noncancelable operating leases consisted of the following at December 31, 2004:

	Capital Lease	Operating Lease
2005	$1,000,000	$117,000
2006	1,000,000	41,000
2007	1,000,000	6,400
2008	1,000,000	0
Thereafter	4,657,700	0
Total	$8,657,700	$164,000

Amounts representing interest   3,264,224

5. Related Party Transactions

The Company has a management consulting service agreement with ABC Associates, a firm owned by a certain stockholder of the Company. Payments to ABC of $65,000 and $50,000 were made in 2004 and 2003, respectively.

6. Income Taxes

Income tax expense differed from that computed on income before taxes at the current statutory federal income rate as follows:

	2004	2003
Statutory federal income taxes	$1,130,695	$819,323
State income taxes	231,114	152,935
nondeductible business expenses	42,455	11,687
Other	(8,640)	(5,421)
	$1,395,624	$978,524

Components of income tax expense are as follows:

	2004	2003
Current		
Federal	$1,185,262	$794,258
State	236,989	157,541
	1,422,251	951,799
Deferred		
Capital lease	9,658	8,740
Accelerated depreciation	(45,781)	(69,655)
Vacation and bonus pay	(21,779)	(18,253)
Other	2,605	11,053
	(55,297)	(68,115)
Total (current and deferred)	**1,366,954**	**883,684**

The Company made income tax payments of $1,452,247 and $901,865 in 2004 and 2003, respectively.

7. Export Sales

Export sales were approximately 15% and 14% of the Company's gross sales for 2004 and 2003 respectively.

Notes

1. Herbert J. Muller, *The Uses of the Past: Profiles of Former Societies* (New York: Oxford University Press, 1952), quoted in Robert W. Kent, ed., *Money Talks: The 2500 Greatest Business Quotes from Aristotle to Delorean* (New York: Facts on File, 1985), p. 43.

2. It is possible for an asset to have a negative or credit balance. One example is if a company uses float in its bank account to write checks for more than what has been deposited. Rather than being printed on the right side of the balance sheet, the account remains listed on the left, but with a negative balance.

3. This calculation can be done in aggregate, not item by item. For example, if a few marketable securities drop in value but the entire portfolio's value rises, no entry is made.

4. Sidney Davidson, Clyde P. Stickney, and Roman L. Weil, *Intermediate Accounting* (Hinsdale, IL: Dryden Press, 1980), p. 15-4.

Debit | Credit

Chapter 4

Accounting Workflow

The higher mind has no need to concern itself with the meticulous regimentation of figures.

—Winston Churchill[1]

The Accounting Flow

YOU MAY THINK THAT MOST ACCOUNTING IS DONE AT THE END OF a period when your accountant sits down to record adjustments, allocations, and accruals needed to prepare financial statements. However, most accounting data is gathered in a daily stream of routine, repetitive transactions.

Every time you pay a bill, write an invoice, or issue payroll checks, you generate an accounting transaction. The quality and integrity of information in your accounting system is derived from day-to-day processing.

An accounting system should mirror the natural flow of activity in a business. For example, a customer order moves from a salesperson to fulfillment, invoicing, collections, and customer service. At each step, transactions are generated. These flow through the accounting system, allowing each department to have current information about the order while simultaneously updating financial records.

At the end of an accounting period, the routine does get interrupted so that financial statements can be produced. Cutoffs are observed, accrual entries are made, and inventories may be taken to ensure that revenues and expenses are booked to the proper period. But, just as the work of the company doesn't stop, the day-to-day routine of the accounting system quickly resumes. This chapter discusses how the daily information from your business is collected and summarized. Topics discussed include:

▶ General and subsidiary ledgers;

▶ Month-end closing cycles and procedures; and

▶ Year-end closing procedures, including audits.

A critical, but often missed, first step to having numbers by which to manage is making sure the right information is collected.

A critical, but often missed, first step to having numbers by which to manage is making sure the right information is collected. By choosing the right chart of accounts, you can develop a versatile account structure that provides you with the right information. After you have determined the kinds of information you need, you will then want to establish when you should receive it.

In addition to supplementing the knowledge you've gained about financial accounting in the previous chapters, this chapter will show you how to overcome the roadblocks to getting accurate and timely inputs.

The General Ledger

The heart of the accounting system is the general ledger (G/L), as illustrated by the flowchart at the top of the next page. A ledger is simply a group of accounts listed in an organized fashion. The accounts that make up the G/L, collectively referred to as the *chart of accounts*, are used to produce the financial statements of a business.

The G/L is the highest summary level of financial information. Detail supporting the numbers is supplied and maintained by subsidiary ledgers or records. For example:

▶ The actual detail on unpaid customer invoices is tracked by an accounts receivable (A/R) system. Transactions summarizing A/R activity are posted to the G/L. If you compare your accounts receivable aging report with the G/L, the total of outstanding invoices should match the

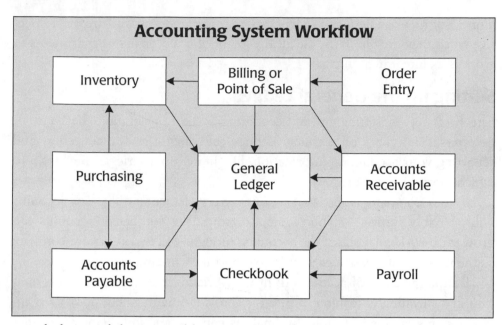

balance of the receivables account on the G/L.

▶ All checks are recorded in a register. During the month, the activity is summarized and posted to the G/L. Bank reconciliations ensure that the cash balance on the G/L is accurate.

▶ Purchases and shipments of inventory are posted to the G/L through purchasing and billing transactions. Either through a perpetual inventory tracking system or periodic physical counts, the value of stock on hand is compared with the G/L total.

Except for very small companies, there are usually distinct functions, even departments, for billing, payables, payroll, and inventory control. Each has independent routines and reports that can seem autonomous, but they actually form a network of activity. Each takes information from other areas, generates additional transactions, and then shares the results with other departments and the general ledger.

If you have shopped for accounting software, you will recognize how the modules in the software mirror the workings of an accounting department, with modules for payables, billing, G/L, inventory, and payroll. Even all-in-one accounting software will have separate data entry windows, reports, and lists for these functions.

Not all companies will need each function and many modules can stand

Except for very small companies, there are usually distinct functions, even departments, for billing, payables, payroll, and inventory control.

alone. But they are designed to work as an integrated unit and are most effective when they do. Similarly, the ideal way for your company's departments to work is as integrated units.

Setting up the General Ledger

The first step in setting up an accounting system is defining the chart of accounts. The chart of accounts defines the categories for collecting and reporting your accounting information, like lining up a series of buckets into which information is dropped.

The chart of accounts defines the categories for collecting and reporting your accounting information, like lining up a series of buckets into which information is dropped.

If your company is just starting out, a very elementary chart of accounts will probably suffice. As your company grows, the number of accounts can grow with it. The layout of the accounts, though, will become more complex as the number of departments and the reporting structure change.

Define the chart of accounts to fit your organization and report information in a meaningful fashion. If information is too aggregated, poorly organized, or misclassified, meaningful analysis can become impossible. Consider the following example:

A jewelry maker operated three distinct businesses under one roof. One business manufactured colorful beads, pins, and earrings; the primary value added for these products was the labor-intensive painting process. The second business had a line of pins and earrings that used purchased metals and stones, doing only polishing and packaging in-house. The third business was an independent subsidiary in a corner of the plant; this subsidiary shared some of the labor, but none of the materials.

Unfortunately, the company had an overly simple chart of accounts: single accounts for sales, purchases, and labor. This structure was adequate for GAAP reporting, which only requires that aggregate sales and expense information be reported. But trying to analyze what each line of business contributed to net income was impossible. The information was so mingled that sales and costs could not be broken down by product line. When the company fell on hard times, it was impossible to accurately say which, if any, of the product lines was profitable.

Defining your accounts is only part of the battle. Once the structure is in place, data has to be put in the right buckets.

One of the best techniques for coding expenses is to push as much as possible out to department heads and line managers and not leave it all to accounting. The advantage of this tactic is that many expenditures may be foreign to the accounting clerk being asked to make an entry. For example, a supplier invoice may only say that you bought part number XYZ-60. Was this a raw material or a supply? Was it used in manufacturing or in new product development? An accounting clerk can take a guess, but the person ordering the item will know for sure.

While some managers may resist the added clerical task, others will recognize that it serves their own interests. They want to know how to better manage their departments and may be evaluated on performance versus budget. Not only do they want accurate information on how money is being spent, but assurances that expenses for other departments aren't being billed to them by mistake.

Requiring managers to include the accounting code on purchase orders for items and services will greatly assist your accounting department. When the invoice and purchase order are matched, the accounting clerk can see the proper coding. If no purchase order exists, have the appropriate manager approve the invoice and indicate the proper coding at that time. You or your controller should review all coding, as a routine procedure, when reviewing vouchers prepared for payment or when signing checks.

Requiring managers to include the accounting code on purchase orders for items and services will greatly assist your accounting department.

Chart of Accounts

Defining your chart of accounts is generally the first major step in setting up an accounting system. This is a key step that requires some advance planning, as your account layout should fit your company's structure and reporting needs. Since the setup comes before you have processed transactions or seen any reports, the process can seem daunting, but it doesn't need to be.

A sample, located at the end of this chapter, shows a basic chart of accounts. While assigning account numbers is as much art as science, the basic numbering convention illustrated is fairly standard. Assets, liabilities, equity, sales, cost of sales, and operating expenses are grouped and numbered in distinct sequences: assets start with "1," liabilities with "2," and so on. Note that this sequence corresponds to the typical order in which the balances are presented on the financial statements. If your company is just starting out, you may be satisfied with a chart of accounts very close to this.

Accounts are often structured in a hierarchy. Usually, only the lowest level of accounts—often called *sub-*, *posting*, or *child* accounts—can have transactions posted to them. Their balances are consolidated and summed into various higher-level accounts—often termed *parent* or *summary* accounts. In the sample chart of accounts, for example, the balance in the raw materials account is aggregated into inventory, then into current assets, and finally into total assets.

The length and structure of account numbers vary by company. Many companies find four-digit numbers adequate, while others have numbers more than 10 digits long or may even vary the length from account to account. Some companies segment the number to contain distinct department or company codes. While account numbers are easier to remember when there is some logic to the numbering and digits have consistent definitions from category to category, it is not a requirement.

Your software package will probably impose some constraints. The length of the numbers may be defined and certain digits or segments may take on specific meanings—such as department codes. Don't get locked into an inadequate numbering scheme. Decide on your account structure first, and then select a software package that can handle it. Some accounting packages, such as QuickBooks™, have eliminated the need for account numbers provided each account has a unique name. However, they still group accounts by asset, liability, expense, and so on.

Most software packages also come with sample or default charts of accounts. Although using the sample charts provides a shortcut to getting started, resist the urge to use these as is. Take the time to tailor an appropriate account structure, either by starting from scratch or by editing one of the samples provided. Be sure to do this before posting any transactions, since it can be difficult to delete or rearrange accounts that have activity posted to them.

Take the time to tailor an appropriate account structure, either by starting from scratch or by editing one of the samples provided.

Technical Tips

A basic philosophy in setting up a chart of accounts is to define as many accounts as you want as long as they have distinct meaning to you. For instance:

▶ Should advertising and promotion be separate accounts?

▶ What about travel and entertainment?

▶ Is it useful to distinguish sales by product line?

▶ How about by territory?

▶ Should personnel, payroll, and accounting be separate departments?

If the differences have meaning to you, or you think they might in the future, then set up additional accounts.

Your accounts should be sufficiently detailed to allow reporting by each significant entity. For example, if you need profit information by product line and by territory, create as many detail accounts as you need. However, you do not need to duplicate details that can be obtained via your billing, payroll, and payables systems. For example, sales information by salesperson or customer can usually be pulled from your billing system; they do not have to be separate general ledger accounts. In addition, tax laws may influence your choice of some accounts. For example, tax laws treat meal and entertainment expenses differently from other travel costs. Separating these expenses up front can save work at year-end.

When setting up your accounts, a little imagination can give you a way to capture some extra views of your data. If it is important to know how much inventory is purchased each month, do not book both inventory coming in and inventory going out to the same account. If a manufacturing company, for example, has just a single raw materials account, all issues and receipts get mixed in together during a month. In this case, if you want to know how much was purchased, you cannot determine it quickly. However, you can easily have this information by setting up a structure similar to the following:

When setting up your accounts, a little imagination can give you a way to capture some extra views of your data.

Account #	Account Description
1300	Purchases
1301	Offset to purchases
1310	Raw materials

Each purchase is debited to the purchases account; all deductions are charged to the raw materials account. At month-end, the offset account (1301) is credited for the monthly balance in the purchases account and the raw materials account debited. Accounts 1300 and 1301 net to zero but you know your purchases for the month just by looking at the 1300 account.

You can use a similar scheme to capture expenses for employee benefits. What if you want to know the totals spent for health insurance or FICA, but still be able to bill each department its share? Rather than divide each bill as it comes in or throw all costs into one operating department, set up a department to just capture each individual benefit expense, such as:

Account #	Account Description
7500	FICA
7510	FUTA
7520	Health insurance
7599	Offset to employee benefits

At month-end, if the total in accounts 7500-7520 is $1,000, make an entry for $1,000 in the offset account (a credit) and allocate the expense to your operating departments (a debit). The benefits department now has a net of zero, but each line item is intact, so you can see at a glance just what was spent on health insurance or FICA. The same scheme works for expenses related to occupancy. Accumulate rent, insurance, and utility expenses in their own accounts before doing allocations.

Journal Entries

Take the time to tailor an appropriate account structure, either by starting from scratch or by editing one of the samples provided.

While most data comes to the general ledger through subsidiary ledgers, some adjustments are posted directly to the G/L with journal entries. These are typically adjustments made at month- or year-end and not routine transactions like those discussed above.

Here are some examples of where journal entries are used:

▶ Correcting an error, such as a purchase posted to the wrong expense account;

▶ Recording monthly depreciation and amortization expense;

▶ Establishing a bad debt or inventory reserve; or

▶ Accruals (discussed in the next section).

In addition to preparing journal entries, like those above, your monthly and year-end closings include a number of important routines and procedures to ensure that information is captured in the proper periods. You will also want to make sure that you receive financial statements on a timely basis. The next section discusses these period-end procedures.

Closings

Most companies close their books on a regular basis, producing annual and either monthly or quarterly financial statements. Part of the closing process is ensuring that expenses and revenues are booked in the proper period, requiring some modification of the day-to-day processes.

First, proper cutoffs must be established with a strict line between transactions that take place on the 31st and those on the 1st of the next month. You have to watch out for transactions processed in one fiscal period that actually relate to another. For example, goods shipped December 31 are generally considered December revenue even if invoiced on January 2. Or, you might pay January's rent during the month of December.

Accruals

To ensure that entries are posted to the correct month, an accountant will book a series of accrual journal entries. An accrual is an entry that records increases or decreases to revenue or expense, even though no cash transaction has occurred. The accountant analyzes actual and anticipated transactions and makes any needed adjustments. Some typical accruals include the following:

- ▶ Sales commissions, earned on the current month's revenues, but usually not paid until the following month;

- ▶ Liability for payroll taxes and employee benefits that are incurred when wages are earned, but may not be paid right away; or

- ▶ Property taxes, service contracts, and insurance that may be billed quarterly or annually, but should be allocated equally to each month's statements.

There is no need to finish one month's payables and receivables processing before starting the next unless your software requires it, which is true of some older packages.

There is no need to finish one month's payables and receivables processing before starting the next unless your software requires it, which is true of some older packages. If you do need to close one month before starting another, holding the old month open for three to four days is enough time for most bills to arrive. Bills received after the cutoff date for payables can be accrued on a journal entry.

Expense and revenue accruals are best done using reversing entries. If you accrue an expense one month and reverse the entry the next, the reversal creates a negative expense that is exactly offset once the invoice is processed by accounts payable. The result is that, while accounts payable processed the transaction routinely in the second month, the expense is recorded in the first.

For items like utility bills that recur monthly for about the same amount, a simple approach is to record them the month they come in. Even though these bills usually cover the prior month, it is more important that one electric bill get entered each month than to precisely allocate usage to the proper month.

In recording expenses, timing issues are among the most common sources of errors in the financial statements of smaller companies. One quick method for detecting omissions or overstatements is to compare total expenses for a month side by side against prior months or the year-to-date balances. If two rent payments slip into the same month or no electric bill was booked, there will be a readily apparent swing. This type of trend analysis is also one of the best ways for you to spot unusual expenses, shifts in performance, or changes in accounting. A good practice is to question any significant changes, so you understand whether changes are permanent or temporary. In turn, you can also explain them to investors.

Smoothing, Spreading, and Estimating

Many accrual entries are made to spread large expenses evenly over several months, rather than taking an unusually big hit the month a bill arrives.

Many accrual entries are made to spread large expenses evenly over several months, rather than taking an unusually big hit the month a bill arrives. For example, annual expenses, such as legal, audit, and insurance can often be estimated, but the bills may roll in irregularly. To smooth their impact, many companies choose to book a flat expense each month. As the actual bills come in, no additional expense is booked. This is accomplished with entries to a balance sheet account, which is debited when a bill is received and credited when the monthly or quarterly expense is booked. Periodically, actual bills should be compared with the estimated annual total and the estimate revised, if needed.

Finally, a lot of numbers must simply be estimated. Accruals should be made regularly to allow for taxes, sales returns, bad debts, and inventory write-downs. You have to make a choice of how aggressive or conservative to be as a range of reasonable estimates is usually possible.

Closing Cycle

Whether your company is large or small, closing your books should be completed within five to 10 business days from the end of the month or quarter. At year-end, this may take longer, due to the added precision that is often desired. At that time, a preliminary close within the usual five to 10 days and either a final close or the start of an audit within four to five weeks are good targets.

Any precision gained by taking longer than five to 10 days at month- or quarter-end usually isn't worth letting the statements get stale. If anything, a number of companies choose to go in the other direction, closing their books in fewer than five days. This sacrifices some precision in order to get information faster and eliminates much of the added effort of a rigorous period closing. For example, if the deadline for posting June transactions is July 1, a fair number of vendor invoices related to June expenses will arrive after the cutoff. However, since the same pattern will likely occur each month, the impact of transactions being deferred from June to July will be roughly offset by those deferred from May to June. Provided monthly swings are fairly minor, this type of accelerated closing may be satisfactory.

Regardless of the timing, establish a regular closing schedule in order to keep the closing on track. A sample 10-day schedule for a company with subsidiary units to consolidate is shown below.

Typical Monthly or Quarterly Closing Schedule

At the end of the month or quarter, send all shipping documents to billing and send all receiving documents to accounts payable. Close checkbooks and complete all entries affecting cash.

Day 1—Complete all billing. Run final receivables reports. Run sales reports. Begin processing new period.

Day 3—Cut off payables entry. Run final payables reports.

Day 4—Accrue payroll expense for days unpaid at month-end. Accrue commissions.

Day 5—Deadline for submission of sales and expense figures from subsidiaries.

Day 7—Final close. Print all reports. Begin preparing financial analysis, such as variance reports and updates of budget to actual.

Day 10—Deadline for submitting statements and supporting schedules to management committee.

The closing schedule should include procedures for each department. Each will have a deadline for cutting off transactions, reconciliations and cross-checks to perform, and a list of reports to run.

If you do find it taking longer than five to 10 days to close, at least report on key indicators earlier than that. If you know things like sales, bookings, headcount, receivables aging, and cash balances, you should have a strong feel for financial results even without final accounting statements.

Day-to-Day Cutoffs

Cutoff and closing issues apply to day-to-day processing as well. In many companies, the most important information provided by the accounting system is not in financial statements, but statistics needed to run the company every day, such as the number of an item in stock or the amount of a customer's balance. The need for this information creates its own demands for accuracy and timeliness that cannot be met by an accountant's journal entry.

For systems to work, users need to understand that if they make information demands on a system, they must be prepared to input data on a timely basis.

For systems to work, users need to understand that if they make information demands on a system, they must be prepared to input data on a timely basis. Consider the following example:

At one used car dealership with more than 30 locations, salespeople had the ability to see the inventory on hand at all the other lots. This included cost information critical for setting resale prices. When a car was added to stock, it usually needed servicing before being sold. The service expenditures were added into the cost of the car. The accounting department promised same-day turnaround on processing paperwork so that the cost figures online would always be up to date.

Problems arose when the service department allowed paperwork to stack up and did not submit it to accounting. A car would be sold for what seemed like an $800 margin—and then a $400 repair bill would float into accounting after the sale. Not only was the car priced too low, but the salesperson found out after the fact that his or her commission was halved. Even though the service department was responsible, accounting got the blame.

Sometimes getting cooperation requires a careful explanation of how the pieces fit together. The following example illustrates how a careful explanation can pay off.

At the same car dealership, there was a clerk who made numerous inaccurate entries and failed to understand why these errors were important. Rather than fire the clerk, the CFO sat down one day and asked the clerk to figure out how much inventory of a particular new car model to order for the next two months. First, the employee realized some sales history was needed to predict future sales—information that came from an accounting report. The next step was to see how many cars of that model were on hand. At this point, the clerk said, "Hold on. I have to make a few adjustments first." It turned out the prior day's incoming shipment had not been entered yet and the report was five cars short. The clerk realized that, without the updated figures, the company would have over-bought. Suddenly, the importance of the clerk's job was apparent.

If reports are unreliable or not timely, people stop using them and may start inventing personal systems, as shown in the next story.

At an apparel manufacturer, the production manager stopped using daily computer reports and started keeping manual notebooks to plan each day's production. The reason was that the manager planned production at the start of the day at 6:00 a.m. Accounting, though, collected the prior day's production reports at the end of each day and didn't start processing them until the staff came to work at 7:00 a.m. Updates on the computer system were available only in mid-morning, too late for the production manager.

The problem was corrected by collecting production reports by 2:00 each afternoon, so data entry could be finished by 5:00 p.m. Because of the earlier cutoff time, reports were on the production manager's desk at the beginning of the day.

People responsible for data entry must also understand the context of their entries and the materiality of any problems. A $400 error may be inconsequential to a financial statement, but a $400 error entering the cost of a used car could result in setting the resale price too low, costing the dealer money. Over time, these errors can add up, particularly if the source of errors isn't found and corrected.

Fiscal Periods

Along with daily and monthly cutoffs, a company must choose a fiscal year. Most opt for a calendar year, since this is the simplest to think about and the easiest to coordinate with payroll tax filings. However, it isn't necessary to report on a calendar year for either financial reporting or income taxes. Many companies select fiscal years that align with the anniversary of their founding or they time their year-end to match the seasonality of their business. For example, many retailers choose a January 31 year-end to allow completion of the holiday season.

You also have a choice over how you define fiscal months. Though most companies use calendar months, others prefer to always have a fiscal month end on Saturday. They accomplish this either by dividing each quarter into two four-week months plus a five-week month (4-4-5) or, less commonly, by dividing the year into 13 four-week months. Note that because each normal year only has 364 days under these schemes, every few years a fiscal year will have a 53rd week added to it so that year-end remains the Saturday closest to the last day of the fiscal year.

GAAP requires that financial statements be prepared on an annual basis; public companies generally must file quarterly statements as well. Otherwise, you have some freedom on when and how often interim statements are prepared. Whether you close quarterly or monthly depends on your need for information or investors' demands for reports. One ski mountain operation used weekly closes to stay on top of operations.

Open Book Management

Should financial results be shared with employees? Many business owners and managers consider this information, particularly how it relates to money taken out of a business in salary or distributions, highly confidential. Others worry that this information could land in the hands of competitors, be used against them to demand raises, or be beyond what employees can understand. However, others swear by the benefits of having their employees understand cost drivers and the overall financial picture.

In the book, *The Great Game of Business*,[2] author Jack Stack credits the turnaround of his company, Springfield Remanufacturing Company, to engaging all employees in improving results. This included giving employees both a voice in how the company was run and a stake in the results. Sharing financial data and educating employees in underlying cost drivers were central to this approach.

Advantages to sharing information include the ability to set a common and known set of financial goals and track progress against those goals. In addition, employees often hold misconceptions about what it costs to run a business, how profitable a company is, and what managers take out in pay. Sharing financial data can dispel some myths. Shared financials can also be a tool toward team building and encouraging employee input into improving operations. Information can help employees make better decisions and understand what a company can afford for bonuses or pay raises.

Educating employees is key to an effective open-book program. Most people won't understand accounting numbers without training or, worse, they may misinterpret information. Simplifying the numbers, focusing on major cost categories, and holding regular meetings or classes can help ensure comprehension. If sharing financials would allow employees to discern sensitive information such as management compensation, consider withholding or hiding some of the numbers.

Year-End Procedures

Fiscal year-end is sort of a grand finale to the accounting cycle. At this time, the books get their greatest scrutiny and additional steps are taken to ensure their accuracy. The fiscal year-end also places the greatest workload of the year on the accounting department.

Part of the work may be an audit or review by an independent CPA, as discussed in Chapter 2. Companies with outside investors are usually required to submit to an annual audit or review by outside CPAs. Knowing what is involved can help your company prepare and may even lower your audit fees.

An audit is not an adversarial process. Remember that the auditors are hired to provide assurance to you, your management, and investors that the financial statements have been prepared fairly and consistently and are reliable. Auditors often provide useful feedback on internal controls and interpretation of the numbers.

Fiscal year-end is sort of a grand finale to the accounting cycle. At this time, the books get their greatest scrutiny and additional steps are taken to ensure their accuracy.

The objective of an audit is not 100% accuracy, but to ensure that financial statements are not materially misstated, meaning an auditor can work with a statistical sampling of data. The size of the sample is basically a function of the level of confidence the auditor has in the internal controls of the company and the magnitude of any discrepancies found. Typical items tested include:

▶ **Cash**—Ensure company records are reconciled to bank statements.

▶ **Receivables**—Request a confirmation of selected account balances shown on the company's aging directly from the customers.

▶ **Inventory and fixed assets**—Observe and test counts performed by the company.

▶ **Payables**—Review the aging, as well as payments, made several weeks beyond year-end.

▶ **Loans and leases**—Request confirmation of balances and terms directly from the lender.

▶ **Capital stock**—Match to legal records.

Where documentation is requested from outside parties, the auditors will insist that all correspondence be addressed directly to them, to ensure the integrity of the responses. You will be asked to assist in requesting responses and in following up after any delinquent replies. You will also be asked for a written representation letter, signed by either you or your top financial manager, covering a wide range of financial and operating issues relevant to forming the audit opinion.

The auditors will also ask any questions needed to comply with full disclosure or to deal with uncertainties and contingencies. These include possible lawsuits or other contingent liabilities, future obligations under contracts and leases, outstanding stock options or warrants, and any possible concerns to be resolved about the company's viability.

Audit Techniques

Audits are biased toward detecting possible overstatement of net income and net worth rather than understatement. The reason for this is mainly because financial reporting serves the needs of investors who are more concerned about inflated instead of understated earnings. Another factor that shapes audit procedures is the use of outside parties. Vendors and customers from whom confirming data is sought have an incentive to report information in a manner consistent with their self-interest.

Audits are biased toward detecting possible overstatement of net income and net worth rather than understatement.

For example, confirmation letters are sent for receivables balances, but not payables. Management has little incentive to understate receivables and is more likely to want to overstate them—and therefore show higher sales and assets. In contrast, a customer is almost sure to point out any overstatement of amounts owed on a confirmation—but may keep quiet if invoices are omitted. The confirmation letters, therefore, can detect inflated receivables, but cannot be relied on to catch understatements.

For payables, the primary concern is that a company will understate them. Invoices may be omitted, and the auditor cannot send confirmations on invoices if there is no record of them. If payables are overstated, vendors who see an error in their favor cannot be relied upon to report it. Instead, auditors will generally examine checks issued in the 45-60 days following year-end to see if any of the expenses paid should have been accrued prior to year-end.

For the same reason, auditors diligently observe inventory and fixed asset counts and confirm bank balances. They do not go searching for assets that may have gone unreported. However, they will seek evidence that no liabilities have been omitted or understated. This task is, perhaps, the most difficult part of the audit and may involve a review of invoices received and checks issued following year-end; letters of inquiry to the company's attorneys; and careful review of contracts, leases, and loan agreements.

Audit Timing

Preparation for the audit usually begins a few weeks before the end of the fiscal year. The auditor starts planning the audit procedures and gets updated by management about events during the year. At this time, the auditor may also evaluate internal controls, identify areas of audit exposure, and review any other items that impact the scope of the audit.

The auditor will also want to get a head start on correspondence needed for the audit, including requests for cutoff bank statements, minutes of board meetings, and letters to the attorneys concerning legal issues.

Generally accepted auditing standards (GAAS) require that auditors observe the taking of physical inventories, which for most companies occurs at year-end. Where internal controls are adequate, inventories can actually be taken on dates other than year-end, which may be desirable if a year-end physical would be costly or require a business shutdown. Fixed assets may be counted at the same time. To ensure that proper cutoffs are observed, the auditors will likely request copies of shipping and receiving logs immediately prior to and following year-end.

The bulk of the audit work comes after a company has prepared a preliminary closing statement, typically three to six weeks after year-end. Even for small companies, this work may take one to two weeks; a review would take less time, perhaps only a few days. Depending on how many reconciliations and schedules you can prepare before the beginning of this round of fieldwork, you could reduce the cost and difficulty of the audit. Work that can save you money includes:

The bulk of the audit work comes after a company has prepared a preliminary closing statement, typically three to six weeks after year-end.

- ▶ Preparation of lead and supporting schedules—fairly simple spreadsheets that list the income statement and balance sheet totals and trace the balances back to detail accounts,
- ▶ Bank reconciliations,
- ▶ Agings of accounts payable and receivable that match the balances on the general ledger,
- ▶ Listings of fixed assets and other assets that all tie to the general ledger,
- ▶ An orderly summary and pricing out of the physical inventory, and

> ► Ensuring access to important records, such as payroll registers, journal entries, contracts and leases, and cash disbursement journals.

Once this fieldwork is complete, the auditors will finish and review their work off-site. You may be required to do additional follow-up, such as pursuing confirmations that have not been received. Preparation of some footnote information, such as outstanding lease obligations and stockholder information, may be held off until now. Also, your financial statements must disclose any material events that occur after the close of the year, but before the issuance of financial statements. You will be asked to discuss these, if any.

The auditors will issue draft statements and discuss them with you to ensure their accuracy and resolve any outstanding issues. You may have preferences on how information is presented and how footnotes are worded. Some last-minute negotiation may occur over the figures themselves, particularly judgment items, such as reserves for bad debts or inventory markdowns.

For public companies, audited statements are usually incorporated into the annual report. Auditors will generally provide bound copies of the audited statements to private companies for distribution.

Management Letters

An audit is intended to formulate an opinion on a company's financial statements.

An audit is intended to formulate an opinion on a company's financial statements. Frequently, auditors are also requested to write a management letter. In this letter, which has no special format, the auditors discuss weaknesses in the accounting systems and any operating problems noted in the course of their work.

Although you should investigate and respond to the comments contained within the management letter, you are not required to do so. Have the auditors review the management letter directly with top management. Because the letter reports on the effectiveness of the financial systems, this type of review provides an internal control on the controller or CFO.

If No Audit

Even if you choose not to have an audit or review, year-end is a good opportunity to clean up the books. Here are some items you can take care of at year-end.

> ► Ensure that bank accounts are reconciled and long-standing reconciling items researched.

- Tie accounts receivable detail to the general ledger and write off or reserve for any questionable items.

- Take a physical inventory and revise standard costs for the new year.

- Count and tag all your fixed assets and update your perpetual listing of these assets.

- Recompute depreciation entries for the new year.

- Research the balances for prepaids, such as insurance or miscellaneous receivables from employee or insurance claims, and either write them off or list them on a supporting schedule.

- Reappraise any reserves, such as for bad debts or inventory write-downs.

- Match accounts payable aging to the general ledger total.

- Make sure that miscellaneous liabilities, such as payroll, income and sales taxes, commissions, and contributions to employee benefit plans, are in line with actual liabilities. Other accrued liabilities may also need to be recomputed. These include accounting and legal fees, employee vacation time accrued and not taken, warranty and returns reserves, royalties, and any possible surcharges for items such as common area fees or insurance premiums.

- Ensure that balances for principal owed on leases or loans agree with amortization schedules.

More than an accounting exercise, these reconciliations and examinations ensure that amounts owed by or owed to your company are not lost in the shuffle. You will also be confident that when the records show a balance for payables or receivables, it is accurate and backed up by supporting detail. Of course, you don't have to wait for year-end. You can routinely verify that this supporting detail exists by asking your controller or accountant for reconciliations and agings.

What Is Ahead?

The material discussed in the previous three chapters, including audits and closing the books, relate to financial accounting. As is stressed throughout this book, this is just one aspect of financial management. A clean audit opinion, for example, does not ensure your reporting system is complete or sound.

We have discussed how your external reporting needs are satisfied. The next chapter looks at how financial accounting, used alone, can fail you and your company. Chapter 5 will look at some of the weaknesses in GAAP reporting. Particular discussions will focus on how companies can manipulate financial reporting and why even properly prepared statements can be misleading. Later, Chapter 7 covers why management accounting is needed to supplement the information developed using GAAP.

Exhibit 4-1. Chart of Accounts—Sample

Account Numbering

Unless your accounting software limits your choices, account numbers can be any length; however, four to six digits are usually sufficient. Extra digits may be desired to track multiple divisions, subsidiaries, or projects. Some industries, like automobile dealers, have a standard chart of accounts. Most companies, though, are free to design their own. Typically, account numbers are grouped as follows:

First Digit	Type of Account
1	Assets
2	Liabilities
3	Equity
4	Revenue
5	Cost of Sales
6	Operating Expenses
7-9	Nonoperating Expenses, Taxes

Computerized systems usually require you to set up a hierarchy in which accounts either can be posted to (child, posting, or subaccounts) or contain subtotals summing the accounts below the hierarchy (parent or summary accounts). This helps format printed financial statements.

Account No.	Account Description	Type of Account
1000	Current Assets	Summary
1100	Cash	Summary
1150	Cash on hand	Posting
1160	Checking account	Posting
1200	Receivables	Posting
1400	Other current assets	Summary
1420	Deposits	Posting
1450	Prepaid insurance	Posting
1500	Inventory	Summary
1510	Raw materials	Posting
1520	Work in process	Posting
1530	Finished goods	Posting
1600	Noncurrent Assets	Summary
1610	Fixed assets	Summary
1630	Equipment	Posting
1640	Building & improvements	Posting
1650	Office furniture	Posting
1710	Depreciation	Summary
1730	Accumulated depr, equipment	Posting
1740	Accum depr, bldg & improvements	Posting
1750	Accum depr, office furniture	Posting
1800	Land	Summary
2000	Current Liabilities	Summary
2100	Trade payables	Posting
2200	Accrued payroll and benefits	Summary
2210	Wages & commissions payable	Posting
2220	State taxes payable	Posting
2230	Federal taxes payable	Posting
2240	Accrued benefits	Posting
2300	Other current liabilities	Summary
2320	Sales tax payable	Posting
2340	Customer deposits	Posting
2400	Short-term debt	Posting
2600	Noncurrent Liabilities	Summary
2700	Long-term debt	Posting
2800	Other noncurrent liabilities	Posting

Account No.	Account Description	Type of Account
5000	Cost of Sales	Summary
5100	Direct labor	Posting
5200	Overhead	Posting
5300	Purchases	Posting
5350	Inventory change	Posting
6000	Operating Expenses	Summary
6100	Sales and marketing	Summary
6110	Salaries, commissions, benefits	Posting
6130	Supplies	Posting
6150	Travel	Posting
6170	Advertising and promotion	Posting
6300	General and Administrative	Summary
6310	Salaries and benefits	Posting
6330	Supplies	Posting
6360	Professional fees	Posting
6380	Rent and insurance	Posting
7000	Other Income and Expenses	Summary
7100	Interest income	Posting
7200	Interest expense	Posting
7500	Other nonoperating	Posting
9000	Taxes	Posting

Notes

1. Quoted in the *Manager's Book of Quotations*, Lewis D. Eigen and Jonathan P. Siegel, eds. (New York: American Management Association, 1991)
2. Jack Stack, *The Great Game of Business* (New York: Doubleday, 1992).

Chapter 5

Financial
Reporting Pitfalls

Accountants are the witch doctors of the modern world.
—J. Harmon[1]

Figures are not always facts.

—Aesop[2]

FINANCIAL ACCOUNTING IS EFFECTIVE IN PROVIDING OUTSIDE investors with relevant, objective information. Boiling down the complex operations of entire companies to a few simple statements that have a consistent presentation across companies and industries is an impressive feat. At the same time, major shortcomings in GAAP reporting severely limit its usefulness. These are some of those shortcomings:

▶ GAAP reporting is intended to meet the needs of external decision-makers, not internal managers. Though properly structured statements can be useful to you, much of the information is too aggregated or not timely enough to help with business decisions. Management accounting is the accounting discipline that provides

Balance Sheet Pitfalls

The ideal balance sheet would reflect the value of your company at a given point in time. Your assets would be valued according to their future earning power and their ability to be converted into cash. In turn, your liabilities would fairly state all your company's future obligations.

Unfortunately, the balance sheet does not come close to attaining this goal. Instead, it has a strange mix of historical, current, market, and depreciated values. The totals and ratios that result from these numbers often have little meaning on their own.

To illustrate this amalgamation, examine how the various asset and liability accounts are valued.

▶ Current assets such as cash, marketable securities, or receivables are generally carried at current value.

▶ Inventory is recorded at the lower of either cost or market value. In addition, there are several acceptable methods for valuing inventory that can yield disparate figures.

▶ Equipment, furniture, and fixtures are valued at historical cost, less some fraction for depreciation. The value can vary greatly based on the write-off method chosen. Fully depreciated assets have zero accounting value, even though they may remain in service.

▶ Land is valued at historical cost. The bookkeeping entry will usually differ greatly from market value when land is held for many years.

▶ Intangibles, such as patents and goodwill, are recorded only if purchased and are ignored if internally generated. They are reviewed annually and written down if their value is deemed to have been impaired.

▶ Liabilities are generally listed at market value. Liabilities may be difficult to value for obligations arising from events that are anticipated but have not taken place.

Ratios and Book Value

Accounting statements add together all of the figures for the above-listed accounts to arrive at numbers such as total assets and net worth. Given the mix of valuation methods used, the totals by themselves have little meaning. They represent neither what was paid for assets nor what they could be sold for. While the individual accounting methods may be very logical and objective, combining figures, unless properly interpreted, is dangerous.

Even one of the most common tools of financial analysis, ratios, can be inaccurate. Outside analysts, such as lenders, place a high emphasis on ratios to judge a company's performance and make credit decisions. Loan covenants often specify earnings or liquidity ratios a company must meet. In addition, many business magazine articles instruct business owners to pay attention to certain ratios as key indicators of the financial strength of their companies and even suggest certain parameters these ratios should fall within.

While ratios, particularly changes over time, are useful, they also mix valuation methods and, therefore, can yield misleading results. For example, an earnings-to-book-value ratio uses earnings, stated mostly in current values, and book value, which mixes several cost bases. The same is true of return on investment (ROI), return on assets (ROA), and debt-to-equity ratios.

While ratios, particularly changes over time, are useful, they also mix valuation methods and, therefore, can yield misleading results.

Short-term measures of liquidity—the *current ratio* or the *quick ratio*—are more useful to you, since all the inputs are valued currently. The current ratio is determined by dividing current assets by current liabilities. The quick ratio, also called the acid test, divides highly liquid assets—such as cash, receivables, and marketable securities—by current liabilities.

Finally, whether discussing ratios or the balance sheet in total, remember that the balance sheet is simply a snapshot at a point in time. Individual elements, particularly cash, can fluctuate greatly from day to day. As was discussed in Chapter 4, the timing of transactions close to the end of an accounting period can impact elements of the balance sheet. Events, such as whether a large receivable is collected or a loan payment is made on December 31 or January 2, can affect the reported condition of a company.

Valuation Pitfalls

In addition to dealing with a mixture of costing methods, when reading a balance sheet, you must also be aware of different valuation assumptions and judgments that go into some of the figures. Even where a balance is valued objectively, an accountant has a choice of accounting methods. In addition, when accounting for future events, such as contingent liabilities or bad debt reserves, either a conservative or aggressive approach can be adopted.

For most current assets and liabilities, there is little problem with valuation. Assets are either cash or quickly convertible to cash, and liabilities will likely be settled at their face value.

Reserves

Reserves present a different problem, especially the establishment of a bad debt reserve. As discussed in Chapter 3, reserves are estimates of anticipated losses that are then recorded as expenses. The bad debt reserve may be based on specific troubled accounts or as a percentage of total receivables based on experience. Although the reserve only reduces the book value of receivables and does not mean collection efforts have been abandoned, business owners often are reluctant to record bad debt expenses. Even though, statistically, some accounts are likely to be uncollectible, particularly those aged beyond 90 days, as long as you are actively pursuing collection and feel the full amount is due, you may be reluctant to record a reserve.

As is covered in more detail in Chapter 8, the largest variable for manufacturing, retail, and distribution companies is usually inventory valuation. For example, because a company can make one of several assumptions about the flow of its purchases and sales, this choice can greatly affect the accounting value given to inventory. For example, the last in, first out (LIFO) method assumes a company sells its newest inventory first, so that the oldest units are still in stock. This inventory is valued at the prices in effect when this type of inventory was first purchased, perhaps five or 10 years ago. In contrast, the first in, first out (FIFO) method assumes a company sells the oldest units first, leaving the most recently purchased units in stock, valued at reasonably current prices. In an era of rising prices, a large disparity can exist between LIFO and FIFO values.

As with receivables, reserves are generally established to anticipate the likelihood that some inventory is slow moving or will become obsolete. Again, you may be reluctant to admit that more than a small part of inventory may require a reserve and the final number is largely a judgment call. Usually, external readers will not know the basis of the reserve.

Inventory is subject to a lower-of-cost-or-market test, which can be applied on an item-by-item basis or in aggregate. Not only is there a lack of consistency, because asset values may be at historic cost, market value, or a combination, but determining market values for inventory is highly subjective.

Noncurrent Assets

For noncurrent assets, the spread between accounting and economic value can be very wide. This spread is a recognized but not easily reconciled issue. In a 1993 speech, Walter Schuetze, the SEC's chief accountant, said:[3]

The cost of many assets does not represent anything close to the "probable future economic benefit" to be derived from the asset. For example, the probable future economic benefit of a successful, direct-response advertising campaign may be many multiples of the cost. The future benefit of a discovery of mineral deposits generally bears no relationship whatsoever to the costs of finding the deposits.

One issue creating disparity is that many assets decline in value over time. To account for this, equipment, furniture, and fixtures are carried at historical value, less some fraction for depreciation. While the concept of depreciation is sound, the application can be troublesome. Just as there are several methods of inventory valuation, several methods of depreciation may be chosen. If your company bought a truck with an expected useful life of five years, there is no trouble deciding that the cost should be spread over the five years of service. But how should the depreciation expense be distributed?

One choice is for you to depreciate an equal amount each year using the straight-line method. While this is the simplest technique, accelerated depreciation would recognize that better service is given early on—and would probably better approximate the actual resale value of the truck. In theory, depreciation could also be calculated based on new appraisals each year or on the basis of mileage.[4]

At the end of five years, the truck may very well still be in service or have a considerable resale value—yet the book value would stand at zero. Once again, there would be no mechanism for writing the value up to market value. Many traditional manufacturing companies have factories full of working machines carried at low or zero book values. Conversely, plants and equipment that are underutilized may have little economic benefit, yet are carried at historic cost. For this reason, the stock of public companies sometimes sells below book value and may be a sign that write-offs are looming.

Land probably has the largest disparity between book and market value. While no depreciation is taken, neither is any adjustment made for appreciation. As the value of land tends to rise steadily over time, companies that have held property over several decades will seriously understate the value. Note that if a company owns a building, the value will be divided between the land and the building itself. The cost of the building and any improvements will be depreciated, while the value assigned to the land will remain constant.

Intangible assets rarely have any relation to economic value. Goodwill, for

The cost of many assets does not represent anything close to the "probable future economic benefit" to be derived from the asset. For example, the probable future economic benefit of a successful, direct-response advertising campaign may be many multiples of the cost. The future benefit of a discovery of mineral deposits generally bears no relationship whatsoever to the costs of finding the deposits.

One issue creating disparity is that many assets decline in value over time. To account for this, equipment, furniture, and fixtures are carried at historical value, less some fraction for depreciation. While the concept of depreciation is sound, the application can be troublesome. Just as there are several methods of inventory valuation, several methods of depreciation may be chosen. If your company bought a truck with an expected useful life of five years, there is no trouble deciding that the cost should be spread over the five years of service. But how should the depreciation expense be distributed?

One choice is for you to depreciate an equal amount each year using the straight-line method. While this is the simplest technique, accelerated depreciation would recognize that better service is given early on—and would probably better approximate the actual resale value of the truck. In theory, depreciation could also be calculated based on new appraisals each year or on the basis of mileage.[4]

At the end of five years, the truck may very well still be in service or have a considerable resale value—yet the book value would stand at zero. Once again, there would be no mechanism for writing the value up to market value. Many traditional manufacturing companies have factories full of working machines carried at low or zero book values. Conversely, plants and equipment that are underutilized may have little economic benefit, yet are carried at historic cost. For this reason, the stock of public companies sometimes sells below book value and may be a sign that write-offs are looming.

Land probably has the largest disparity between book and market value. While no depreciation is taken, neither is any adjustment made for appreciation. As the value of land tends to rise steadily over time, companies that have held property over several decades will seriously understate the value. Note that if a company owns a building, the value will be divided between the land and the building itself. The cost of the building and any improvements will be depreciated, while the value assigned to the land will remain constant.

Intangible assets rarely have any relation to economic value. Goodwill, for example, does not represent any measurable asset. It is simply the premium paid over and above the net value of the assets in the acquisition of a company. Goodwill presumably reflects the value of things such as employee talent, market reputation, and technology. Until recently, goodwill was amortized over time. Starting in December 2001, the accounting changed so that goodwill stays on the books for the original amount unless the fair value of the acquired assets is judged to be "impaired." (See the discussion on accounting for acquisitions later in this chapter.)

A similar accounting treatment is used for patents. If purchased, they are carried for the purchase price. However, the research and development costs of internally generated patents, no matter how valuable, are expensed as they occur.

Liabilities

Unlike assets, which are mostly carried at historic cost, liabilities are generally carried at current values. Most of the difficult issues affecting liabilities are when to account for events that are anticipated but haven't taken place and how to judge the future cost. In other cases, a firm may have incurred a future obligation, but because the expenditure benefits those future periods, no liability is recorded. When you read financial statements, be aware that significant exposures may have been omitted or disclosed only in footnotes.

Where either the probability of a loss cannot be determined or the loss cannot be reasonably estimated, contingent liabilities are not recorded. This is the reason major exposure for environmental cleanups, product recalls, or outstanding lawsuits may not appear on the balance sheet.

Long-term lease obligations are another liability that can be kept off the balance sheet, even though rules for leases have been tightened over the years. For example, leases that cover most of an asset's useful life are treated as if money were borrowed to purchase that asset. A month-to-month computer rental usually is not considered a liability while a four-year computer lease probably is. Yet, a four-year lease on a building is not considered a liability, because the useful life of that building is much longer. However, the total of all lease obligations is disclosed in footnotes. To make the balance sheet appear as healthy as possible, companies often try to structure financing in such a way that the liability can stay unrecorded. (See the sidebar on off-balance-sheet financing for more on this topic.)

Goodwill, for example, does not represent any measurable asset. It is simply the premium paid over and above the net value of the assets in the acquisition of a company.

Leases and Off-Balance-Sheet Financing

Though the rules on leasing, enacted in 1976, may seem complex, they ended a period in which companies regularly used leases to keep financing "off the balance sheet." They were such an accounting dilemma that eight of the first 30 FASB Statements dealt with leases.

Essentially, capital leases are accounted for as if a company borrowed money to purchase a fixed asset. To qualify as a capital lease, at least one of the following four conditions must be met:

1. Ownership of the asset transfers to the lessee.
2. The lessee can buy the asset at a bargain price at the end of the lease.
3. The lease term covers at least 75% of the asset's life.
4. The present value of lease payments exceeds 90% of the asset's fair market value.

If a lease doesn't meet any of these conditions, it's considered an operating lease. Rental expense is recorded as payments are made and the future value of lease payments must be disclosed in footnotes. However, the balance sheet is not affected. Because companies prefer to reduce the amount of debt they report, many go to great lengths to structure leases in a way that keeps them from having to appear on the balance sheet.

Is keeping leases off the balance sheet worth the effort? The benefit is that the balance sheet shows less debt and better leverage ratios can make it easier and cheaper to borrow additional funds. However, constructing a lease just so it qualifies as operating could introduce unnecessary transaction costs. Further, since lease commitments get disclosed in footnotes and, perhaps, in other filings, will anyone be fooled?

Enron and other companies took off-balance sheet financing in other directions. Enron established separate entities in which it held part ownership and whose obligations it secured. However, it failed to record the liabilities on its balance sheet and disclosed them in footnotes that even security analysts couldn't unravel. Other companies secured the debt of unrelated entities, such as manufacturers extending credit to distributors and retailers, to ensure purchase of their products. New FASB rules have closed both loopholes, requiring special purpose entities to be consolidated and companies to record as liabilities the market value of any guarantees.

Another variable concerning liabilities and the balance sheet arises because companies usually use different accounting methods for income taxes and financial reporting. A controversial GAAP requirement is that the difference between financial statement tax liability and that on the tax return be carried as a liability. The assumption is that the tax savings one year will be offset in following years. This is true, for example, of depreciation where an accelerated method for tax purposes will reduce income in early years, but cause higher income later. However, a strong argument can be made that in many companies the liability will never be paid and has no place on the balance sheet; in a growing company, the liability is likely to continue to build as new assets with high depreciation outweigh older assets.

Liabilities concerning partially funded employee pension plans may also be stated inaccurately on the balance sheet. Companies often set up employee pension plans that obligate them to make payments to employees after retirement. If an employer has set aside at least 100% of the cash needed to fund the expected liability, then the plan is considered to be fully funded. If not, the pension liability is only partially funded. Partially funded employee benefit plans have many accounting complexities and create liabilities that are complicated to measure. Suffice it to say that this category is likely to be misstated.

Partially funded employee benefit plans have many accounting complexities and create liabilities that are complicated to measure.

Income Statement Pitfalls

While the balance sheet represents a snapshot of a company's value at any point in time, the income statement summarizes the flow of activity between two such points. Net income is the change in reported value during an accounting period. So, you can see how problems in valuing balance sheet accounts simultaneously affect the income statement.

Several balance sheet valuation issues have an impact on income. When depreciation is recorded, half of the entry reduces assets and the other half is an expense. Selecting an accelerated depreciation method, as discussed in Chapter 3, not only reduces assets earlier, but also increases expenses in earlier years.

For inventory, using the first in, first out (FIFO) method of valuing inventory uses more recent prices to value inventory. But while FIFO seems to make the balance sheet more current, it has the opposite impact on the income statement. FIFO results in sales being booked at current prices, but expenses—

inventory shipped—at older, historical costs. During periods of rising prices, FIFO will tend to inflate profits. By contrast, the last in, first out (LIFO) method ensures that both revenues and expenses on the income statement are at current values, but causes the balance sheet to reflect outdated values.

The argument of whether assets and liabilities should be written up or down as market values change often revolves around the impact these entries would have on reported net income. While adjusting the values would help the balance sheet be more reflective of the actual value of a company, the adjustment would require that income and expense be recorded, even though no transaction has taken place.

At times, the current rules protect investors by limiting management's latitude in assigning asset values and recognizing unearned income or expense. At other times, the rules have the opposite effect. For example, requiring land to be carried at historic value, rather than market value, understates a company's net worth.

The argument of whether assets and liabilities should be written up or down as market values change often revolves around the impact these entries would have on reported net income.

Stock Options

Stock option accounting is a controversial topic. Qualified options became a popular compensation vehicle in large part because they require no upfront cash outlay by employees or the company, allow employees to share in the upside potential of a company's stock, and are tax-deductible. However, the key factor may be that GAAP does not require any expense to be recognized when options are granted or exercised. So, unlike wages or bonuses, employees can be given something of value without expending cash or affecting earnings.

Many people feel that options should be treated the same as other compensation and that the favorable accounting treatment encourages excessive option grants while hiding the information from investors. A number of major corporations have agreed and now voluntarily expense stock options when granted. Opponents argue that footnote disclosure of option grants is sufficient and that because the impact of options is dilution of shareholders, and not a cash outlay, no expense is incurred. They worry that making options less attractive to companies will reduce the number of grants and hinder recruiting of employees.

This type of controversy highlights both the variability of accounting earnings and the effects of accounting rules on management behavior.

The Matching Principle

Another income statement pitfall concerns the timing of revenue and expense transactions. One key accounting principle—the matching principle—dictates that revenues are not recorded until all or a substantial portion of the services has been completed and objectively measurable compensation has been received. A company may substantially increase its earnings power during a period by developing products and services, booking orders, or partially completing a sale, but no revenues or associated expenses are booked until a sale is actually consummated.

Complicated timing issues and occasional period-to-period swings also affect reported income. The income statement is driven by the desire to match the revenues in a given period with the expenditures that supported and produced them. If a product is built in one year but not sold until the second year, the costs of making the product are carried as an asset at the end of the first year, when the product still has earnings potential, and then expensed in the second year, when the related revenue is realized.

The income statement is driven by the desire to match the revenues in a given period with the expenditures that supported and produced them.

But how are period expenses and costs with a future benefit distinguished? Consider sales and marketing expenditures, including advertising. A strong argument can be made that these expenses carry a significant future benefit. However, because of the difficulty in sorting out the present and future benefits and matching specific efforts to product sold, accountants choose to expense these types of costs in the period when they are incurred.

Likewise, general and administrative expenses are period expenses, since they cannot be closely associated with product sold. But how about research and development expenses? Unsuccessful R&D has little future value, but R&D that results in significant new products and patents enhances a company's value. Yet, because of the uncertainty of the future value, GAAP requires that all R&D expenses be recorded as period expenses.

On the other hand, manufacturing expenses are included in the value of inventory and expensed as cost of sales. As discussed in more detail in Chapter 8, depending upon the assumption made about the flow of goods, the amount of cost of sales can vary significantly, leading to further potential inaccuracies on the income statement.

detailed information on internal operations. Management accounting is discussed in Chapter 7.

▶ Financial accounting measures can be accurate, yet inadequate or misleading. Accounting concepts, such as profit, historic cost, and conservatism, are not the same as cash flow, market value, and accuracy. Many changes in a company's financial position or outlook are simply not fully recorded under GAAP. Accounting often fails to capture the true impact of events on a company's value or support current decision making.

▶ Creative accounting is a reality. Through methods that range from simply aggressive to fraudulent, companies can shape their financial statements. The reader of statements must beware.

Given the complexity of accounting issues and the different needs of internal and external readers, any sets of rules are a compromise.

Weaknesses in GAAP are not merely academic concerns. Investors must rely heavily on financial statements to make decisions. In addition, even though managers have other decision-making tools at their disposal, they often let financial accounting be the tail that wags the dog. Rather than just reporting on a company's performance, the accounting actually influences it.

For example, management compensation tied to accounting measures can provide inappropriate incentives. Trying to "make the numbers" each month or quarter can chew up management time, create artificial deadlines, and cause long-term goals to be compromised. Standard financial analysis, used for decisions on credit and investment, places a lot of emphasis on ratios, earnings, and book value, even though these measures are often flawed. And creative accounting often masks poor management and distorts decisions by investors and creditors.

These faults do not mean GAAP should be replaced. Indeed, the need for objective and consistent financial reporting is clear and GAAP meets this need. Given the complexity of accounting issues and the different needs of internal and external readers, any sets of rules are a compromise. However, the rules should not dictate how business owners operate or limit them from developing additional sources of information. The key is for both internal and external users of financial statements to be aware of the limitations of GAAP reporting and put it in proper perspective.

Costing methods, valuation, judgment, and creative accounting are factors that can create both intentional and unintentional distortions of the financial facts. This chapter concentrates on those factors and how they can affect your perception of a business.

Using Income Statements

So what is the "bottom line" on the bottom line? Is it a useless muddle of values or can it be of value?

Like any financial accounting statement, interpreting an income statement requires an understanding of the assumptions and judgments that went into it. However, compared with the balance sheet, fewer items distort the income statement. Because income is a flow of revenues and transactions during an entire period, the income statement is more representative of your company than a snapshot on a single day—as you have with the balance sheet—and less subject to shifts at the end of a period.

Income statements have fewer valuation issues: most expenses are incurred and settled within the same period, so the basis of valuation is known. As a result, period-to-period and trend comparisons also have more meaning. Nonetheless, as is discussed below, substantial room still exists for manipulation of net income, so investors reading financial statements must still be cautious.

Earnings before interest and taxes (EBIT) more accurately captures the earning power of a company by excluding the impact of taxes and capital structure.

While most people are only concerned with net income, the very bottom line that encompasses all activity in a period, some lenders, investors, and managers focus on slightly difference measures. Earnings before interest and taxes (EBIT) more accurately captures the earning power of a company by excluding the impact of taxes and capital structure. For example, a company that finances its operations with some debt rather than all equity will incur interest expense a peer company might not. Similarly, S corporations will not show any income tax expense, making their net income appear more favorable than for C corporations that do report income tax expense.

Earnings before interest, taxes, depreciation, and amortization (EBITDA) has become a very popular measure. By excluding depreciation and amortization expense, which do not consume cash, this measure presumes to capture the cash-generating power of a company, independent of capital structure and taxes. However, a weakness with EBITDA is that it ignores capital spending altogether. For a business that makes significant investments in equipment, buildings, and other fixed assets, ignoring the impact of this spending greatly overstates the cash flow generated.

Operating income is another refinement of EBIT, which excludes all nonoperating items such as investment income from an unrelated business. A recent trend has been for businesses to present pro forma earnings. Businesses will strip away nonrecurring expenses and items unrelated to ongoing operations to try to show the underlying business is profitable. Such numbers can be very misleading, since there are no rules controlling what management can and can't include. In addition, so-called nonrecurring or unrelated expenses have a way of recurring or being replaced by a new set of unanticipated expenses.

If you go to sell your business, you'll find out that investors often want to see earnings stated "before owners' compensation." Owners' pay and perquisites vary widely and to outsiders can be a significant unknown impact on the bottom line. To get an idea of what earnings will look like after the sale, buyers want to adjust accordingly.

Some common ratios are used to evaluate income. For public companies, earnings per share (EPS) is often the only measure widely quoted. For companies with options and convertible securities outstanding, this measure can get complicated. However, it is basically just net income divided by the number of common shares outstanding. Return on assets (ROA), which is net income divided by total assets, and return on investments (ROI), net income divided by owners' equity, are also frequently used. However, because the denominators in these two ratios come from the balance sheet, they are subject to the same weaknesses as other balance sheet ratios discussed earlier in the chapter.

Emphasizing Profit

Confucius is quoted as saying, "The wise man understands equity; the small man understands only profit."[5] Indeed, a perfect income statement would reflect the period change in a company's true net worth. This change, though, would be a subjective measure taking a long-term view of a company—a look that investors try to take when evaluating companies and business owners often recognize instinctively. But accounting relies on capturing transactions, not subjective measurement. Net income will often fail to record the true impact of events on a company, particularly in the short term.

Worse is the high degree of reliance managers put on short-term profits. There is a lot of pressure to meet quarterly targets and fast-track managers may change jobs every few years, which can lead to accounting methods that favor current reported income. Focusing on short-term profits can also weaken incentives to make necessary investments in R&D and other long-term programs.

Focuses on short-term profits are reinforced further by compensation plans that pay bonuses based on current income. The bonuses and financial

There is a lot of pressure to meet quarterly targets and fast-track managers may change jobs every few years, which can lead to accounting methods that favor current reported income.

99

rewards give added incentive to boost current income and to devote unnecessary effort to attempting to manage profits.

Cash Flow

While profit is an important measure, it is still an accounting concept. Equally important and often critical is cash flow. A company showing a profit or positive book value can run out of cash and fail but, as former MCI Chairman William McGowan once said, "No company has ever gone bankrupt because it had a loss on its P&L."[6]

*W*hile profit is an important measure, it is still an accounting concept. Equally important and often critical is cash flow.

Cash flow has another key advantage as a measure of performance—it is an extremely objective measure. Cash flow can be precisely measured and verified, without a need for accruals and other judgment calls. Simply put, unlike net income, cash flow won't lie. Cash flow is discussed in more detail in Chapter 9.

Creative Accounting

Did you hear the joke about a CEO who asked candidates interviewing for a job the question, "How much is 2 + 2?" The man who used lengthy equations and finally deduced the answer as "4" was hired as the mathematician. The woman who drew a graph with intersecting curves and answered "5" became the economist. The last prospect drew the curtains closed and whispered, "How much do you want it to be?" This person became the new accountant.

Anyone who has worked long with financial statements or has noted the many judgment calls that must be made in accounting will not be surprised that there are many opportunities to finesse the numbers. A difficult but all too common dilemma for accountants is handling requests from the boss to improve the appearance of the income statement or balance sheet. Almost always, changes in estimates or procedures can be made to boost net income and yet stay within GAAP. A common perception is that any controller or accountant worth his or her weight always has money tucked away that can be used to dress up the financial statements.

Outside CPAs are not immune to this pressure, either. In part, their resolve to get tough about accounting issues is tempered by knowing that the client pays their salary. Even with new rules that limit the scope of nonaudit work a CPA firm can provide and the spin-off of consulting divisions, audit and tax fees are still sizable and can create pressure to go along. The ability to push back is also tempered, because accounting rules often get stretched rather than broken or a questionable item is not material to the overall statements. Finally, a CPA often is forced to rely on the word of the client and is not in a position to contradict an opinion on the salability of inventory or creditworthiness of a slow-paying account.

In reaction to shareholder lawsuits, SEC pressure, and the accounting scandals at companies like Enron, CPAs have clamped down on much creative accounting. Even so, only annual statements of public companies are required to have audit opinions. Significant decisions are based on monthly and quarterly financials as well as statements of private companies. These can escape independent review—at least temporarily.

Accounting Gimmickry

A popular cartoon from several years ago can help illustrate how the bottom line can be manipulated. The cartoon shows an executive addressing his management team saying, "I am glad to report that once again we broke even on operations and pulled a profit on accounting procedures."

Accounting gimmickry is not a new phenomenon and, in fact, seems to run in cycles. One peak came during the 1960s. Switches in accounting methods, run-ups in unfunded pension liabilities, and assorted other tricks temporarily inflated reported earnings. Eventually, FASB and SEC rulings closed these gaping loopholes. One article cited 1970 as "the year of the big bath," when, in a single week, 60 companies reported write-offs and write-downs to their earnings.[7]

Another surge was experienced in the 1990s and into the 2000s. In a high-profile speech in 1998, well before the scandals at companies such as Enron, WorldCom, and Tyco surfaced, SEC chairman Arthur Levitt assailed the quality of reported earnings. Citing the pressure of managers to meet expectations and manage earnings growth, Levitt specifically cited some of the most common accounting games and initiated action at the SEC to crack down on these. These tricks include "big bath" write-offs, acquisition accounting, "cookie jar" reserves, and premature revenue recognition. These and other games are discussed more fully in the sections below.

One legitimate reason to manipulate income is for tax purposes, where it is desirable to choose accounting methods that reduce reported income. In the United States and most Western countries, it is perfectly legitimate to maintain two sets of books—one for financial accounting and one for taxes.[8] The benefit of doing this, however, will vary from company to company.

Ironically, some companies choose to pay higher taxes in order to report higher net income—a strategy that only makes sense if reporting lower income or losses would jeopardize operating needs, such as the ability to raise financing.

Manipulating Reserves

The most common weapons in the creative accountant's arsenal are various reserve accounts. These include establishing reserves for potential bad debts, inventory loss or obsolescence, or accruing for various potential liabilities. Because these reserves require considerable judgment, they are also prone to abuse.

Management can be under pressure to meet expectations and achieve smooth earnings growth. One way to do this is to increase reserves and accrued liabilities when times are good. Accelerating the expenses may take pressure off future periods or create a "cookie jar" of reserves that can be dipped into as needed. For example, by adopting less conservative standards for estimating bad debts or identifying obsolete inventory, future earnings can be propped up. Even when no cookie jar has been built up, aggressive accounting that limits write-downs and reserves can defer recognition of bad news for quite some time.

Write-Offs

The decision of when to actually write off an asset is another variable in creative accounting.

The decision of when to actually write off an asset is another variable in creative accounting. Generally, an accountant will wait for an opportune moment to take a write-off that reduces income. As long as a plausible case can be made for an asset having a future value, the asset may be allowed to stay on the books. A common example is inventory of slow-moving products. The inventory may be first quality and, therefore, potentially salable, but if no one is buying or future products threaten to obsolete it, the inventory should be written off. Yet, if a case can be made that the inventory could be sold within one year, it may be allowed to stay on the books at or near full value.

When bad news hits, companies often prefer to take their lumps all at once. This so-called "big bath" approach holds that, if you are going to deliver bad news to investors, you may as well make it a disaster. At this point, write-downs that have been deferred are taken and reserves that have been depleted get restored. By putting the bad news behind and claiming the large write-off is an extraordinary event, a company can claim that future earnings look bright and also establish a set of reserves to cushion those future periods.

Acquisition Accounting

Acquisitions create another opportunity to take one-time charges and write-downs. In an acquisition, the assets and liabilities of the company being acquired are revalued, including estimated costs of closing the deal. These should reflect current market value and not necessarily the existing book value, so there is judgment involved. Any difference between this net book value and the purchase price is recorded as goodwill. If assets are deliberately undervalued, if the acquired company is asked to accrue all sorts of liabilities prior to the deal date, or if unrelated costs are categorized as "deal costs," goodwill simply increases without penalizing earnings. Should the company be able to sell some of the assets above the new book cost or avoid recording expenses because they were accrued to prior to acquisition, profits are artificially boosted.

In an acquisition, the assets and liabilities of the company being acquired are revalued, including estimated costs of closing the deal.

Another aspect of this is that the acquirer has up to 12 months to determine the market values. If during this time the acquirer decides, for example, that certain inventory is not salable, the acquirer can simply write it down as of the acquisition date instead of recording the expense in the current year, as would normally be done.

Until recently, another loophole existed. If merging companies were of roughly equal size, they were allowed to use the "pooling" method, in which the balance sheets of the two companies were essentially added together. A part of this accounting allowed premiums paid above book value to be attributed to the value of ongoing research and development. This created a large write-off at the time of the acquisition, rather than goodwill. The benefit of this is that, similar to "big bath" write-offs, the acquiring company could take a one-time earnings hit so that future earnings would be unencumbered by goodwill amortization expense.

Once again, accounting rules drove business behavior. Companies abused the "in-process R&D" write-offs, working hard to squeeze acquisitions in under the pooling rules and walking away from deals that wouldn't qualify.

Pooling was eliminated, but only after a compromise solution was reached. Goodwill is no longer amortized, but instead is carried at full value as long as the underlying asset is not impaired. This keeps future earnings from being impacted by the cost of an acquisition, at least as long as the impairment test is met. At some point, the goodwill will be written off, but this may be in one lump sum, again allowing management to take all its lumps at once and keep projected earnings unharmed.

Revenue Recognition

P robably the most signifi- cant accounting issue, and the one most subject to abuse, is revenue recognition.

Probably the most significant accounting issue, and the one most subject to abuse, is revenue recognition. Chapter 3 discusses some of the complicated rules surrounding this issue. The addendum at the end of this chapter also describes how some companies have abused the rules.

There are permissible ways to control earnings through the timing of sales near a period-end. Most companies go through a push at quarter- or year-end to sign deals or ship as much as possible. Companies can also defer revenue by choosing to ship on January 1 rather than December 31. Similarly, companies may defer expenses or refuse incoming shipments to shift expenses to the next period.

Some companies, though, run afoul of the rules by keeping months open, shipping several days after month-end but predating invoices. Others make deals with customers to ship at month-end with an agreement that delivery not be completed, or that payment can be deferred, for a week or more. A popular technique, "channel stuffing," calls for shipping goods to distributors and recording revenue even though the distributors have the right to return any unsold product. Even worse, some companies have simply shipped to their own warehouses or loaded goods temporarily on trucks at year-end and counted these as sales even though no end customer exists.

Timing of Transactions

Timing the sale of fixed assets is a commonly used method to manipulate income. GAAP does not permit companies to write up the value of assets when the market value has appreciated; assets that have declined in value must be written down to market value, however. A company that bought land 20 years ago may have a sizable, unrecognized gain. That gain is booked when the land is sold, thus having an impact on the financial statements.

Using a related method, some companies refinance to show profits. If a company has issued debt and market value has declined below book value due to rising interest rates, the company can buy back the debt on the open market—or swap it for equity—and book a profit by retiring the debt.

Balance Sheet Management

Managing the balance sheet at year-end can greatly enhance a company's appearance. Most of the procedures that boost net income will also improve the appearance of the balance sheet. Higher sales increase receivables, a current asset, helping both net worth and various financial ratios. Higher inventory values and slower depreciation keep assets on the books, while limiting accrued expenses keeps current liabilities off.

Managing the balance sheet at year-end can greatly enhance a company's appearance.

Some shifting among balance sheet accounts can also occur. Most common is boosting cash balances by holding off paying vendors until just after year-end or by encouraging early customer payments. Deliveries can be refused in the few days before year-end to keep both inventories and payables down. Last-minute borrowing, particularly if the debt is classified as noncurrent, can improve stated cash positions.

As discussed earlier in this chapter, leasing assets, instead of buying them, can give firms the opportunity to do "off-balance-sheet financing." In recent years, companies have exploited these rules, aggressively keeping property off the books using a technique called *synthetic leasing*.

Case 1: IBM in the '80s and '90s

The difficulty of making accurate decisions using financial statements and the considerable leeway management has in choosing accounting methods is illustrated by the history of International Business Machines (IBM) in the late 1980s and early 1990s. In an article in *The Wall Street Journal* on April 7, 1993, considerable evidence was presented indicating that IBM adopted increasingly aggressive accounting methods to prop up reported earnings during a period when business was deteriorating.

Although the article asserts that none of the changes were illegal or affected any of the underlying business problems, IBM's day of reckoning was probably delayed. During this time, executives were awarded large raises and bonuses that were partly tied to earnings, while investors who bought shares near their peak in 1987 saw the stock plunge more than 70% by 1993.[9]

The changes in IBM's accounting practice fell into three broad categories. The first involved revenue recognition and determining when a sale was actually complete. While some high-technology companies wait until a system is installed and running at a customer site, IBM chose to book revenue upon shipment.[10] In some cases, but only when installation at a customer was expected within 30 days, it even booked shipments to its own warehouses as sales. Another revenue issue was how to account for various sales gimmicks that offered customers liberal return policies or price protection refunds if prices later fell. IBM critics contend that full revenue was being booked at shipment, despite evidence that payments received would be less.

The second category was the treatment of leases. Many of IBM's leases had revenue streams that fell short of GAAP requirements for capital leases. Instead of qualifying as sales when the contract was signed, with all the expected revenue booked at once, they would have to be treated as rentals, with the revenue only booked as payments were received. In an extremely unusual transaction, IBM purchased insurance that guaranteed the value of the computers at the end of the lease. This residual value, when added to the payments from the customer, met the GAAP test and allowed IBM to recognize the sales immediately.

Finally, starting in 1984, IBM began to reduce the estimated cost of its retirement plans and to spread the costs of its factories further into the future. Though these changes were fully disclosed in IBM's financial statements and were common at other companies, critics maintained they were a shift away from IBM's traditionally conservative accounting.

How large an impact the accounting changes had on IBM's earnings is unclear. The company asserted that its actions were appropriate and agreed to by its auditors. Nonetheless, analysts seemed shocked when IBM announced layoffs and nearly $5 billion in losses in 1992 and its stock fell sharply.

If IBM, with traditionally conservative accounting practices, can be tempted to adopt aggressive methods to boost earnings, how many other companies are acting similarly? If the analysts who closely scrutinize IBM's books can be surprised, how cautious should a small business lender or investor be when analyzing accounting statements? And did IBM's officers fool themselves into thinking things were better than they were based on the accounting numbers? If so, they may have missed their chance to turn the company around.

Summary

The weaknesses in GAAP, the reality that accounting figures can be manipulated, and the pressure on managers to meet earnings expectations create very real operating problems that go well beyond the high-profile issues of shareholder lawsuits and investments in scandal-ridden companies. For example:

- ▶ A manager whose bonus is tied to accounting figures or feels pressure from investors or lenders to meet earnings expectations
- ▶ A controller asked by his or her manager to change an accounting treatment to help meet targets
- ▶ Having to analyze the books of another company in making credit or acquisition decisions

Within limits, some maneuvering is normal. You don't need to be unduly conservative, some "window dressing" at period-end can legitimately improve how your financial statements appear to outsiders, and your presentation to outsiders can focus on the numbers that put your company in the best light. When computing tax income, there is every reason to attempt to minimize income within the legal limits and no reason you can't choose different accounting treatments for tax and financial accounting purposes where allowed.

Questionable accounting tactics, though, lead down a slippery slope, even where fraud is not involved. Aggressive accounting generally can prop up earnings for only so long before deterioration shows up in another business barometer or the accumulated sins become too much to overlook. Even in fairly steady times, the artificial increase in one period's profits only detracts from the next period.

The situation only becomes worse if management uses inflated profits to delay operating action, including hiding issues from investors or lender—ostensibly to work out problems without interference. Open communication and "no surprises" are keys to good relations with investors, and the financial statements are generally the centerpieces of communication.

If you do decide to play small games to smooth earnings or window-dress the balance sheet, do not end up fooling yourself. You need to be aware of the real operating trends and issues, regardless of reported income. As Mark Twain said, "Get your facts first, and then you can distort them as much as you please."[11]

Addendum to Chapter 5: Deconstructing Enron and Other Accounting Scandals of the Early 2000s

The accounting scandals at Enron, WorldCom, and other major companies made headlines throughout 2001 and 2002 and helped trigger one of the most severe declines ever seen in U.S. stock markets. What were some of the accounting games used by these companies?

Enron created a large number of "special purpose entities" that carried a lot of debt, much of which was secured by Enron stock. Because of Enron's ownership interest, most of these should have been consolidated into Enron's financial statements, which would have added billions of dollars of debt and a similar reduction in equity. Though some of these relationships were disclosed in footnotes, the structure was so massive and involved that few people understood the extent of the debt. When Enron stock tumbled, so did the ability to make good on the debt guarantees and the financial structure fell like a house of cards.

Enron also inflated revenues by acting as a broker in sales of energy and counting the gross transaction volume as revenue rather than just the broker's fee. Enron also issued equity in exchange for notes receivable and recorded the notes as assets rather than reducing equity as called for by GAAP.

WorldCom paid fees to local carriers for line capacity and, rather than expensing those costs as required by GAAP, capitalized them. By depreciating the costs over time, WorldCom deferred billions of dollars in costs and inflated current profits. Prior to this, WorldCom also engaged in aggressive acquisition accounting. In 1996, WorldCom wrote off $2.14 billion related to acquired technology acquisitions and added another $600 million in other reserves.

Global Crossing, along with other communications companies, was accused of swapping capacity, with both companies recording sales revenue even though no money changed hands. Global Crossing is also accused of recording revenue up front on contracts where it still had significant future obligations and making misleading use of pro forma financial statements.

Xerox settled a suit filed by the SEC claiming profits were overstated by $3 billion over four years. Xerox was accused of recording excessive revenue up front on lease-or-buy contracts, despite future obligations and customers' rights to cancel.

Adelphia was accused by the SEC of shifting $2.3 billion of debt to the books of unconsolidated subsidiary companies. The company also diverted company funds to pay for personal investments and expenses of insiders and made misleading statements about the number of cable system subscribers.

Notes

1. J. Harmon, Jurist, Miles v. Clarke, quoted in *The Manager's Book of Quotations*, p. 4.

2. Aesop, "The Widow and the Hen," quoted in *The Manager's Book of Quotations*, p. 386.

3. "FASB Asset Definitions at Odds with Historical Cost Model," *Accounting Today*, 7 June 1993, pp. 13-15.

4. Howard Ross, *The Elusive Art of Accounting: A Brash Commentary on Financial Statements* (New York: Ronald Press, 1966), p. 44.

5. Confucius, quoted in *The Manager's Book of Quotations*, p. 3.

6. William McGowan, quoted in *The Manager's Book of Quotations*, p. 6.

7. Louis V. Gerstner, Jr. and M. Helen Anderson, "The Chief Financial Officer as Activist," *Harvard Business Review*, September-October 1976, p. 100.

8. James McNeill Stancill, "Managing Financial Statements—Image and Effect," *Harvard Business Review*, March-April 1981, p. 181.

9. Michael W. Miller and Lee Berton, "As IBM's Woes Grew, Its Accounting Tactics Got Less Conservative," *The Wall Street Journal*, 7 April 1993, p. 1.

10. In 1987, the SEC filed suit against another computer manufacturer, Storage Technology Corp., for recognizing revenue when product was shipped rather than installed. The SEC also charged that a major transaction had been backdated in 1983 to turn a loss into a profit. The suit was settled with no admission of wrongdoing.

11. Mark Twain, quoted in *Apollo Book of American Quotations*, Bruce Bohle, ed. (New York: Dodd, Mead & Co., 1967), p. 148.

Part Two

Beyond Financial Accounting

Debit | Credit

Chapter 6

Controllership: Managing with the Numbers

The change from the spelling of the word 'comptroller' to 'controller' is in some mysterious way related to a change in the corporate status of the controller.

—Jerome Bennett[1]

STRONG FINANCIAL CONTROL DOES NOT MEAN TRYING TO RUN A COMpany by the numbers—not many companies could succeed doing that. The key is being able to run a company with the numbers. This means putting a system of controls in place that protects a company's assets and the integrity of information. Numbers can help you navigate, but they cannot be the only factor in operating decisions.

Financial managers play a critical role in running a company, but it is a supporting one. Their role, it has been said, is similar to brakes on a car: you need them to keep from going over a cliff, but they can't be in charge or you will never go anywhere. Robert Townsend, in *Further Up the Organization*, agrees:[2]

When accounting runs the operation (and this happens a lot), the situation must be changed. Accountants can be smarter than anyone else or more ambitious or both, but essentially they are bean counters—their job is to serve the operation. They can't run the ship.

Of course, controllers should not be excluded from management or be satisfied with just being bean counters. Quite the contrary: from providing information to supporting operating decisions, ensuring adequate cash flow, and identifying cost savings, controllers should be dynamic, proactive forces in their companies.

To be positive forces, two major prerequisites must be met. First, the controller's duties have to be properly defined, particularly the distinction between simply doing accounting and being a controller. Then, the person who fills that job must have the appropriate background, perspective, and attitude. This chapter explores the differences between accountants and controllers and then redefines the job description for your company's controller.

The distinction between an accountant and a controller is more than just education or a title. The two terms imply a different breadth and perspective in financial management.

Controllership or Accounting

As mentioned earlier in Chapter 1, there is a big difference between a controller and an accountant or bookkeeper. A large part of a controller's job is, indeed, accounting and most controllers are accountants by background. In many smaller companies, the top accountant is simply referred to as the controller regardless of the actual job description. To add some confusion, the synonymous, but relatively outmoded term "comptroller" is sometimes used to describe the same position.

The distinction between an accountant and a controller is more than just education or a title. The two terms imply a different breadth and perspective in financial management:

▶ Accounting is bean counting. It is little more than recording financial transactions and tallying the results. A controller, on the other hand, can interpret the numbers and provide meaningful feedback.

▶ An accountant accumulates historical information, while a controller is both historical and forward-looking in perspective.

▶ An accountant is usually happiest working with figures and may rarely set foot outside of the accounting department. A controller is usually plugged into activity throughout a company and works regularly with managers in all departments.

▶ Accounting is concerned only with transactions that can be measured in dollars. But, a controller may also be interested in developments that may not be actual financial transactions, such as the impact of potential lawsuits or price changes, as well as nonfinancial measures, such as productivity and quality.

▶ An accountant is overhead—that is, much of the work is routine and dictated by accounting conventions and tax laws, and the less that work costs to perform, the better. A controller will pay for himself or herself many times over by finding pockets of potential savings, supporting key decision makers, and anticipating problems. The controller's office can often be a true profit center.

The Traditional Role

Unfortunately, the qualities that make a good accountant don't necessarily make an effective controller. Some of the best controllers don't even have strong accounting backgrounds; others are accountants who can make a transition to looking beyond the numbers and embracing a management perspective. According to an article in the *Journal of Accountancy*, "Controllers whose experience is entirely accounting oriented may lack the expertise to establish appropriate operational and administrative controls."[3]

Perhaps the foremost reason for this lack of expertise is that accountants usually receive most of their formal training in financial accounting and tax, which are certainly important topics. All publicly held companies and many private ones must prepare financial statements that conform to GAAP; all must file tax returns. But, as is discussed below, while these chores make up the bulk of a CPA's work, they are only one part of controllership.

The emphasis on financial reporting can tilt both accountants' skills and their perception of their job toward reporting—and away from operating issues. Without exposure in school to broader management topics or significant on-the-job training, accountants are poorly prepared for or even unaware of the responsibilities of controllership.

When emphasis on financial reporting is the case, accounting reports can become ends in themselves instead of a means to help management. And, not surprisingly, managers often complain that accounting reports contain mean-

Some of the best controllers don't even have strong accounting backgrounds; others are accountants who can make a transition to looking beyond the numbers and embracing a management perspective.

ingless information. They observe that financial statements are generally completed well after the end of a period and contain highly aggregated information.

While GAAP statements can and should be useful, one problem is that GAAP principles assume that the readers of financial reports are knowledgeable in accounting. Therefore, statements rarely disclose the many conventions and estimates that go into their preparation, making them difficult for the lay reader to interpret properly. These conventions and estimates are discussed in greater detail in Chapter 3.

Of course, the person best qualified to interpret a statement is an accountant, particularly the preparer. Yet, in many companies, the accountant hands off the completed financial statement to management and returns to day-to-day processing, preparing for the next month's closing. By leaving interpretation to the reader, an accountant leaves managers stranded and increases the communication gap between accounting and management. Effective controllers do not lose interest in financial statements once they have been prepared. They recognize that part of the job is interpreting the results and communicating the information to both top management and outsiders.[4]

The personality traits that attract people to accounting and make them effective are not always desirable traits in a controller.

Personality Traits

The personality traits that attract people to accounting and make them effective are not always desirable traits in a controller. The stereotype of accountants, of course, is that they are humorless, boring, nitpicking types, wearing green eyeshades, spending their workday hunched over ledger books adding up figures. While the green eyeshades have disappeared and computers have replaced ledger books, the role many accountants play in smaller companies remains isolated, narrow, and routine.

Accountants tend to be detail-oriented and very precise. Comedian Bob Newhart, a former accountant who defies this stereotype, describes his view of accounting as a "strange theory of accountancy": "if you got within two or three bucks of it," it was OK. As he says, "This never really caught on."[5]

Accountants need to have an affinity for working with very detailed information. However, a problem arises when they lose the forest for the trees and become overly precise. An intern in a government agency once had a summer job where the first month's assignment was locating a $14 discrepancy in accounts receivable dating back several months. While this example is extreme, many accountants will spend hours, even days, looking for the last dollar needed to balance a reconciliation.[6] In addition, accountants are frequently uncomfortable in providing estimates—or even rounded figures—when asked quantitative questions.

A controller needs to understand when precision is meaningful and when it is simply a number-crunching exercise. Precision can pay off when determining money owed or due—not just shifts between accounts—or where it sheds light on a chronic problem. Precision becomes costly, though, when it chews up valuable time that could be spent better on other tasks.

A controller needs to understand when precision is meaningful and when it is simply a number-crunching exercise.

Because so much of accounting is imprecise, that so much time is spent concentrating on minute details is ironic. Balance sheets will often have items accurate to the dollar next to estimates, such as for bad debt and inventory reserves, that may only be accurate within tens of thousands of dollars. And cost accountants often show unit costs to four or more decimal places when the actual precision is nowhere close to that.

Negative Goals

Accountants are often criticized as plodding, probably because accounting is such a cautious and mechanical field. For example, accounting has the negative goal of avoiding anything that might be misleading, as opposed to the positive goal of being informative. GAAP even has a conservatism convention (as discussed in Chapter 3), which says that when equally acceptable methods exist for valuing a transaction the one that results in the lowest net income must be used. You might wonder why conservatism, and not accuracy, is a convention.

Accounting leans away from subjective valuations in favor of objective numbers, often conflicting with the information needs of management.[7] Take some examples of valuing balance sheet accounts discussed in Chapters 3 and 5. The values of many assets fluctuate over time and with market conditions. Yet, because GAAP requires objectively measurable valuations, nearly all assets are shown at acquisition costs. This method of valuation works fine when assets turn over frequently, such as with accounts receivable, but introduces great distortion when applied to buildings and land held over many years. These conservative conventions can discourage accountants from thinking creatively about financial values.

Much of accounting is mechanistic. The work is performed by rote, without any real management perspective. So, the wider issues of controllership involve a significant shift. In contrast to preparation of financial statements, management accounting, asset management, planning, and internal controls deal with current operations and may not have any preset rules. The objectivity, precision, and negative goals that apply to GAAP reporting must be set aside.

Management Support

CEOs and other nonfinancial managers must support and encourage the impetus of financial staff to take on a broader range of financial issues. If your management style is seat-of-the-pants, you may obstruct this goal. Without a willingness to step back from daily operations to set direction or analyze options, it can be difficult to implement effective planning or management accounting.

Without a willingness to step back from daily operations to set direction or analyze options, it can be difficult to implement effective planning or management accounting.

A more common problem is that you may view accounting as a necessary evil. You may expect little else from your controller or accountant than producing monthly statements, paying the bills, and filing tax returns. As a result, minimal resources are allocated for the controller's area.

If your financial department is understaffed, broader controllership duties will get passed over. The controller may not have the time to concentrate on issues beyond day-to-day processing. Or, if you own a smaller business and your controller is little more than a bookkeeper, that person may be efficient at handling daily transactions and monthly closings, but be unable to produce very little else.

Substantial resources and effort must be devoted to financial management. In return, a strong, well-rounded controller can provide the controls, analysis, and decision support needed to avoid crises and identify opportunities to boost the bottom line.

What qualifications should your controller have and what should his or her duties be? The remainder of the chapter spells out a job description for the controller. The areas of responsibility discussed here also provide an outline for the material in the remainder of the book.

Beyond the Numbers

The job description of a modern controller demands an individual who is forward-looking and management-oriented. Accounting, particularly GAAP reporting, is just one part of the job. Too often, financial reporting diverts a controller's attention from the things that actually make money or can cause trouble.

Similarly, when hiring a controller, look for someone who can bring a management perspective. Financial reporting is mechanistic; finding someone who can do that task is relatively easy. What is rarer and more valuable is someone who can go beyond the numbers.

The job description below lists the objectives and areas of responsibility for the ideal controller. Specific tasks for each of the eight main areas of responsibility are explored further immediately following this job description.

Model Job Description for a Controller

Objectives

▶ Provide relevant and timely information throughout the organization and comply with outside reporting requirements, including financial, tax, and regulatory statements.

▶ Communicate financial results to investors and creditors and establish internal planning and feedback loops.

▶ Serve as the guardian of a company's assets and establish a system of internal controls, as well as protect liquidity.

▶ Manage the accounting staff and perform a number of administrative tasks.

Main Areas of Responsibility

▶ Financial and tax reporting
▶ Management accounting and decision support
▶ Planning and budgeting
▶ Monitoring
▶ Cost control
▶ Asset management
▶ Internal controls
▶ Administration

Financial and Tax Reporting

The routine recording of transactions and preparation of financial statements in accordance with GAAP are the most familiar aspects of the controller's job. These tasks extend to SEC reporting for public companies, preparation for year-end audits, and any special reporting requirements imposed by regulatory agencies, corporate partners, or investors.

While coordinating tax planning and preparation is a responsibility of the controller, he or she does not have to be a tax whiz. This expertise is available from an outside CPA. Tax regulations are complex and change regularly, and the time and cost needed to stay current—beyond maintaining a good working knowledge—are something few smaller company controllers can afford.

As discussed earlier, it is not sufficient to simply prepare a financial statement, hand it off to management, and then return to day-to-day processing. Part of financial reporting is interpreting the results and communicating the information to top management and outsiders. The controller best understands the complexities of GAAP and the assumptions that went into preparing the financial reports and so should be involved in analyzing the results.

An effective tool for communicating this information to management and outside investors is a brief write-up accompanying the actual financial statements. This write-up can discuss operating trends and variances and highlight key, but nonfinancial events. Outsiders, in particular, usually appreciate this direct line of communication with the "numbers person." In addition, discussions of financial results are an important part of quarterly and annual reports issued by public companies.

The controller must also choose the proper level of detail and organization for reports. While the minimum requirements may be a consolidated income statement and balance sheet, breakdowns of the information are usually desirable. For example, a company with several divisions probably should have a separate, pro forma income statement for each division. Breakdowns by product line or geography may be desirable. Department managers will demand information for their own activities.

In many cases, satisfying the needs of management will require special and even one-time-only reports. Your controller will need skill in extracting and manipulating detailed information that is captured, but not routinely reported by the accounting system. The controller must ensure that sufficient detail is captured and be adept in consolidating and organizing the data into useful reports.

Management Accounting and Decision Support

Financial accounting is only part of the reporting picture. While financial accounting primarily satisfies the needs of outsiders for consistent and objective historical information, management accounting is designed to satisfy

While coordinating tax planning and preparation is a responsibility of the controller, he or she does not have to be a tax whiz.

operating managers' needs for timely and detailed information about internal costs and operations as support for decision making.

Unlike tax and GAAP reporting, management accounting is not required. In addition, the form it takes is entirely up to the discretion of management. While some companies will find that the added detail is not worth the expense of collecting the data, others depend on having current cost and operating statistics. And, no matter how strong it is, a financial reporting system is not a substitute for management accounting.

In a manufacturing setting, for example, the management accounting system may be used to determine standard product costs. Operating information can be collected on how actual costs compare with the standard costs, as well as on productivity and machine utilization. In a service setting, profitability by project is crucial and individuals might be measured against sales quotas or productivity. Almost any company would like to know profitability by customer or by product, measurements that likely require breaking down sales and expense information in more detail than the general ledger.

Unlike financial reporting, which must conform to GAAP, management accounting is unregulated.

Unlike financial reporting, which must conform to GAAP, management accounting is unregulated. Whatever information is required by management, reported as frequently and in as much detail as needed, can be part of a management reporting system. The controller must not only understand the operations of a company, but also be adept at communicating with line managers and be responsive to their needs for information.

Planning and Budgeting

Seat-of-the-pants operating styles and the pressures of day-to-day operations can keep managers from doing formal planning and control. However, planning is more than an academic exercise. It is the process through which companies establish goals, communicate these goals to managers and outsiders, and identify potential problems and opportunities.

Plans and budgets should reflect the strategies and objectives of top management. The controller's job is to ensure that these plans exist, coordinate their preparation at all levels, and test them for reasonableness. The controller then monitors actual results against plans, provides feedback, and helps with any needed updates. At least three types of plans should be prepared.

A long-term model covering two to five years. The model should provide pro forma income statements and balance sheets by month for at least one year, by quarter for another year, and annually after two years. This type of plan typically is contained in a company's business plan and should be updated at least once a year.

An annual line item budget. Before the start of each fiscal year, the targets for that year should be translated into specific departmental and detailed account budgets. The controller often helps managers prepare their budgets by supplying trend data and other analyses, compiling the figures, and then tracking and reviewing any variances from the plan.

A rolling current year forecast. Expectations and plans change as a year unfolds. Keeping a current forecast broken out by month that includes actual results for closed months and updated projections for the remainder of the year is vital. Current year results are often what top management and investors are most focused on and this forecast generally provide the most current snapshot of the trends and expectations for the year.

*U*ltimately, cash flow—not profit—determines the fortunes, even survival, of a company.

Ultimately, cash flow—not profit—determines the fortunes, even survival, of a company. If liquidity is an issue, a separate *cash flow forecast* is also essential even if a company already has budgets and forecasts. Cash flow can fluctuate greatly within accounting periods and may not move in tandem with net income. The relevant time frame for cash flow forecasts depends on the stability of a company and can be as short as week-by-week or built into the long-term plan.

Monitoring

To be effective, planning and management accounting must include monitoring of results. The setting of goals and standards is not fully meaningful without evaluating progress made and using that information to improve operations. Just collecting data and issuing reports is insufficient. Active review and analysis, followed by action, provide meaningful feedback.

The controller is the logical choice to perform the review and analysis, because this person is most familiar with how the numbers were prepared and probably is the most numbers-oriented staff person. Analysis can be a time-consuming task and, just as day-to-day concerns can push planning aside, the monitoring process can get shortchanged.

In analyzing results, the controller's focus should be forward-looking. The goal is not simply to provide a scorecard, but to identify problem areas and suggest improvements. Correcting a variance or having an early warning of a potential cash crunch are more important than measuring the amount of a shortfall.

Cost Control

In addition to monitoring results, a controller should always be proactive in holding costs down. This does not mean harassing employees over expense reports, though establishing a sensible travel policy is a good idea. But nonfinancial employees are unlikely to have the same motivation to look for savings as a controller.

Cost savings include finding ways to save on routine expenditures like supplies, travel, and phone service. Rates in any of these areas can creep up over time and need to be reexamined and renegotiated periodically. Market rates for things like recruiter fees, rents, and insurance can fluctuate greatly, depending on economic conditions and the controller needs to recognize opportunities to negotiate discounts. Duplicate and unnecessary expenses can sneak in over time and a controller needs to weed these out.

On a different level, a controller needs to be involved in decisions to commit to larger expenses, such as hiring staff, leasing new space, and setting compensation plans. The forecasts and plans provide the controller knowledge on future growth and what a company can and can't afford. Without unnecessarily restraining growth, the controller needs to ensure that spending is prudent and speak up if spending commitments risk being out of line with revenue.

Asset Management

The controller is the guardian of a company's assets. From cash disbursements to credit policy, from inventory control to capital expenditures, the controller is involved in managing the movement and integrity of company assets. Often, asset management is where the controller makes the most direct impact on the bottom line.

Both physically and figuratively, the controller controls the checkbook. Ensuring proper authorization for all cash disbursements and managing cash flow—the timing of both expenditures and receipts—are jobs of the controller. A controller also works hard to squeeze cash out of assets, such as receivables and inventory, while stretching payments to the greatest degree possible.

Accounts receivable can tie up large amounts of cash and expose a company to bad debt losses. By establishing and enforcing a credit and collections policy, a controller can achieve timely collections and reduce potential write-offs.

From cash disbursements to credit policy, from inventory control to capital expenditures, the controller is involved in managing the movement and integrity of company assets.

Inventory, for companies that carry it, usually is the greatest control risk. Not only is it expensive to carry, but any on-hand stock is subject to obsolescence, theft, and damage. Through physical controls, reporting systems, and sharp analysis, a controller can work to improve turnover, while ensuring a proper mix of materials and finished goods.

Internal Controls

The accuracy and integrity of financial systems and data depend on having a system of internal checks and balances. The controller must be familiar with basic controls and implement them.

While fraud is one target of controls, the actual incidence of fraud is quite slight. For example, restricting physical access to assets and ensuring that at least two people must authorize any transaction that expends an asset are simple but often sufficient controls against fraud.

Two more important targets of controls are reducing errors and ensuring proper accountability for transactions. Many companies suffer from redundant processing, costly errors and omissions, or double-checks that could be avoided with an orderly system of checks and balances.

A controller will often find resistance to the work that goes with enforcing controls. When pressure rises to push work out, shortcuts that bypass the control process often slip in. The controller must be able to explain the need for controls and enforce adherence. Support by top management is especially important in this area.

Administration

A controller in most companies is asked to handle a wide range of administrative tasks. The exact mix will vary from company to company, but these are some common areas:

- ▶ Legal and contract issues
- ▶ Human resources and employee benefits
- ▶ Computer and office equipment selection and upkeep
- ▶ Insurance
- ▶ Office management
- ▶ Payroll
- ▶ Records management

The size of a company and whether it has additional managers for personnel and treasury will determine the breadth of the controller's job. But even if the controller doesn't have primary responsibility, his or her input will typically be sought on these matters.

Controller as Ombudsman

In addition to these eight main areas of responsibility discussed above, your controller should be available to act as your company's ombudsman. The controller is most likely the person with the greatest overlap into the various functions within your company and often knows more about a company's operation than anyone except the very top managers. Because so much information flows through the controller's department and from nearly all areas of a company, the controller often has a better overview of the total operation than others on the management team.

The controller is most likely the person with the greatest overlap into the various functions within your company and often knows more about a company's operation than anyone except the very top managers.

Show all business proposals to your controller to ensure they make economic sense. Your controller must be prepared to ask questions about how projects will be funded, raise legal questions, or ensure that proper milestones are established. Within limits, the controller's job is to be a cynic. Not to unnecessarily beat on managers or be a pessimist, your controller's job is to make sure the tough questions get asked and the numbers get run about planned projects or past performance.

Working Together

Clearly, the traditional bean counter role for a controller is inadequate. The job calls for a dynamic, management-oriented person who can play a key role in setting and achieving the goals of your company.

The job may also require an additional investment in staffing the accounting department. The controller's slot demands a highly skilled and experienced manager, a person harder to find than a technically skilled accountant. And because the duties are also expanded, additional support staff may be required. However, these investments in the controllership function will pay off.

To repeat, no matter how skilled the controller or large the support staff, his or her job is to support management, not run the company. To return to the airplane analogy, the controller provides the instrument panel, but is not the pilot. The controller's job is to provide accurate, timely, and relevant information. He or she can flash warnings, suggest action, and even make some minor corrections directly. But the ultimate decision making rests with management.

For managers and the controller to understand these roles and work closely together is crucial. Managers need both useful information and assurance that day-to-day transactions are accurate and complete. Conversely, the controller needs feedback on what information is needed and support to enforce compliance with policies and procedures.

Desired Background

Just as the notion of the controller as bean counter is obsolete, so is the idea that an effective controller can work in the isolation of the accounting department. The controller must get into the trenches and work with managers throughout a company. The term "shirtsleeve controller" is often used and appropriately connotes someone who works hands-on and who is able to communicate through informal, as well as formal channels.

An effective controller in a smaller company should not just be adept at figures. He or she must have management savvy and the forcefulness to get things done throughout an organization.

An effective controller in a smaller company should not just be adept at figures. He or she must have management savvy and the forcefulness to get things done throughout an organization. Prior smaller company experience is important; the orientation of larger companies is very different and the transition from a larger to a smaller company more difficult than it appears.

Should the controller be a CPA? It doesn't hurt, but it should not be a prerequisite. The CPA designation means proven expertise in financial accounting, audit, and tax. But, the CPA designation says nothing about management experience and, therefore, is greatly overrated as a qualification for company controller candidates. In fact, a certified management accountant (CMA) may be a more appropriate designation to look for.

In addition, many highly skilled accountants choose to bypass the certification process or have passed the CPA exam but simply lack the public accounting work experience or continuing education necessary for the CPA designation.

A controller could even be a nonaccountant. Technical accounting skills should take a back seat to management skills and hands-on experience.

Controlling the Controller

Simply redefining the controller's job description is not enough. Managers must take an active role in accounting issues and, in short, control the controller. Just as the controller must have management savvy, nonfinancial managers can benefit from a working knowledge of accounting.

The remainder of the book explores further several of the areas of controllership described above. By understanding the objectives and practices in each area, you can ask better questions of your financial managers and work more effectively with them. The next chapter focuses on how to satisfy your internal needs for information.

Notes

1. Jerome V. Bennett, *Administering the Company Accounting Function*, second ed. (Englewood Cliffs, NJ: Prentice-Hall, 1981), p. 38.

2. Robert Townsend, *Further Up the Organization* (New York: Alfred A. Knopf, 1984), p. 2.

3. Monroe S. Kuttner, "Putting the Controller in Control," *Journal of Accountancy*, May 1993, p. 89.

4. Howard Ross, *The Elusive Art of Accounting: A Brash Commentary on Financial Statements* (New York: Ronald Press, 1966), p. 14.

5. Bob Newhart, "Retirement Party," *The Best of Bob Newhart* (Warner Brothers Records, 1963).

6. There is an element of validity here. Even though a reconciliation may be out of balance by only a dollar or two, there is no guarantee that the difference is trivial. The error could consist of two large transactions, one a plus and one a minus. In addition, tracking down a $50 difference in some accounts may uncover a billing or payment error that translates into cash for a company. In these situations, the cost of the time needed to reconcile and the potential benefit should be compared.

7. Ross, *The Elusive Art of Accounting*, p. 12.

Chapter 7

Management Accounting

> If you can't measure it, you can't manage it.
> —Anonymous[1]
>
> Tell me how you measure me and I will tell you how I will perform.
> —Eli Goldratt[2]

SPORTS IS A COMMON METAPHOR FOR BUSINESS AND, IN THE CASE OF how information is used, a correlation exists between the needs of business and baseball managers. In baseball, a handful of accepted measures of performance are used: batting averages, earned run averages, saves, and runs batted in, to name a few. Specific rules about how each is calculated limit the use of individual judgment. Having these rules ensures that games in different cities are accounted for in the same way, making statistical comparisons valid across the league and across seasons. Knowledgeable fans are also aware of how the accounting is done and can interpret a box score or an individual player's statistics.

The baseball manager, however, quickly finds these popular measures insufficient. Information may be needed on how a batter does against a particular pitcher or in "clutch" situations. Does the manager "play the percentages" and change pitchers? Order a bunt? How should fielders be positioned for a hitter? The manager needs statistics specific to these decision-making needs.

The manager also needs certain information almost as fast as it is available. By the time the box score is published the next morning, the statistics are too late to help. Watch any baseball telecast and the availability and proliferation of statistics is evident, attesting to the desire for information beyond that supplied by traditional performance measures.

Information Needs

Information needs in business parallel the needs in baseball. Financial accounting is akin to traditional baseball statistics, providing a consistent and fair method of keeping score, while primarily intended to serve the needs of outsiders. But often, this traditional information isn't enough and you need additional information that is tailored to support decision-making and provide meaningful feedback. The information must be more detailed, timely, and focused on internal operations than GAAP reporting. Management accounting—also known as *cost accounting*—is a separate discipline, or perhaps more of a mindset, designed to meet this need for internal, operating information.

Financial accounting is akin to traditional baseball statistics, providing a consistent and fair method of keeping score, while primarily intended to serve the needs of outsiders.

Though often thought of in connection with inventory or project costing, management accounting refers to a broad range of internal decision support tools from complex manufacturing systems to basic tracking of key indicators. Running numbers on the basis of product, project, or unit supports decision making in a way aggregated GAAP statements can't. As one manager says,[3]

> Without a good cost accounting system, it's management by anecdote. Salespeople regularly make passionate pleas for price relief on specific orders. When I press them, they say "threat of competitive entry." What choice do you have in the absence of cost data except to go by your judgment of the salesperson's credibility?

Financial vs. Management Accounting

The major differences between financial and management accounting can be summarized as follows:

Financial Accounting	Management Accounting
Financial accounting is required	Management accounting is optional
Financial accounting is governed by GAAP	Management accounting is unregulated
Financial accounting reports only on monetary measures	Management accounting can report on nonmonetary measures
Financial accounting reports only on the past	Management accounting can report on the present and take future events into consideration
Financial accounting often aggregates figures	Management accounting is detail-oriented and more likely to focus on segments of a business
Financial accounting uses defined fiscal periods	Management accounting can report over any time period deemed relevant

Management accounting is often referred to as a fairly recent development. However, at least two influential writers, Robert Kaplan of Harvard Business School and H. Thomas Johnson of Portland State University, convincingly argue that management accounting practices flourished in 19th- and early 20th-century businesses.[4] Unencumbered by the need to report to outsiders, business owners kept tabs on key operating factors, secure in the knowledge that, if these were in order, profits would take care of themselves. According to Kaplan and Johnson, the increasing use of outside financing in the early 1900s led to the dominance of financial reporting and squeezed management reporting out of many companies.

Management accounting can address your information needs about internal operations that are unmet by financial reporting. The information you receive should provide detailed and timely feedback on the efficiency of your operations, plus provide a measure of your product costs. This chapter covers the basic issues of management accounting that arise in practice.

What to Measure

Management accounting is often taught as an inventory valuation tool. However, the concepts of collecting nonfinancial information, calculating profitability by project or customer, tracking key ratios like sales per square foot, and computing many more measures not covered by GAAP reporting can be applied across a broad range of organizations and activities. The key is getting timely and useful information, in any format you desire, unencumbered by the conventions of financial accounting. To effectively operate your business, you want whatever it takes to get a handle on key indicators of success, whether it is the true contribution to profits of various products and activities or an alert to possible problems. Examples of important nonfinancial feedback you could choose to receive include the following:

▶ Quality might be measured by parts rejected, customer returns or complaints, scrap, or a teacher-to-student ratio.

▶ Productivity is indicated by units produced, sales per salesperson, and transactions processed. The information could be used in manufacturing, sales, and general and administrative departments (G&A), respectively.

▶ Capacity utilization is very important for industries with a fixed capital plant. Hotels measure vacancy rates, airlines watch the percent of capacity, and manufacturers track plant and machine utilization.

▶ Efficiency can measure how quickly assets turn over. Grocers track stock-outs and spoilage; credit managers watch average days receivable. Inventory turns are often key indicators.

▶ Absenteeism and turnover rates may give insights into morale problems.

▶ Overtime hours may indicate activity or how smoothly work is scheduled.

▶ The number of new leads generated and percentage of sales closed may be key for a sales organization.

Key Indicators

Though the cost of a significant management accounting system may be beyond some companies, even the smallest businesses can benefit by identifying and tracking key indicators.

Key indicators will vary from organization to organization. Some managers like to focus on their top-line products. High-tech manufacturers often track bookings, backlog, and billings. Other managers may want to simply know total cash in and out. Most of the nonfinancial measures mentioned earlier—such as those that measure quality, productivity, efficiency, and capacity utilization—could qualify as key indicators.

You may find it useful to ask your controllers or bookkeepers to develop daily or weekly flash reports that track these kinds of vital numbers. Most of the information is easy to gather and, therefore, can be available on a timely basis. And best of all, the format can be simple to read and understand. Rather than dig through printouts, you can get a one-page report that keeps you on top of business trends. Here are examples from two CEOs:

You may find it useful to ask your controllers or bookkeepers to develop daily or weekly flash reports that track these kinds of vital numbers.

Ron Friedman, CEO of a 75-person accounting firm, says, "Every morning by 9:30, I receive a printed report that tracks certain key results from the day before. That's a tremendous management advantage. I can respond immediately to any problem signals. Think of all the time and money you lose when you find out about problems only at the end of the week or the month. Depending on the type of business you're in, the numbers you need to watch this closely will be different. Small fluctuations are only natural, but once you track daily results for a while, you'll get a feel for those fluctuations that are more troubling."[5]

Norm Brodsky, a veteran entrepreneur, says this about his records storage business. "I've learned over the past 13 years that our sales rise in direct proportion to the number of new boxes we add in a given period. Tell me on September 1 how many new boxes came in during August, and I can tell you our overall sales for August within 1% or 2%."

He adds, "The best businesspeople I know all have key numbers they track on a daily or weekly basis. It's an essential part of running a successful enterprise. Key numbers give you the financial information you need to take timely action. Business moves too fast to wait for the monthly, quarterly, or annual statements."[6]

Make sure, though, that your key numbers are the right ones. Author and entrepreneur Jack Stack tells of a hotel manager who focused on reducing expenses when his key number should have been occupancy. No matter how low his costs were, he simply wasn't filling enough rooms to make money.[7] Another company adopted the trendy economic value added (EVA), a complicated number that blends several factors into a single measure. While the number may have been relevant, no one understood it. As a result, no corrective actions were taken.[8]

Traditional Cost Accounting

What is often taught as management, or cost, accounting has its roots in manufacturing companies and the costing of inventory. However, classic cost accounting methods can apply to other types of businesses, including companies trying to determine profitability of projects or product lines or comparing actual results with budget. Below is an overview of terminology, practices, and methods of traditional management accounting.

Terminology

Usually, management accounting systems are concerned with determining what products or services should cost, tracking actual costs, and examining any differences. Below are some of the terms accountants use to describe these processes.

Standard cost is the predetermined estimate of what a product or service should cost. It can be a target or average against which performance can be gauged. Standard cost usually refers to a unit cost.

Variances are the difference between actual and standard cost. The term is also commonly used to express the difference between budgeted and actual results. Where performance is better than standard, such as lower costs or higher margins, a *favorable* variance results. If performance is worse, the variance is termed *unfavorable*. By convention, accountants generally show unfavorable in parentheses, e.g., (10) regardless of whether actual result is numerically higher or lower than budget.

Variances may be analyzed further to isolate cost drivers. For example, a product's unit cost could be impacted by changes in labor hours, labor rates, the price of purchased components, volume, and total overhead costs. Therefore, accountants may break down a variance into pieces such as a purchase price variance or labor rate variance.

Variable costs or **direct costs** are those expenditures that change proportionately with each unit produced or each hour billed. The material that goes into making and packaging a product and the labor used to assemble and transport it are all variable costs.

Fixed costs are expenses assumed to be constant, or at least constant over a certain time period. Fixed costs may also be referred to as *overhead*, *burden*, or *indirect* costs. Heat, rent, and equipment are examples of fixed costs. Adding one additional unit of output would not change the expenditure on these items.

It's important to recognize that no costs are totally fixed. Given a large enough change in volume or passage of time, all costs are subject to change. One can't project significant increases in revenue without allowing for at least some increase in so-called fixed costs or overhead.

Semi-variable costs vary in discrete steps, where producing one additional unit would not change costs, but adding 100 units might. These costs could include supervisory time, machine repairs, or customer support. Sometimes, semi-variable costs are treated as a separate category. More frequently, companies distinguish only between fixed and variable costs, forcing a decision on which group these costs belong to.

Joint-product costs arise from processes that contribute to multiple products simultaneously; they are the costs incurred in shared processes. These costs pose a particularly difficult accounting problem—though they may vary directly with total volume, they cannot be traced directly to a single product.

Allocation of costs is the apportionment of expenses or revenues, according to a basis other than direct measurement. For example, if a software company has multiple products, it may try to allocate computer server and work-group software cost based on headcount; a retailer may allocate rent to departments based on square footage. Cost allocations are issues in almost any exercise determining costs and profitability of products, services, and offices. As discussed in more detail later in this chapter, allocations also have numerous pitfalls.

Full cost or **fully absorbed cost** is the sum of all the costs of production: direct costs plus an allocated portion of indirect costs.

Gross margin is the difference between a product's selling price and the full acquisition cost. It factors in any production or shipping overhead but not selling and administrative costs. Note how this differs from direct margin.

Direct margin or **contribution margin** is the difference between selling price and direct costs. It represents profit before considering any overhead costs.

Job costing tracks costs by project or production run rather than by individual unit of product. For example, a consulting firm or building contractor may be more interested in the profitability of jobs than a cost per hour.

Incremental cost and last dollar pricing is a concept expressing the belief that, in setting prices for incremental orders or products, you should consider only the variable costs involved. Many orders that may appear to produce a loss if an average overhead factor is tacked on may actually be profitable as long as direct costs are covered.

Opportunity cost involves the idea that taking one course of action or using up a resource may preclude another option. In this case, the true cost of an action may not be what was spent but rather what profits were missed by not pursuing the alternative activity.

Setting Standards

Standard costs are the basic measures of management accounting. They provide a basis for valuing products and services and targets against which performance by your company and your employees can be measured. Because feedback is often provided in comparison with a standard, you must decide how easy or difficult standards should be to achieve. You have three basic choices for setting standards:

▶ **Historical performance standards.** Standards based on historical performance have the advantage of being objectively measurable and will highlight trends in operating performance. However, this method has the weakness of ignoring changes in processes, volumes, and product design. Past inefficiencies are also built into current targets.

▶ **Engineered standards.** Standards set by looking at how, in theory, a job can or should be done. These may end up being more a set of ideals than reality, as problems under actual operating conditions may not be factored in. Nonetheless, these targets may provide a good standard against which to measure variances.

▶ **Attainable standards.** Setting attainable standards is a popular technique that recognizes the inevitability of some inefficiency, such as down time or equipment failures, but often sets standards more challenging than historical performance. These standards should be set tough enough to provide meaningful targets but reasonable enough to keep employees motivated.

Which method you choose will depend on your use of the standards. A mix may be appropriate, as can be seen from the following example:

One company that produced disposable medical devices that were packaged into kits used a very effective mix of standards. Historical standards were applied to machine time used in molding and extruding high volumes of cups, syringes, and tubing. This provided times that were realistic—since no machine upgrades were planned—and easily measured. Since little labor was involved, the lack of an incentive to boost output was immaterial.

Engineered standards were used for component and packaging materials, where product specifications were tight with little tolerance for variances. Attainable standards were an integral part of the labor standards for packaging. Employee compensation included individual incentive pay for meeting and beating standards. Standards that were unattainable led workers to give up or leave the company due to low pay. Unattainable standards also understated a product's cost, since standard labor hours were too low. Standards that were too easy were costly to the company. Once the company revised its standards to a rate slightly below what the very best workers could do and adjusted further for normal down time, productivity rose and standard costs better reflected actual production costs.

Operating Ratios

Often, measurements of key indicators take the form of ratios: gross margin, sales per salesperson, sales per square foot, and billable vs. payroll hours.

Often, measurements of key indicators take the form of ratios: gross margin, sales per salesperson, sales per square foot, and billable vs. payroll hours are typical measurement ratios. Ratios are useful for comparing results from different periods or benchmarking against other companies. You can look for information on other companies in the same industry or with similar growth patterns. Trade associations can be a good source of standard ratios for your industry. Try to find other companies of similar age or capital structure. A company that outsources much of the operation will look very different from one that does everything in house. Young, emerging companies may operate quite differently from more mature competitors.

The actual value of a ratio is often less important than the change over time. You will want to investigate any changes in your ratios. Here's an example:

One company that was growing, but slower than forecast, noticed that sales per salesperson were decreasing. The cause turned out to be that older salespeople had to spend much of their time training new ones, which kept them from calling on customers. The company, which had to make long-term advance commitments for capital equipment and, therefore, needed accurate sales forecasts to avoid unnecessary spending, was able to adjust its sales expectations and bring its expenditures in line.

Analysis Pitfalls

Common pitfalls exist across a broad range of product, unit, or project analyses. The following illustrate some do's and don'ts of financial analysis and management accounting.

Don't Tie into GAAP

Management and financial accounting should coexist, one geared toward internal decision making and the other done in accordance with GAAP and intended for outsiders. Where many companies get in trouble is forcing cost figures and reporting to tie into financial reporting.

The conventions, definitions, and timing of financial reporting are simply inappropriate for management reporting. Management accounting is not simply a subset or rearrangement of financial accounting data; it is a separate discipline, requiring a different approach and mindset. GAAP concepts that can lead to problems include the following:

Management and financial accounting should coexist, one geared toward internal decision making and the other done in accordance with GAAP and intended for outsiders.

▶ Being tied to fiscal periods for reporting. Management reporting doesn't need to report in months, quarters, or years. It can be weeks, days, or even hours. Also, reporting can be more frequent and timely with no need to wait until a fiscal month is closed.

▶ Ignoring nonfinancial measures.

▶ Sharply dividing production from selling, administrative, and R&D. This can lead to excluding direct costs, such as royalties and commissions, from product costs while feeling the need to allocate all indirect production costs.

▶ Assuming that costs deferred for financial reporting, such as fixed asset purchases, must be deferred for cost accounting or that expenditures such as advertising or R&D must be treated as expenses even if they have future value.

▶ Aggregating data rather than looking at unit, product line, or location costs.

▶ Assuming that historic cost is the only available measure. Current market values, incremental cost, or opportunity cost may also be appropriate.

Ignore Sunk Costs

In management decision making, sunk costs are usually irrelevant. Past expenditures for equipment, advertising, or goodwill cannot be altered, so you must focus on making best use of your current resources. At the same time, you will realize that some current and future expenditures will provide a long-term benefit, while others provide only an immediate return.

Once again, GAAP rules may not align with these decision-making criteria. Many sunk costs, such as equipment purchases, goodwill, and pension benefits for prior service, must be spread over future periods. At the same time, other expenditures with possible future benefit, such as R&D and advertising, are expensed immediately.

Avoid Simplistic Allocations

Most companies have a large pool of expenses that do not appear directly related to the cost of producing products, delivering services, or selling. In many companies, this may even be the vast majority of expenses, including overhead, such as managers' wages, utilities, marketing, insurance, and rent.

When a unit is truly stand-alone, such as a company with just a single retail store or subsidiary producing and selling a single product, total profitability can be captured fairly, as all overhead costs relate to the same activity. But when multiple products, locations, or operating units contribute to a shared overhead cost, determining how much of the cost belongs to each gets extremely imprecise.

Deciding on what measure of input to base an allocation can get sticky. At the medical device company mentioned above, some packaging operations were manual, while some were machine-based. Each operation had a different number of required workers. On what basis should expenses be allocated? Total units produced? The value of the units produced? Total machine hours? Total labor hours? Dollars of direct labor? The space occupied by each operation? In this situation, many manufacturers blindly choose labor hours as the basis of allocations. This scheme makes sense when production is labor-intensive; however, as processes are increasingly automated, many such allocations have become outdated. The best allocation scheme is one that traces costs as closely as possible to their source.

The math of computing allocations can be very straightforward. It's easy to divide rent expense by headcount, but does headcount really drive rent expense? In *Relevance Lost*, authors Thomas Johnson and Robert Kaplan present an example of a company that mistakenly relied on such an allocation.[9]

> The company had incurred a large expense for prior service pension costs. Under GAAP accounting, these costs are capitalized and amortized over time. The company, quite logically, allocated the expense to different plants based on years of service of the workers. This allocated most of the expense to the plant with the older workforce. Even though this plant was actually more efficient than newer plants with younger workforces, the numbers made it seem more expensive to operate and, as a result, it was shut down. The problem, as explained earlier, is that these pension costs were sunk costs; they had nothing to do with current operations, yet were accounted for as if they did.

If overhead expenses are not driven by the activity being measured or the allocation scheme seems indirect, it may be better not to do any allocation at all. It may be better to simply focus on the contribution margin of a product or a group, considering only direct costs, and set targets high enough so that it's clear that overhead costs will be covered.

Note that for manufacturers this could be a difference from GAAP accounting, where all manufacturing expenses are allocated to inventory costs. However, GAAP conventions for inventory valuations do not need to be applied to other analysis.

Control Overhead Expense

One danger of allocating away overhead expenses or calling them "fixed costs" is that one may believe they neither change nor need to be controlled. These can represent 60%, 80%, or more of a company's costs, so ignoring them in favor of direct or more easily measured costs like labor can be a mistake. Consider the following points:

▶ Allocating overhead expense based on labor can make direct labor seem more costly than it really is and the allocations can make it seem that overhead is actually a function of labor hours.

▶ If overhead is allocated out, managers may not feel compelled or able to control those costs, especially if they arise in other departments. Worse, they may have an incentive to reduce the direct costs on which overhead expenses are allocated, but no incentive to reduce overhead itself.

► Costs may not be as fixed as often assumed. Although one additional unit of output won't change what is spent in the short term on rent, insurance, or management, these expenses can change and do bear a relationship to activities. Three months, a year, or five years may pass, but all expenses become variable at some point.

Rather than create the illusion that volume or production efficiencies can change overhead, a better option is budgeting and controlling overhead expenses separately. For example, if the cost of the human resource department cannot be traced to individual products, establish an operating budget and hold the department manager responsible for it. Perhaps, you can develop measures for efficiency, such as cost per applicant. If costs change, the results are reported for just the department; the difference does not have to be absorbed by other departments or individual products.

Down Time and Economies of Scale

Picking up and putting down a product and starting and stopping processes add costs. Yet, a cost accounting system may look only at volume of production.

Costs are accrued not just when a piece of manufacturing equipment is in use or an employee is working on a billable client project. Part of any process is setup and down time and, if these are not accounted for, a cost accounting system can make one run of 100 hours look as costly as 100 runs of one hour each. Better instead to look at elapsed time from the start of one job to the start of the next.

Related to this, renowned management consultant and writer Peter Drucker asserts that actual costs are in proportion to the number of transactions an operation generates.[10] Picking up and putting down a product and starting and stopping processes add costs. Yet, a cost accounting system may look only at volume of production.

Drucker also talks about the cost of product clutter. Customers increasingly expect choices; gone are the days where consumers are offered "any color, so long as it is black." According to Drucker, this can be very costly, because in most companies, a 90-10 rule exists: 90% of the profits come from 10% of the products. When looking at costs, a system must be able to distinguish the very real cost differences that arise from volume production, higher sales turnover, and learning curve efficiencies enjoyed by mature or popular products and services.

The following example illustrates some of the issues in this section.

A medical device company's management accounting system showed that it was losing money on every unit of three of its 10 top-selling products. Over the protests of the sales manager, the company tried raising prices— only to see volume sink in the highly competitive market. After restoring their prices, management took a closer look at the standard costs. They discovered that overhead was allocated based on inputs, such as standard machine and labor hours. Standard cost per unit was the same whether a typical production run was 1,000 units or just one. This application of standard costs ignored efficiencies that large production runs of these popular products generated, such as reduced setup and handling time. As a result, the best-selling products were being assigned a disproportionately high amount of overhead expenses. Contrary to the accounting reports, all of the top products were actually profitable.

Overburdening

Without the effort to uncover the true relationship between activity and cost, the time spent devising allocation formulas will succeed in spreading overhead costs, but will say nothing about what actually drives them or how you can control them. Even worse, you may rely on this faulty cost information to make critical decisions.

The use of direct labor to allocate manufacturing overhead is a prime, and common, example. While this may have been a reasonable basis 30 or 40 years ago, many manufacturers have become increasingly automated over time. Automation reduces the labor pool over which to spread overhead expenses and makes labor seem increasingly expensive. Automation also makes departments that are labor-intensive seem increasingly expensive by comparison.

The results can be appalling. Companies, seeing their fully burdened labor cost rise, have been led to outsource work in search of less expensive labor, only to find they have been led astray by the accounting system. Although labor costs may seem to decline, outsourcing adds a very large overhead expense in purchasing, shipping, inspection, accounting, and top management time and money. And if the accounting system ignores or fails to properly allocate these expenses, the outsourcing option will continue to look good. Even worse, since the internal labor pool has shrunk further, burden rates become even higher, making in-house production look even less attractive.

Similar distortions can occur in decisions to shift work among departments within a company. Any system that does not reflect true cost relationships will result in cross-subsidies among products. Profitable products assigned excessive overhead costs can end up being eliminated or priced out of the market. Allocating on a basis other than labor may not solve the problem, since the issue often is the decision to allocate costs in the first place.

Excessive Detail and Precision

Just because data can be collected does not mean you should collect it all. Accountants are very comfortable with detailed, precise information and, left to their own devices, may design an overly elaborate system.

Accountants are very comfortable with detailed, precise information and, left to their own devices, may design an overly elaborate system.

Another issue is that a measurement can only be as accurate as each component. If labor costs can be precisely tracked but material costs cannot, the combined total will be only as good as the material costs. Efforts in capturing labor costs may be wasted.

A problem in manufacturing systems is that cost data tend to be very precise—or at least appear that way. A product's cost may be broken down to its minutest components or carried out to four decimal places. The latter occurs because components are bought in bulk and labor or machine output is often tabulated in units per day or hour. For example, if you buy 20,000 screws at a time for $75 and use two per product, your cost is $0.0075 per unit of finished product. Or, if one person making $12 per hour can process 130 pieces per hour, the labor cost for that operation is $12 divided by 130 or $0.0923 each. The use of four decimal places results from the arithmetic used and does not necessarily mean that you should have confidence down to one-hundredth of a penny.

In fact, that very precision often masks a high degree of uncertainty. How many managers, looking at a cost carried out to four decimal places, would suspect that the numbers *before* the decimal could be wrong? What if production in the example above ranged from 100 to 150 pieces per hour and there were 100 such operations per finished product? Total labor costs could be as high as $12 or as low as $8. A unit cost carried out to four decimal places would give no hint of the wide variation possible.

Even where a high degree of precision is possible, it is usually best not to sweat the small stuff, as the example below illustrates.

At a circuit board assembly company, the person preparing kits for production always counted out the 10 nuts and screws that went into each product. This practice lasted until the owner walked by and recognized the inefficiency of counting such low-cost parts. The owner reached over, grabbed a handful of nuts and screws, tossed them into the kit and said, "That's 10."

Other Concepts

Last Dollar Pricing

As mentioned earlier, last dollar pricing expresses the idea that, in setting prices for incremental orders or products, you should consider only the variable costs involved. Many orders that may appear to produce a loss if an average overhead factor is tacked on may actually be profitable as long as direct costs are covered.

This is a very simple, yet powerful idea. A company with excess capacity can ill afford to turn away sales that generate cash just because the margin doesn't cover a somewhat arbitrary fair share of the overhead. An enlightened approach is to ignore sunk costs—unrecoverable prior expenditures—and concentrate on the added benefit a job can bring.

Many orders that may appear to produce a loss if an average overhead factor is tacked on may actually be profitable as long as direct costs are covered.

However, you can very easily go overboard with this approach. Rarely are overhead costs truly fixed. Rather, they simply tend to move in discrete steps. Utilities and supplies, for example, often increase on a unit-to-unit basis, but not always proportionately. The changes may also be impractical to measure. And while it is fine to accept the incremental order that covers only its direct cost, somewhere along the line a company's pricing must be set to cover overhead as well.

A clothing manufacturer that was losing money and had excess capacity took on contract manufacturing from another company. The money made exceeded standard labor costs and it appeared the added work would add to the bottom line. However, the new work clogged the factory and contributed to production problems with the manufacturer's standard lines. Furthermore, the standards of the new customer were different and significant rework was required, wiping out the already thin margins.

A commonly heard expression is that incremental sales help absorb overhead. This term seems to downplay two important facts:

▶ First, in aggregate, for a product's price to simply exceed direct costs is insufficient. The product must be profitable after all costs are considered. The price must not just absorb overhead but cover it.

▶ Second, the phrase implies that overhead is fixed and somehow beyond control and that any profit must be derived from increasing direct margins. In truth, overhead expenses are often as controllable as direct costs.

The bottom line is that if an order is truly incremental business, then you are correct to consider only incremental costs—which may include direct and semi-variable costs. Long-term decisions must take overhead into account. After all, in the long run, all costs are variable. In addition, if accepting one piece of business affects your company's ability to take on other business, the lost profit is part of the incremental costs.

An innovative approach to pricing made popular by Texas Instruments for products such as digital watches and calculators is to take advantage of learning curves.

Learning Curves

An innovative approach to pricing made popular by Texas Instruments for products such as digital watches and calculators is to take advantage of learning curves. Empirical evidence points out that, for new products or processes, costs decline as experience increases. At least one study has shown cost reductions from 20% to 30% for each doubling of cumulative production. Machine-intensive operations show lesser, but still significant reductions.[11] This approach suggests that it may be profitable to drop prices below current costs if doing so buys sufficient market share to increase volume and move down the learning curve to lower costs.

Not every business should rush to cut prices and pump up volume. But you should realize that costs are not static and that pricing decisions require an understanding of business dynamics.

Activity-Based Costing

If relationships among overhead expenses and specific activities can be traced and if tracking the costs is important enough, a company may want to consider activity-based costing (ABC). ABC is a fairly recent development in management accounting that traces all indirect costs back to the products that generated them. ABC recognizes the problems traditional cost systems have with allocating overhead and with ignoring selling and administrative expenses, even though these may vary with sales or production volume.

In addition to trying to more accurately record both product costs and the relationship of activity to overall expenses, ABC looks at seemingly fixed costs as resources and examines how efficiently they are used. For example, if a purchasing manager can process 2,000 transactions a month, but handles only 1,500 this month, there is excess capacity of 500 transactions.

ABC can show department managers how they are using the purchasing manager, the economics of having excess capacity, and what would happen if the number of transactions increased. Since in the long run the amount spent on purchasing managers and other overhead departments will adjust to volume, the future impact on these costs can be determined.

While ABC improves the quality of management accounting information, it often uses the same accounting information as traditional systems. The underlying data must be sound or ABC will just be a rehashing of those figures. More importantly, ABC also takes only quantitative measures into consideration. Critics argue that accounting-based systems cannot tell you about quality, customer satisfaction, and other nonquantitative concerns. To the extent that these are critical success factors, even the most sophisticated accounting system will come up short.

Flexible Budgets

What if your company establishes expense targets based on $100,000 of sales per month and actual volume is $120,000 or $200,000? Some expenses, such as rent, will likely be unaffected by the increase in volume, but will decline on a percent of sales or per unit basis. Many other costs will increase with volume and, perhaps, exceed originally budgeted levels. If sales fell to $80,000, the reverse would be true. How valid can ratios, standard costs, and budgets be if sales volumes fluctuate from projected levels?

One common tool for capturing these relationships is the flexible budget. Rather than pegging budgeted expenditures at fixed levels, the budget for each variable expense is expressed as a function of the activity that drives it. These activities that drive expenditures may be sales volume, units produced, sales calls made, or number of clients seen.

Once these relationships are determined, the flexible budget can adapt to

Some expenses, such as rent, will likely be unaffected by the increase in volume, but will decline on a percent of sales or per unit basis.

any level of activity. More information about flexible budgets is provided in Chapter 12.

For managers trying to stay within budget, a flexible budget means having the freedom to hire more people as volume increases or pressure to cut costs if activity declines. Rather than going through the roof when travel expenses exceed budget, top managers can relate travel costs to the number of sales calls made. In fact, some of the most valuable and quick tests you can make are ratios between costs and total activity. These ratios might include sales per salesperson or employee, sales per square foot, and direct labor cost per unit produced.

Computing Labor Costs

A common issue for companies as diverse as manufacturers trying to determine labor cost per unit and professional firms trying to price services is calculating labor costs. Payroll taxes, fringe benefits, holidays, and down time can easily add 40%-60% over and above basic wages.

Take as an example an employee earning $20/hour. Over 52 weeks and 40 hours per week, gross pay is $41,600. However, assume that the employer must pay the following payroll taxes:

Tax	Sample Rate	Annual Cost
FICA and Medicare	7.65%	$3,182
State Unemployment	3.5% on first $10,800	$56
Federal Unemployment	0.8% on first $7,000	$378

Now add in other common fringes:

Benefit	Sample Rate	Annual Cost
Holiday Bonus— Two Weeks' Pay	4%	$1,664
Health and Dental Insurance	$600/month	$7,200
401(k) Match	1%	$416

Others: Tuition assistance,
  stock options, profit
  sharing, charitable
  contribution match, etc.
	$1,000	$1,000

These bring out-of-pocket compensation costs up to $55,496, a 33% boost over base pay. Now look at the hours worked. An employee may average 15 vacation and sick days plus 10 holidays, reducing the hours worked from 2080 to 1880. Dividing this into $55,496 yields hourly compensation of $29.52, a premium of 48% over the base pay of $20/hour.

Other factors can also drive up the hourly or daily cost of labor. There is always a certain amount of down time in a day for breaks, meetings, or administrative tasks. The number of billable or productive hours in a day may be only two-thirds of the hours paid for. The numbers above are also before overhead costs associated with employees, such as computers, office space, supplies, and phones. The fully loaded cost of an office employee is often close to double his or her base wages.

Influencing Behavior

Management reporting systems not only report on performance but, because they provide feedback and incentive, they also influence behavior as well. Your measurement system must be in line with the strategic goals of your company. These goals can be both financial and nonfinancial.

In financial accounting, success is generally measured by profits—or a related criterion, such as ROI. One problem with this standard is that profit is basically a short-term yardstick. Unfortunately, short-term profits can rise while the long-term health of a company declines. Slashing expenses, such as advertising or R&D, boosts profits but sacrifices future returns; a sharp increase in inventory hurts cash flow, but has no impact on profit.

One of the most difficult tasks facing top executives as an organization grows is keeping managers focused on long-term, strategic goals. Management accounting opens the door to measures that report on progress toward these long-term goals, not just short-term profit. Management accounting provides a chance to report on the health of operations, not just the balance sheet.

Conclusion

Management accounting is more than just an extension of the financial accounting system or an attempt to allocate expenses to activities. As defined here, it encompasses a broad range of reporting, from a simple key indicators report to profitability by product or job to full-blown cost systems. These analyses and measures provide managers feedback and decision support tools that go beyond traditional GAAP reporting.

Managers should work with their accountants to define measures and how frequently they need to be reported. The task should not be simply left to the accountants. For one, management accounting is largely common sense and lack of accounting training is not necessarily a hindrance. Furthermore, accountants may be out of touch with managers' needs or their thinking may be constrained by traditional accounting definitions and reporting cycles. Combining management common sense with the analytic and data-gathering skills of your controller, you should be able to come up with the instrument panel of numbers that help you steer your company.

Notes

1. Anonymous, quoted in *The Manager's Book of Quotations*, p. 394.

2. Eliyahu M. Goldratt, *The Haystack Syndrome: Sifting Information out of the Data Ocean* (Great Barrington MA: North River Press, 1991), quoted in the newsletter of the Boston Chapter of Institute of Management Accountants, October 1993.

3. Benson P. Shapiro, V. Kasturi Rangan, Rowland T. Moriarty, and Elliot B. Ross, "Manage Customers for Profits (Not Just Sales)," *Harvard Business Review*, September-October 1987, p. 106.

4. H. Thomas Johnson and Robert S. Kaplan, *Relevance Lost: The Rise and Fall of Management Accounting* (Boston: Harvard Business School Press, 1987), p. xii.

5. Ron Friedman, quoted in "A Daily Dose of Numbers," *Inc.*, January 1998. Reprinted at www.inc.com/articles/1998/01/10147.html.

6. Norm Brodsky, "The Magic Number," *Inc.*, September 2003, pp. 43-46.

7. Jack Stack, quoted by John Case in "Troubleshooting Your Critical Numbers," *Inc.*, December 1999, from *Open Book Management: Bulletin*, www.inc.com/articles/1999/12/15980.html.

8. Bill Fotsch, quoted by Case in "Troubleshooting Your Critical Numbers."

9. Johnson and Kaplan, *Relevance Lost*, pp. 199-200.

10. Peter F. Drucker, *Managing for Results: Economic Tasks and Risk-Taking Decisions*, reprint edition (New York: HarperBusiness, 1993), p. 241.

11. John S. Hammond III and Gerald B. Allan, "Note on the Use of Experience Curves in Competitive Decision Making" (Boston: Harvard Business School, 1975).

Part Three

Managing Your Assets

Chapter 8

Inventory Management

A FAVORITE INTERVIEW QUESTION OF THE CORPORATE CONTROLLER at a *Fortune* 1000 manufacturing company used to be "What asset should a financial manager devote the most effort to controlling?"

The right answer was inventory. Cash is certainly precious, but it is easy to protect and account for with basic internal controls such as bank reconciliations. Receivables tie up great amounts of capital, but the only risk is whether they are collectible. Fixed assets are stable and, though they can get damaged, are hard to steal without detection. Inventory is, by far, the asset that is the most difficult to control and value.

Control of inventory involves multiple, difficult issues, including:

▶ Preventing physical losses such as theft, damage, and obsolescence;

▶ Valuing inventory, both in aggregate for financial statements and on a unit basis for pricing decisions and other analysis;

▶ Freeing up cash by keeping inventory from sitting on the shelf while balancing the need to keep adequate stock to meet customer demands;

▶ Maintaining accurate records of stock on hand to ensure smooth production and improve purchasing decisions.

The Walk-Through

The quickest way to gain insight into the quality of inventory management is to walk through a plant or warehouse.

The quickest way to gain insight into the quality of inventory management is to walk through a plant or warehouse. A tour usually provides a number of visual clues about the amount and quality of inventory, which in turn signal operating problems and potential cash drains. Consider the following examples:

A medical products manufacturer's warehouse was filled to near capacity. Forklifts were busy shuffling boxes around to make space for new production. Though most of the inventory was current, some locations contained stacks of boxes covered with dust, damaged by forklifts, or crushed under the weight of other boxes. It was quickly apparent high stocking levels were creating costs from obsolescence, damage, and simply having to store product.

A heating, ventilation, and air conditioning repair and installation business had replacement parts and duct components stored in all corners of its shop. This provided a clear sign that there were no controls over the amount or movement of materials.

A jewelry company that generally made items to order had a roomful of unsalable finished goods. These items were production overruns from orders for a major customer that did not accept excess goods. Further investigation revealed that the manufacturer routinely overproduced to cover for reject goods that resulted from poor quality control.

An apparel manufacturer and retailer had products up to 20 years old stashed in its basement. Because the business was sensitive to fashion, the old inventory lost value quickly, while the quantity on hand increased regularly. This was a clue that a strategy was needed to liquidate excess merchandise.

As these cases show, observing the amount, age, condition, and storage of inventory can tell you if problems exist. The answer is not as simple as stripping the shelves of inventory or changing buying habits. For example, excess inventory is often a sign of deeper structural problems that must be resolved as a prerequisite to reducing inventory levels.

This insight is illustrated in this drawing. Stocking excess inventory provides a buffer against a multitude of problems, including long lead times, bottlenecks, obsolescence, and poor quality. Put another way, system weaknesses force managers to keep excess inventory on hand to compensate. Since many of these issues and their solutions are in accounting and control systems, a controller and all levels of management must work together to correct them.

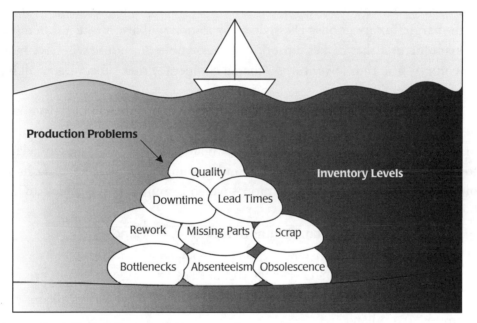

Analyzing Inventory Levels

In addition to inspecting the inventory, what numbers can you look at to tell you how effectively it is being managed?

A popular and quick measurement of inventory levels can be accomplished by looking at turns—the ratio of the annual cost of sales to on-hand inventory, also referred to as a *turnover ratio*. This measure compares average on-hand inventory with cost of sales to gauge how quickly stock turns over. Although turns can be calculated for individual items, they are usually stated for the company as a whole. The less inventory your company needs to support a level of sales, the higher the turns ratio. A high turns ratio is usually considered indicative of more effective management.

To calculate turns, divide your cost of sales—not sales, but the cost of goods sold for the period, including manufacturing cost, storage, and certain overhead costs—by your average total dollar amount of inventory on hand. For example, if you started a year with $90,000 of inventory and ended with $110,000 of inventory, your average inventory was $100,000. If your annual cost of sales was $400,000, your turns ratio was four ($400,000 / $100,000).

Compare your turns ratio number with those of similar companies to see how you are doing. How often inventory turns over will vary by industry. Supermarkets, for example, turn inventory over more quickly than sellers of high-margin luxury goods. The style of operation will also make a difference. A manufacturer that makes most of its subassemblies in-house will have more inventory—and thus fewer turns—than a competitor that subcontracts all but the final assembly.

Sometimes, you will hear people discussing months of inventory on hand instead of turns, particularly when discussing individual items. The months of inventory measurement, illustrated by the formula below, is closely related to turns. To determine how many months of inventory you have on hand, divide 12 months by your turns ratio—which is annual cost of sales divided by inventory.

A trade-off to high inventory turns is that lean inventories run the risk of stock-outs—inability to fill customer orders.

Equation: Months of Inventory on Hand

months of inventory on hand =
12 months / (annual cost of sales / inventory)

If inventory turns four times per year, on average, you have three months of inventory on hand.

On-Time Delivery

Other numbers you will want to take a look at in your analysis of inventory are the percentage of customer orders shipped on time and the average time needed to fill backorders. A trade-off to high inventory turns is that lean inventories run the risk of stockouts—inability to fill customer orders. Shooting for 100% on-time delivery may be too costly, but you can establish a target, such as 95% or 98%. Then, if you fall behind, it may indicate that some inventory quantities should be raised.

Balanced Inventory

Another number to examine in your analysis, even more important than the level of inventory, is whether inventory is well matched or balanced. In aggregate, you may have two months of inventory but be out of one material while carrying a two-year supply of another. For example, a clothing retailer may find itself stocking odd sizes and colors. Likewise, most of the old products on the shelves of the medical products company discussed in the examples at the beginning of this chapter were low-volume, specialty items. While the overall turns level may have looked healthy, the ratio was driven by the movement of the top-selling products.

Not only does a poorly matched inventory risk having overstocked items go stale, but you may need additional spending to bring the inventory into balance if you need to fill out a product line in order to market it. Additional spending may also be necessary if component parts have value only when converted to finished goods. Test your inventory regularly, item by item, to ensure a matched inventory.

Shrinkage

Inventory shrinkage is basically a way to say there is less inventory on hand than there should be. Even though differences between book and actual inventory may build slowly over time, the problem may only come to light when a physical inventory is taken, perhaps as infrequently as once a year. By the time the losses are discovered, it may be impossible to accurately trace the cause. In addition, a large discrepancy can turn a profit to a loss or at the least provide a nasty surprise. As one small business owner described it:

> I thought we were doing really great. Then, at year end, I was shocked by a write-down of $66,000 in inventory that offset about a quarter of our pretax profits. I felt like I'd been kicked in the stomach. My illusion of having established control was shattered.[2]

The big question for both managers and controllers is "Is inventory, as reported on our statements, really all there?" In one study, over 95% of the companies surveyed reported inventory discrepancies. For smaller companies, these differences averaged between 2.5% and 4.5% ($60,000-$100,000) of inventory on hand. Both gains and losses against book were reported, although losses were roughly two and one-half times more common.[3]

Inventory shrinkage is basically a way to say there is less inventory on hand than there should be.

155

The study also strongly indicated that accounting weaknesses are to blame. Only 1% of the discrepancies were blamed on theft. Errors—such as unreported scrap, inaccurate standards, or misreported production counts—accounted for over 80% of the variances.[4]

How do you avoid a year-end inventory surprise? Here is a partial list of suggestions:

- Record scrap as it occurs or create adequate reserves. This is particularly important if the only way on-hand inventory is reduced is when an item gets shipped. You need a procedure for subtracting items that are damaged, rejected, or thrown out or the accounting system will continue to report them as on-hand.

- Check incoming shipments and invoices for price and quantity discrepancies—the number of errors is often surprising. You will save money by spotting, and getting credited for, undershipments, as well as improve the accuracy of your records.

- Deter theft by physically restricting access.

- Physically control component parts, so that employees must complete requisitions for repairs or assembly. A major source of shrinkage is employees simply pulling parts they need off the shelf without completing any paperwork.

- Invoice all shipments.

- Have accurate bills of material (BOMs)—listings of component parts and quantities needed for higher-level assembly—so that inventory is properly relieved for production and shipments. At one company, a shortage of one part forced them to use a substitute item in assembling several products. However, the BOMs were never updated, leading to negative quantities of the first item (which, to compound the problem, were usually adjusted back to zero) and overstated amounts of the substitute.

- Watch reported production, especially for employees on incentive programs. Make sure that rework is not double-counted.

- Check for parts with similar descriptions or prices being confused in billing and receiving.

- Perform cycle counts—periodic test counts of inventory—to catch discrepancies during the year, not just at year-end.

▶ Book adequate reserves during the year to avoid a year-end hit if specific losses cannot be tracked.

Successful System Elements

After analyzing your inventory levels and the problems that need correction, you should examine your inventory control system. A wide variety of systems exist. Although the shape and form of inventory control systems vary, some basic elements are present in most successful systems.

Software

The most basic element for a successful management system is proper software. Your current accounting software may suffice, especially if your company does no manufacturing or does only some light assembly. Most off-the-shelf packages include an inventory module that can track basic ins and outs. Many also handle a simple bill of material (BOM). When you assemble product, the system can use the BOM to relieve the inventory of component parts.

Manufacturing companies, however, may need additional software specifically designed for inventory and production control. Tracking work-in-process, handling complex bills of material including sub-assemblies, and doing production scheduling are some of the features manufacturers may require. As a starting point, many off-the-shelf accounting vendors can provide you with a list of third-party software compatible with other particular software programs you may want to use. See Chapter 14 for more about choosing financial software.

As a starting point, many off-the-shelf accounting vendors can provide you with a list of third-party software compatible with other particular software programs you may want to use.

Physical Controls

Strong physical controls are also important. As is discussed later in Chapter 15, controls are needed less as a deterrent to theft than to ensure that transactions are recorded properly. Simply locking a stockroom can prevent well-meaning employees from grabbing items they need without filling out paperwork or from misplacing parts they are returning to stock. Securing the receiving area keeps employees from moving items onto store shelves or into production before someone can count and log the incoming shipment.

Administrative Controls

In addition to strong physical controls, tight administrative controls are also needed. From verifying the stated quantities of incoming shipments, to cycle counting the stockroom, checking reported production, controlling key punch errors, and comparing shipping records with invoices, a series of checks and balances is needed to prevent the administrative errors that account for the lion's share of reported shrinkage.

Recording scrap, damage, and other losses as they occur is important. As stressed earlier, failing to keep accurate records loses valuable information on the cost and source of these problems. Also, reported on-hand inventory quantities will likely be overstated.

Commitment

The most important component for a good inventory management system is a high degree of commitment from management.

The most important component for a good inventory management system is a high degree of commitment from management. Implementation of any inventory control system is not an overnight job. Several tries may be needed to get it right. The new system is likely to meet resistance from employees, as well. Thorough training is important so that the information from the system can actually be put to use. Otherwise, employees will be tempted to either ignore the system or develop alternate, redundant procedures to get information.

Inventory Control Techniques

Before the widespread use of computers, a number of techniques were developed to manage materials, particularly the purchasing cycle. Two techniques that are still popular are EOQ and ABC, which are described below.

Economic Order Quantities (EOQ)

Economic order quantities (EOQ) are calculations of the optimum lot sizes for purchasing items. The simplest EOQ models balance sales demand with handling costs, quantity discounts, carrying costs, and lead times—the amount of time from placing an order to receiving it. More complex calculations can add in the variability of demand and the risks of obsolescence and shrinkage.

Companies also establish formal reorder points based on calculations of the minimum level of inventory desired, taking into consideration demand, customers' sensitivity to stockouts, and the turnaround time to acquire additional stock. If inventory drops below the minimum, a reorder is generated. A maximum, using the same criteria, may also be set, creating what are known as *min-max targets*.

ABC Classification

Many companies successfully use ABC coding of parts to gain control over inventory. The ABC classification system codes inventory components according to cost and usage. The coding stems from the 80-20 rule, or the theory that a few parts constitute the majority of expense while a large number of parts are relatively trivial. By focusing the most effort on the relatively few "A" parts, a company can afford to tightly control its most valuable inventory, while removing uneconomical and burdensome controls on less essential items.

A typical breakdown might be as follows:

▶ **A parts** constitute 1%-20% of items but 70%-80% of inventory value. The A classification generally includes expensive, hard-to-obtain, or single-sourced goods. Purchasing is closely controlled to keep holding costs down and ensure adequate supply. A parts are stored in a physically secured location and cycle-counted with relative frequency.

▶ **C parts** are fairly cheap and easy to obtain. C parts may constitute more than 50% of inventory items, but may account for only 10%-20% of the cost. C parts are purchased in bulk and cycle-counted infrequently.

▶ **B parts** are items falling between the two extremes of A and C parts. Usually, A and C parts are identified first, and whatever parts are left are classified as B items.

After inventory is classified as A, B, or C, each class is managed differently according to importance. Segmenting the inventory decreases overall management costs while increasing control where control is critical. ABC coding can be effective in a wide range of settings, from very simple operations to full-blown materials resource planning (MRP) and just-in-time systems, discussed next.

MRP and MRP II

Materials resource planning (MRP) was the first production and inventory control methodology to grow out of the use of computers. MRP is a straightforward method that takes projected demand for final products and "explodes" through the bills of material (BOMs). The MRP system calculates through all levels of assemblies to arrive at the demand for component parts. The MRP system then nets this demand against stock on hand and on order to create a buying plan for what is lacking.

The goal is to drive inventory to zero—or desired safety stock levels—by providing precisely the materials needed to meet production demand.

MRP is simply a tool for calculating inventory needed to meet a given production plan. The system answers a need for breaking through multiple-level BOMs and for scheduling receipts. MRP does not analyze whether shop capacity is sufficient to meet the plan. And while an MRP system computes what purchases are needed, it does not execute the recommended purchase plan.

A more integrated approach, and one that is a logical progression from the basic MRP system is *manufacturing resource planning*, or MRP II. MRP II overcomes many of the shortcomings in basic MRP systems by taking into consideration the human and machine capacity of a plant. By including these functional areas of manufacturing, MRP II can ensure that all operations work off the same plan and provide feedback between these areas. MRP II, however, is highly complex; so, while MRP systems are quite common, MRP II is less so. These are the basic elements of MRP II systems:

▶ Master production scheduling

▶ Capacity planning

▶ Bills of material

▶ Shop floor control

▶ Production accounting

▶ Inventory control

The system starts with the master schedule. The master production schedule is used to determine the quantity and timing of goods needed to meet sales goals. The master schedule is quite comprehensive, taking into account such things as forecasted sales, plant capacity, and the availability of material. The end demands are then exploded through the BOMs to determine the need for component parts. This, in turn, leads to the issuance of purchase orders to vendors and the release of production orders to manufacturing. The progress of these orders is then closely monitored and controlled by the system. Accounting tracks the resources consumed and compares the results with both industry and company standards.

MRP—Problems in Practice

Though MRP systems are capable of dramatic results, research indicates that the majority of systems fail to live up to expectations.[5] Several factors seem critical for successful implementation.

First, MRP works best for manufacturers that produce goods in large batches or repetitive processes where planning of production, ordering and carrying of inventory, and production control are important issues. Job shops may have little use for MRP, since they deal with smaller volumes of production, are less reliant on forecasting, and may use relatively fewer component parts to make a product.[6]

MRP requires accurate recordkeeping. Whatever quantities the system shows for inventory on hand must approximate physical quantities. BOMs must be accurate or order quantities will be thrown off. Production counts must also be correct.

Lead times need to be measurable and kept up to date. Lead times that are unpredictable or inaccurate undermine the production schedule. Overestimating lead times causes overstocking of items. Underestimating lead times can result in stockouts or extra demands on employees to expedite orders or juggle production schedules.

Lead times that are unpredictable or inaccurate undermine the production schedule.

Most importantly, MRP requires a strong commitment from all managers involved. The system requires a large up-front investment of time and money plus continuous monitoring, data input, and adjustment to run effectively. Implementation of a MRP system is a major undertaking.

Given the high failure rate in practice, you will want to consider the benefits you hope to achieve and the commitment level in your company before investing in MRP systems.

Just-in-Time

A more recent development is just-in-time (JIT) inventory techniques. JIT was credited with contributing to much of the success of Japanese manufacturing companies starting in the 1980s. Greatly reduced production lead times and reduced inventory are just two of the benefits JIT is supposed to deliver. But exactly what is JIT and is it truly a remedy for high inventories and other manufacturing problems?

JIT is not simply an inventory control technique; it is more a philosophy. Though JIT seems to mean different things to different people, it seems best described as:

▶ Doing things right the first time;

▶ Eliminating costs that do not add value to the final product; and

▶ Scheduling work on a pull, rather than push, basis.

This last point, pulling instead of pushing, means that production is based on actual orders—not forecasts, as is the case with MRP—with each level of production creating demand for the functions below it.

Some of the underlying concepts of JIT are:

▶ **Quality at the source.** A commitment to 100% quality eliminates the costs of scrap, rework, and complaints.

▶ **No wasted steps.** Processes and designs are simplified, leading to shorter setup times, shorter distances for people and material to travel, fewer production steps and movement, and less paperwork.

▶ **Balanced and synchronized workflow.** Employees are organized into cooperative teams of flexible, broadly skilled workers able to do problem solving.

▶ **Preventive maintenance.** Ongoing maintenance is emphasized, since equipment breakdowns that cause stoppages will interrupt the synchronized workflow.

Notice that none of these concepts say anything about reducing inventory, but a successful JIT system will reduce inventory in several ways. JIT results in companies ordering goods from suppliers only as needed. By shortening lead times, companies can keep fewer of these goods on hand. In addition, finished goods inventory is reduced by cutting down production lead times and by producing to actual orders rather than for stock. Finally, streamlining production means less work-in-process.

Combined, all of these measures lead to lower costs. Carrying costs, rework, handling, inspection time, and paperwork are all lower. Reducing inventory also means that less space is needed for storage and you have less exposure to loss.

Remember that reducing inventory levels or shortening lead times is not the starting point of JIT. Rather, reduced inventory levels result from improvements in the manufacturing process and the adoption of the quality-driven philosophy.

Kanban and Combined Systems

JIT and MRP are not necessarily incompatible—although there is controversy on this point. Some companies continue to use MRP to calculate the need for raw materials for the purpose of planning, but under JIT stop short of actually committing to order materials.

An alternative method for determining reorder points is *kanban*. *Kanban* uses visual signals, rather than reports, to authorize making or buying more of an item. In some systems, a colored card is inserted in a parts bin. Usually, the card is filled in with instructions for replenishing the stock. When parts are used to the point that the card is exposed, the card is pulled and personnel can process the refill order in a routine fashion on the shop floor.

Kanban uses visual signals, rather than reports, to authorize making or buying more of an item.

Other reorder signals can also be used. Some companies use specially marked containers. When the containers become empty, they are routed to the proper department for refilling.

Kanban was developed in Japan and is used most effectively with JIT. However, even where JIT has not been implemented, the *kanban* idea can be effective in generating timely reorders of materials used in large quantity.

The Goal

The Goal: Excellence in Manufacturing is one of the most influential books on production and inventory control.[7] A novel written by Eli Goldratt, an Israeli physicist, and Jeff Cox, *The Goal* is more about an operating philosophy than specific analytical tools. The central theme is that the goal of a company is to make money and that some traditional notions about production efficiency are counter to that goal. Two points in particular bear mentioning.

One is the idea of attacking bottlenecks. When work in process is held up at one point in production, two things happen.

- ▶ Inventory begins to pile up in front of the bottleneck, contributing to higher overall inventory and carrying costs.
- ▶ The entire throughput—the amount of material going through a process in a given time—of the plant is affected as operations downstream from the bottleneck don't get the parts they need to keep running.

Basically, the entire operation is only as effective as the weakest link. Goldratt's answer is to do what it takes to move parts through the bottleneck. Don't let the bottleneck area sit idle. Bring in additional resources, if needed, to increase capacity. Even if the added resources seem costly, like reinstating old, slower equipment or adding workers, the benefit of improving total throughput in the plant will greatly outweigh the higher unit cost at the one operation.

The other key insight of *The Goal* is that trying to be efficient by keeping people and machines busy all the time can cost money if you have no orders for the goods they are working on. Building for stock just to keep a plant busy means that cash has to be spent to buy raw materials. That cash ends up being tied up in finished goods sitting in a warehouse.

Even though down time means higher unit costs of production and what seems like less efficiency, it can enhance the overall welfare of your company.

Converting Excess Inventory

In practice, of course, you are likely to have excess inventory on hand at various times. What steps can you take to reduce stock and generate cash?

A common mistake is thinking that all inventory is good inventory. Don't hold onto slow-moving items because you have one customer who orders them from time to time or because an order for them came out of the blue a few months ago and might again. The items can be in excellent condition or have been costly to acquire, but if they are not moving, they are tying up cash and probably losing value as they sit on the shelf.

If you have excess inventory in the form of finished goods, devise a strategy to sell it off in an orderly fashion.

If you have excess inventory in the form of finished goods, devise a strategy to sell it off in an orderly fashion. Try discounting the goods or paying a higher commission on those items. If they were purchased goods, perhaps the supplier will give you a credit if you return them. Discount chain stores may be willing to take production overruns or seconds. Only as a last resort should you have to offer the goods to a liquidator.

For raw materials, you may need to crunch some numbers to see if you generate more cash by selling off the excess or converting the materials to finished goods before selling them. One thing you don't want to do is put excess materials into production just to keep the plant busy. You will spend cash for labor and any additional materials needed and, if the finished products aren't sold, get nothing in return.

Tracking Inventory

For GAAP reporting, inventory is generally accounted for with one of two methods, perpetual or periodic. The system you choose depends on your type of business and your particular needs.

Perpetual Method

Under the perpetual method, all ins and outs of individual items are recorded as they occur, so that the system always has a detailed record of what goods are on hand. Cost of goods sold is calculated directly as goods are taken out of stock and any inventory losses are captured as they occur.

Most companies with perpetual inventory systems still take physical inventories to verify the accuracy of the book figure.

The perpetual method works best where inventory can easily be measured and tracked in discrete units and where accurate information about on-hand quantities is important. Typically, retailers, distributors, or assembly operations use the perpetual method. Most companies with perpetual inventory systems still take physical inventories to verify the accuracy of the book figure; however, this can be accomplished with cycle-counting rather than a 100% physical inventory.

Periodic Method

The periodic method does not track movement of the components of inventory, relying instead on period-end physical counts to determine stock on hand. Cost of sales is determined via this equation:

Equation: Cost of Sales

cost of sales = beginning inventory + purchases − ending inventory

The periodic method is easier to implement than a perpetual system. Instead of recording each purchase and sale on an item-by-item basis, purchases are recorded in aggregate and the number representing the cost of goods is derived based on ending inventory.

The major weakness of the periodic method is that it leaves you exposed to a year-end surprise if the physical inventory reveals an unexpected shortfall. Similarly, without occasional physical inventories during the year, interim financial statements may be unreliable. The periodic method assumes that any inventory not accounted for at year-end must have been sold. If significant scrap, theft, and other losses have occurred, they will not be detected without a physical inventory.

Overcoming many of the inventory management problems discussed earlier in this chapter will require perpetual inventory systems. However, where the costs of tracking inventory are high or with little benefit and the risks of losses from shrinkage low, the perpetual system can make sense. You can beef up a perpetual system by specifically tracking certain transactions, such as scrap and damaged goods. You can also track units on hand with a perpetual system, but account for costs using the periodic method.

Valuation

Once on-hand quantities are known, the next question is "What is it worth?" What seems like a simple question quickly gets complicated by some of the following issues:

- What is the flow of goods? If you buy goods every month and prices fluctuate, how do you figure out when you bought the units that are still on the shelf and what you paid for them?

- If you add value, such as in manufacturing, what costs do you add in?

- If the market value of the goods changes while they sit on your shelf, should you make adjustments?

To understand some of the many possible complications, consider this example.

> The local stationery store carries a stock of printer ink cartridges. In November, the store buys 1,000 at $10.00 apiece. Sales are good and when the stock on hand drops to 500 pieces at the end of the month, the store reorders another 500. However, there has been a general 10% price increase; in addition, it costs an extra $1.00 per unit to buy a smaller quantity. The new price is now $12.00 each. The store sells another 300 in December. At year-end, the store's accountant must compile a balance sheet. What is the value of the 700 cartridges still in stock?

Of course, the problem is an accounting question, not an operating question. From your management standpoint, the main question is what the cartridges can be sold for and, perhaps, what you will have to pay when you reorder. Only accountants are concerned with historic cost.

Based on differing assumptions and methods, at least five correct answers to the question about the value of the 700 cartridges are possible. The accountant starts by asking how much was paid for the inventory. Immediately, an assumption must be made about the flow of goods. Did the store sell the oldest goods first—in which case it still has all 500 of the cartridges bought at $12.00 and 200 of the original cartridges? Or, has it also sold some of the newer cartridges? Maybe the accountant could tell by looking at the boxes themselves, but with thousands of different items in stock this hardly makes sense. A shortcut is needed.

LIFO and FIFO

What if the accountant assumes that the newer cartridges were sold first? This is called *last-in, first-out* (LIFO) accounting. In this case, only 200 cartridges purchased at $12.00 would remain, plus 500 bought for $10.00, yielding an inventory value of $7,400.

Another possible assumption is that the oldest goods are always sold first, since this is in keeping with good inventory management. This is known as the *first-in, first-out* (FIFO) method. Then, the accountant assumes that the 700 units on hand consist of all 500 bought at $12.00 and 200 bought at $10.00, for a value of $8,000.

From a profit-and-loss standpoint, the assumption that the flow of goods is FIFO ends up with a higher markup of the goods and increased profits.

Forced to make a choice, suppose the accountant decides that FIFO better reflects the condition of the inventory and makes the appropriate entries. From a profit-and-loss standpoint, the assumption that the flow of goods is FIFO ends up with a higher markup of the goods and increased profits. In using FIFO and assuming that in December the store sold only older cartridges costing $10.00 each, the markup, if the 300 cartridges are sold at $20.00 each, is $10.00, yielding a net profit of $3,000. On the other hand, with LIFO, using as the unit cost the $12.00 cost of each cartridge purchased in December, the cost of sales would be $3,600 (300 cartridges times $12.00 cost) and the profit would be $2,400 (300 cartridges times $8.00 markup).

If the flow of goods is deemed to be LIFO—where the most recently purchased goods are assumed sold first—because this better matches current revenues and expenses, then another problem is encountered. How can the 500 cartridges that you carry still be valued at $10.00 each when the same cartridges today would cost at least 10% more? When cartridge prices rose, didn't the value of the cartridges on the shelf rise? By buying smart, in large quantity and before the price increase, didn't the store profit?

According to GAAP, you don't earn a profit until you have actually sold something. Just because prices went up on something you own doesn't mean you actually made money. The same is true if you buy in a large enough quantity to qualify for a price break—you have not made an accounting profit until you have sold the products.

Weighted Average

LIFO and FIFO are not the only choices. A weighted average can also be used. In the example above, the 1,500 cartridges cost a total of $16,000 and both cost of sales and finished inventory could be calculated to yield a cost of $10.67 each.

Standard Cost

Another method is to develop a standard cost, which is an estimate of what purchased or manufactured inventory should cost. Both inventory and cost of sales are computed using the standard cost. Any variances, actual costs that differ from standard, are included directly in that period's cost of sales. In the example, the store might establish a standard of $10.00 per cartridge. The $2.00 per cartridge ($1,000) extra paid in December would be expensed as a purchase price variance and the remaining stock of 700 cartridges carried at $7,000.

Actual Cost

Many things can affect an item's value as it sits on the shelf, such as obsolescence, shifts in market prices, or damage.

For big-ticket items, where each unit of inventory can be tracked separately—perhaps by serial number—you may be able to use the actual cost of each unit, eliminating the need for any flow assumption. Unfortunately, this method does not apply to the low-cost, high-volume items carried by the stationery store.

Reserves and Write-Offs

Many things can affect an item's value as it sits on the shelf, such as obsolescence, shifts in market prices, or damage. How are these events recorded?

Accounting rules require that inventory be carried at lower of cost or market value. As was discussed in Chapter 5, if an item's value rises, the company cannot book a gain; but if the value for which it can be sold—the realizable value—drops below cost, the value must be written down.

Since this rule can be applied in aggregate instead of item by item, normal price shifts, in which some prices rise and others fall, shouldn't require an adjustment. But if an item or a group of items suffers a significant loss in value, this loss should be reflected on the books.

A write-off is made when inventory is determined to have no value, such as in the case of damaged, stolen, or obsolete goods. Usually, though, inventory on hand retains at least some value. Perhaps, it can be repaired or sold at liquidation prices. Instead of writing off the entire balance, an estimate is made of the realizable value and book value adjusted down to it. This is called a *reserve*.

For tax purposes, inventory adjustments and write-offs generally can be deducted only if the inventory is actually disposed of. For financial accounting, a reserve or write-off can be recorded without physically disposing of the inventory.

Since carrying inventory always includes the risk that some losses will occur, many companies prefer to book reserves on an ongoing basis, rather than wait to identify specific losses. For example:

> An apparel manufacturer that was affected by changes in styles from season to season booked a monthly reserve for cloth. They knew that as the product line changed some unsalable material would be left over. At year-end, this amount would be computed and the actual estimated write-down booked. By booking the reserve over time, the hit had already been spread out and a year-end surprise avoided.

Some typical events companies choose to reserve for include expected, but as yet unrealized losses for shrinkage, obsolescence, and damage. Booking reserves is conservative, helps prevent future negative surprises, and often reflects a realistic expectation of losses. However, reserves tell you nothing about the source of the losses.

Inventory reserve entries require a great deal of judgment. Predictions of what a fair reserve for scrap is or what goods will become obsolete may be impossible. In the end, you have a wide range of possible figures. Since the choice will impact the income statement, the reserve entry can give you great variation in reported profit.

For tax purposes, inventory adjustments and write-offs generally can be deducted only if the inventory is actually disposed of.

Value-Added Costs

When valuing inventory, companies with value added—the goods become more valuable through labor, machining, or other operations—have the additional problem of deciding what internal costs should be added to the purchase price of materials. Once the costs are determined, how are they traced or allocated to specific products?

GAAP and tax reporting require that all direct and indirect costs be included in the cost of inventory. This is called the *full absorption cost* or simply *full cost*. For your own internal information needs, you may prefer to look at only direct costs. Direct costs may be more relevant when looking at the incremental impact of pricing or production decisions. Direct costs also avoid any arbitrary impacts of allocating overhead costs. If you require direct costs for analysis, you may need to make a special request from your controller or accountant.

When allocating overhead for full absorption costing, how overhead is allocated to individual items is not regulated by GAAP as long as the method is reasonable. GAAP requires only that the aggregate cost of inventory be correct. Overhead includes virtually all costs of acquiring or converting materials into finished, salable product. For purchased items, whether for resale or as an input to an assembly or manufacturing process, all costs of getting the goods in the door—such as freight and insurance charges and the costs of handling and inspecting the goods—are included.

For manufacturing companies, all costs in the production area are included. The determining factor for GAAP is in what department expenditures occur, not how directly the expenditures vary with production. Operating expenses can cover a broad range, such as tools, packaging materials, rent, and utilities. For some expenses, such as heat and rent, an allocation might be made between production and administrative functions. Labor cost would include assemblers, machine operators, inspectors, and, perhaps, the purchasing agent and the vice president of manufacturing.

The wages of people in other departments, such as R&D and G&A, are excluded even if their work supports production. For example, accounting salaries, even for people who process production paperwork, are not added into the cost of inventory.

When allocating overhead for full absorption costing, how overhead is allocated to individual items is not regulated by GAAP as long as the method is reasonable.

Inventory and Liquidity

If you have ever applied for a line of credit, you will have discovered that banks are reluctant to lend against inventory. At best, you may find that you can borrow 50% of book value and with a fairly tight cap. Yet, the same bank may be willing to lend up to 80% of accounts receivable.

The bottom line is that book value is not a reliable indicator about what inventory is worth, particularly to a lender. Part of this has to do with what the inventory would be worth if the bank called the loan and had to sell it. Without an ongoing business, work-in-process and finished goods may be worth only a fraction of their recorded cost. Purchased goods may be worth only slightly more as suppliers may be willing to buy them back.

The risk of damage, obsolescence, and other losses also cause lenders to depreciate inventory value. Finally, the vagaries of accounting play a role. Bankers realize that what it costs to acquire or make a product may not be what you can sell it for.

Inventory, of course, also ties up cash. Although inventory is classified as a current asset on the balance sheet, it can be highly illiquid—not readily convertible to cash. A company with many current liabilities and a high portion of its current assets tied up in inventory could find itself in a cash crunch.

If you are analyzing financial statements, either your own or someone else's, spend time evaluating inventory. Can you determine whether there is excess inventory, in which case an asset could quickly turn into a write-off and a profit turn into a loss? No matter how healthy the current ratio, is the company liquid? If the company had to be liquidated, how much of the inventory value could be recovered? Plus, as discussed earlier in this chapter, high inventory can be a sign of inefficiency. Looking beyond the book number is likely to reveal insights into the company's true health.

Summary

To review, for nonservice businesses, inventory often represents the greatest area of exposure.

- ▶ Inventory ties up large amounts of cash and excess stock is vulnerable to damage, theft, and obsolescence.

- ▶ Tracking and accounting for inventory is a complex task and it can be costly, and companies frequently are surprised by shrinkage.

- ▶ Accurately computing unit costs is critical for pricing and operating decisions.

- ▶ In many manufactured products, materials typically make up most of the cost, so the potential payback from controlling inventory can be greater than for labor and overhead.

Simply demanding lower inventory levels is not enough. Reduced inventory results from good management, not the other way around. Excess inventory often builds up as a buffer against operating problems; a sudden reduction may expose these problems before a company is prepared to deal with them.

A few quick improvements may be available for both manufacturers and nonmanufacturers. On-hand inventory can be scrutinized for overstocked items that. if sold, even at a book loss, could generate cash. Inventory can be brought into balance and tighter physical controls implemented. An ABC coding can be devised and, for the A parts, EOQs can be calculated or a min-max system can be devised. Many just-in-time practices can be implemented without a full-blown conversion.

More sophisticated manufacturing systems, such as MRP and JIT, require long-term investments and, usually, changes in philosophy. These are definitely not quick fixes and a high level of management commitment is needed to succeed. But, in large and small companies alike, the stakes are high when dealing with inventory management, so the effort can pay off.

Notes

1. Oliver W. Wright, quoted in *Money Talks*, p. 149.

2. Charles J. Bodenstab, "Surprise! Surprise!" *Inc.*, September 1988, p. 135.

3. Il-Woon Kim and Arjan T. Sadhwani, "Is Your Inventory Really There?" *Management Accounting*, July 1991, pp. 37-38.

4. Ibid., p. 39.

5. Ron Fisher and Guy Archer, "MRP: The Problems and Some Solutions," *Accountancy*, May 1991, p. 115.

6. Sheldon Needle, "Microcomputer-Based Manufacturing Software," *Journal of Accountancy*, June 1990, p. 115.

7. Eliyahu M. Goldratt and Jeff Cox, *The Goal: Excellence in Manufacturing* (Croton-on-Hudson, NY: North River Press, 1984).

Chapter 9

Cash Management and Liquidity

Cash is king.
Happiness is a positive cash flow.

—popular sayings

NOTHING MATTERS MORE THAN CASH. WHILE MAKING A PROFIT is nice, cash flow is vital. Many growing companies find themselves strapped for cash just as their business is taking off. Similarly, a struggling company possibly can stay afloat by finding ways to generate cash.

Cash flow is, perhaps, the single most important element of survival for a smaller business. In a survey of the owners of more than 60,000 failed businesses, more than 60% blamed their failure on factors linked to cash flow.[1] And according to a study by the accounting firm of BDO Seidman, 26% of small to medium-sized companies called inability to control cash flow their number-one problem.[2]

Admittedly, cash flow problems are often just a symptom of operating shortcomings. Good planning and effective cash management could prevent many cash crunches and resulting crises and failures. Ensuring adequate cash flow provides a needed cushion for companies in unstable situations and also can allow a company to take advantage of opportunities to reduce costs or make strategic investments.

Good planning and effective cash management can prevent many cash crunches and resulting crises and failures.

Effective cash management requires:

▶ Understanding the critical differences between cash and profit,

▶ Having the ability to forecast your cash needs,

▶ Using strategies to maximize your cash flow, and

▶ Knowing how to react to a cash crisis.

In addition to the skills listed above, this chapter discusses how to work with investors and lenders plus strategies for squeezing cash out of your balance sheet. It also covers how cash flow provides an unbiased performance measure and why even profitable companies can run out of money.

Cash Flow vs. Profit

Cash flow and profit are not the same thing. Profitable companies can, and do, fail for lack of cash flow. Consider the following examples:

A start-up trucking company enjoyed almost immediate success. By its second year, sales topped $1.5 million and net income was $50,000. Though sales grew only slightly the next two years, profits improved to more than $100,000 per year. But, over those two years, accounts receivable more than doubled, to $500,000. The company also moved into a new facility, absorbing $100,000 in prepaid expenses—carried as assets on the books. Despite being profitable, the company's wealth was tied up in noncash assets and it faced severe liquidity issues. With its lines of credit exhausted, when the IRS came looking for $40,000 in back taxes, the company decided to shut down. At the time it went under, the company showed a positive book value of more than $200,000.

A manufacturer of industrial furnaces found itself caught in a frustrating cycle of feast and famine. Most of its jobs were large, up to $1.5 million, and these large and lengthy projects made up a large portion of annual sales, which were growing to about $8 million. Little money was collected on jobs while in progress, so cash flowed out steadily when large jobs were being worked on. The company was repeatedly thrown into crisis. Many times, the president admitted being unsure, when leaving at night, if the power would still be on the next day.

As soon as a job was done and the customer had paid, the company was flush with cash and all obligations caught up. But because each job seemed to lead to more or larger jobs, there never was a cash cushion. Although sales were growing and the company reported steady profits, the roller coaster cash flow put the company's survival in jeopardy. Fortunately, the company finally got over the hump and was able to pay cash out to its investors, but only after about 10 years.

In just its second year, a start-up producer of leather car seats was succeeding in lining up orders from auto repair shops. The operation was capital-intensive, but the influx of orders seemed to prove that the risk taken by investing in equipment would pay off. Fixed costs were high, due to the payments on the equipment, and margins were modest. But if all the orders could be processed, the company would make a solid profit. Unfortunately, the supplier of leather hides put a cap on credit at $100,000 and no banks or other vendors were willing to extend credit. With payments for the finished seats coming in 30-60 days after the hides were paid for, the company could purchase only enough hides to get production up to a breakeven level. The owner estimated that production would more than double if only enough hides could be secured.

What is it about accounting principles that allows companies like these to show seemingly healthy profits while teetering on the edge of insolvency? The basic answer is that cash, while it might be the key to survival, is not the central focus of financial accounting. The bottom line in accounting is net income.

Over the long term, profit and cash flow will tend to be roughly the same, but with significant differences in timing over that period. The differences in timing are a result of the distinction between committing to an expenditure and recognizing an expense, between completing a sale and getting paid.

Over the long term, profit and cash flow will tend to be roughly the same, but with significant differences in timing over that period.

The gap between net income and cash flow can be very wide. If receivables increase due to rapid sales growth, revenues—and probably profit—will increase ahead of the actual cash receipts. Increases in inventory or fixed assets also consume cash but have little immediate impact on the income statement. Most commonly found in smaller, growing companies, these circumstances are the reason why even profitable companies are vulnerable to running out of cash.

Something else to be aware of is that inventory and receivables are classified on financial statements as working capital, but clearly are not equivalent to cash. Conversion of inventory or receivables to cash, particularly of slow-moving inventory items or troubled accounts, is neither assured nor cost-free. Even companies with seemingly healthy working capital balances can be thrown into crisis if cash unexpectedly becomes tight. In addition, as discussed later in this chapter, though you may be able to borrow money based on inventory and receivables, the available credit will be only a modest percentage of your asset balances.

Cash Cows

On the other hand, some companies may incur expenses, but still hang onto cash, even as accounts payable and liabilities are increasing. Expenses, such as depreciation, amortization, and write-offs, do not use cash. Mature companies, which more often have these circumstances, can be lucrative cash cows, generating cash even when showing only modest profit.

When it comes to survival, cash flow is what ultimately matters. As quoted in Chapter 5, William McGowan, the former chairman of MCI, once said, "No company has ever gone bankrupt because it had a loss on its P&L."[3]

Positive cash flow, however, is no guarantee that a company is healthy. Consider the following example:

A general contracting company that built retail stores collected money from its customers in installments. Generally, the contractor received an initial payment of 25%-40% when a contract was signed, two or three progress payments, and then the final 10% when all work was completed and the subcontractors were paid in full.

Margins were very thin, generally 10%-15%, but with close to $40 million in contracts, there seemed to be enough margin to more than cover overhead expenses. Certainly, cash flow was very good while the business was growing. The contractor enjoyed the reverse of what most other growing companies see, with receipts upfront, payments deferred, and new jobs bringing immediate cash.

But the cash flow masked serious underlying problems. During a recession, margins deteriorated due to competition and cost overruns even made some jobs unprofitable. The company started using upfront payments from new jobs to pay off balances due to subcontractors on jobs in process.

This enabled the company to survive as long as there was a steady influx of new jobs. But when business slowed, the cash flow dried up. Subcontractor payments came due with the customers' money long since paid out and few new jobs coming in. Less than a year after celebrating what seemed like a record year, the company was insolvent.

In this case, cash flow was misleading and timely financial statements could have revealed the underlying problems. By matching payments and expenses on each job, the financial statements could have shown how margins were shrinking and even suggested corrective action.

Unfortunately in this case, at the time the crisis hit, the company had gone six months into its fiscal year with no interim financial statements and its auditors were uncovering critical errors in the preliminary statements for the prior year.

Cash Focus

Both cash flow and profit are important measures, working hand in hand to give you a more complete picture of your company's health than either could alone. But because net income is more commonly used, you may need to shift your thinking to give emphasis to cash flow.

Because net income is more commonly used, you may need to shift your thinking to give emphasis to cash flow.

Learning to focus on cash and liquidity may actually be easier for a CEO than for an accountant. If you have ever run a business out of a checkbook, this might be a familiar task. You will already know that, at the most basic level, if more cash comes in than goes out, the company is gaining. As long as cash is in the account, the business is solvent.

Only as the business gets more complex will you need to adopt financial accounting to better classify assets and liabilities and make accrual entries. But the basic practice of keeping on top of the checkbook often remains.

On the other hand, accountants have been trained to focus on net income. They may be less attuned to the importance of liquidity. Therefore, while the accountant should do the work of tracking cash flow and preparing cash forecasts, you may have to take the initiative in getting work on cash forecasts and cash flows started.

Monitoring cash flow also brings an additional and key advantage over just doing accrual accounting. Cash is a very immediate and objective measure. At any point in time, you can know how much cash is on hand. You have no need to wait for a monthly close to get an update.

177

You do not have to contend with timing issues, judgments, or GAAP rules when measuring cash flow. While a dollar of inventory or goodwill on a financial statement could have varied meaning, you know what a dollar of cash is worth. And, while financial statements can be manipulated, cash flow is a tangible, unbiased measure. If you want an immediate barometer of where you stand, without unraveling accounting jargon and rules, cash flow will provide it.

Cash Flow Forecasting

Cash flow is not just a method of keeping score, but a matter of survival for many companies.

Cash flow, of course, is not just a method of keeping score, but a matter of survival for many companies. For others, cash flow may represent the ability to seize expansion opportunities or fund vital product development. Simply reporting on cash flow is not enough. You also need to forecast cash balances and anticipate possible problems.

The cornerstone of cash management is a detailed cash forecast. For most companies, monthly budgets should be done, projecting in advance by at least six to 12 months. As discussed in Chapter 11, a company's budget and forecasts should include a balance sheet and cash flow. For most stable companies, this level of cash forecasting should be sufficient.

Companies in a cash crunch, though, should also do weekly budgets extending eight to 12 weeks. Actual performance should then be tracked against the forecasts to provide warning of potential shortfalls, as well as feedback about the validity of the original assumptions.

The cash forecasts pick up where normal revenue and expense budgets leave off. Projections should be broken down by week to identify swings that can occur mid-month. The forecasts also capture the difference in timing between payments and receipts and the financial accounting recognition of income and expense. A typical format for a cash flow forecast is shown in the sample at the end of this chapter.

Unlike business plans and budgets—discussed in Chapters 11 and 12—which are a mix of forecasting and goal setting, cash projections should strictly be forecasts. The purpose is to anticipate cash needs, not set targets or impress investors. Because the cost of running low on cash is severe, it makes sense to inject some pessimism. You can do this by choosing conservative assumptions or by discounting the results. If a forecast becomes outdated, revise it. To wait for the end of the budget period or to match the cash forecast to the regular budget or financial reporting cycles is unnecessary.

In moving from a regular budget to a cash forecast, many items will be the same. Payroll, freight bills, and cash sales are usually booked as revenue and expense very close to the time when cash changes hands. Items such as rent, utility bills, and service contracts are usually paid once a month. A weekly cash flow would reflect the specific timing of the payments.

For other line items, the difference in timing is substantial. Sales and purchases are often on credit, so the cash impact will lag. Subscription and service contract revenue may have the opposite effect, with cash being received in advance. Inventory purchases, which do not generate an income statement expense until sold, reduce cash flow as soon as they are paid for. Capital expenditures can have a major impact on the cash forecast and, unless assets are leased, cannot be spread out as they are for financial statements. Other expenses that are often smoothed for financial reporting, such as insurance, heat, and taxes, must be adjusted to reflect the actual timing of payments.

Cash needs can also be highly seasonal. Consider the following example:

A manufacturer of gift items experienced close to half its sales in the last quarter of the year due to the holiday season. Cash flow was highest in January and February as customers paid for their holiday orders and production was low. Cash flow turned negative during the summer due to slow sales and a build-up of inventory for fall production. It was essential to understand this pattern to establish a line of credit sufficient to cover the low point in cash flow and to communicate expectations to the lender.

Some of your biggest exposures are outstanding purchase orders and contracts.

When doing cash planning, you might also have to look at items that don't even appear on your balance sheet. Some of your biggest exposures are outstanding purchase orders and contracts. Even if your accounting system doesn't track these obligations—and it probably won't unless your purchasing system is automated and purchase orders are used for all items—you should ask your controller to have this information available at all times. Contingent liabilities, such as lawsuits, are additional off-balance sheet items that may have to be worked into your projections.

Ideally, the cash budget should have the ability to handle "what-if" questions. The "what-if" questions allow you to test different scenarios, while emphasizing that any projection has a margin of error. Try changing your assumptions about sales, the timing of inventory purchases, or the speed of collections to see the impact on cash. Develop contingency plans to deal with any potential forecasted problems.

Maximizing Cash Flow

Good cash management does not have to wait for a crisis. Freeing up cash—whether to invest, pay down existing debt, or take advantage of vendor discounts—brings substantial rewards. Your objective is to wring cash out of your business and keep it out. If you find that you have a potential or actual crisis, you can solve the problem in several ways.

Short-Term Strategies

If your projections indicate a cash shortfall, first ask yourself if you have internal sources of cash that can make up the difference. Start by looking at your balance sheet. Inventory and receivables usually are the biggest cash drains on a company. Both also carry an added risk: the longer they are not converted to cash, the greater the risk they never will be. Issues about controlling and reducing inventory are discussed in Chapter 8. Refer to Chapter 10 for techniques to speed collections of receivables.

Stretch out your cash by waiting at least until the due date before releasing funds.

Payables also offer an opportunity for generating cash. Stretch out your cash by waiting at least until the due date before releasing funds. Additionally, although you must judge how far you can push, particularly with key vendors, payments can frequently be delayed 15-30 days beyond these due dates. Many vendors are willing to accept a reliable, but slow payment schedule. Attempt to get terms on all payments, since this type of financing costs you nothing.

You can use other ways to hold onto cash a few days longer or generate a little extra interest income. Having payments wired or mailed to a lockbox gets cash into your account faster. Put as much cash as possible in an interest-bearing account or short-term investments. Have the bank automatically sweep any excess funds from your checking account into it to generate extra interest income, provided the added income exceeds any fees generated.

Long-Term Strategies

In addition to squeezing the balance sheet, you can use a number of longer-term strategies to reduce cash needs. These include the following:

▶ Lease or rent equipment instead of buying.
▶ Get suppliers to hold parts in their inventory, while charging you only when you order parts.

- ▶ Use sales representatives instead of a dedicated sales force, to save on fixed costs of salaries and a sales office.

- ▶ Use an application service provider (ASP) in lieu of purchasing software and related hardware.

- ▶ Outsource work to outside contractors or reduce employee hours rather than simply cutting headcount outright.

- ▶ Subcontract manufacturing work to a third party to eliminate payroll and overhead costs, plus reduce or defer the carrying costs of inventory.

These strategies can be particularly helpful to smaller companies seeking to reduce upfront outlays, control risk, and preserve cash. However, each also brings a potential cost, such as sharing profits or loss of control over operations. You can work with your controller to develop additional strategies for conserving cash and to weigh alternative approaches.

Keep Cash in the Business

If your company has a healthy cash balance or is generating cash, resist the temptation to distribute it to investors, spend it, or loosen cash management disciplines. Simply having cash in your business is a major competitive advantage. For example:

- ▶ It is generally more economical to buy assets rather than lease.

- ▶ Buying supplies or inventory in quantity may be more economical than in smaller lot sizes.

- ▶ Acquisitions or large-scale jobs may be possible only if there is sufficient liquidity.

- ▶ Employees, vendors, and customers all want assurance that a business is stable. A strong cash balance enhances financial strength. By contrast, delayed payments, bounced checks, and debt send significant negative signals

- ▶ Managing under a tight cash flow can be time-consuming and distracting for management.

Consider the following examples on the impact of having cash in the business.

A software company self-financed its growth. Though modestly profitable and growing around 20% per year, expansion was constrained by available resources. Because new employees generally took several months to get up to speed and contribute tangibly to profits, new people were added only if cash flow at current run rates could cover their costs. While in this operating mode, the company was acquired by a firm with deep pockets. This enabled rapid increases of the sales and consulting staffs and growth the first few years after the acquisition averaged close to 50% per year.

The owner of a small box manufacturer regularly paid out the profits of the company to himself and maintained no reserves, either in the company or personally. This forced the business to lurch from paycheck to paycheck. When an unexpected three-month downturn came, the business was suddenly forced to shut down.

Financing and Investors

As hard as the work might be to generate cash internally, going to outside sources is generally more difficult and more expensive.

As hard as the work might be to generate cash internally, going to outside sources is generally more difficult and more expensive. As the last anecdote above also illustrates, successful fund raising cannot be assumed. Start-ups will find few sources of seed capital and even successful entrepreneurs report spending close to half their time the first year in business trying to raise financing. In addition, selling equity to outsiders raises the issue of valuation and how much control you must surrender.

Once your company is successfully launched, your cash needs may only increase. As discussed earlier, one of the ironies of rapid growth is the creation of greater cash needs. At this point, assuming a company is profitable or close to it, possible investors should show greater interest. However, as earlier examples demonstrated, investor interest is not guaranteed. To reduce dependence on outside sources, you may want to hold down growth to what can be financed with funds generated internally.

Debt is an option for companies with assets—which can be used for collateral—or a history of positive earnings and cash flow. Debt does not dilute ownership, but it does increase the risk of the company. Interest payments on the debt raise your breakeven point and your company must also generate sufficient cash to meet any principal payments.

Capital structure for any financing you seek will depend on:

▶ What ownership percentage you want to maintain,

▶ How much leverage you are comfortable with,

▶ Your tax strategies, and

▶ The availability of money.

The basis for calculating how much financing you need is your cash forecast. Follow your forecast out to find the future point where your cumulative cash flow is the most negative. This point determines the minimum amount of cash needed.

Be conservative in calculating your cash needs, to make sure that you borrow enough. Just as you would tuck away money for a rainy day in your personal savings, you will want a cash cushion for your business. Run a worst-case scenario to see what your maximum cash need might be.

Allow for some unexpected expenditures and for shifts in the timing of transactions. Raising financing now will be easier and cheaper than if you find yourself in the midst of a crisis.

Debt

If you borrow money, as opposed to raising additional equity, it can come in a variety of forms. Banks will generally offer a line of credit. A typical formula might allow borrowing of 70%-80% of accounts receivable up to a maximum. Banks typically are less likely to lend against inventory, as the likelihood of recovering fair value in case of default is substantially less. A typical formula might only allow borrowing on 50% of purchased goods and no borrowing against work-in-process. Banks also will generally ask for all assets to be pledged as collateral, even though the borrowing formula may be limited to receivables and inventory. Though this is a fairly standard request, you should ensure that the request is reasonable. Pledging more assets than you need may limit the ability to borrow additional sums later on. The same caveat applies to personal guarantees. Though frequently required of small business owners, these put a substantial burden on owners: they should be avoided or removed if possible.

Expect your bank to attach covenants to your loan agreement specifying targets for earnings and various liquidity ratios. If you have sufficient cash and don't need to tap into your line of credit, you may still be required to borrow something for periods such as 30 days just to keep it active. On the other side, if your cash flow is seasonal, you will be expected to pay your line down when cash flow allows.

Debt from investors is more likely to be a term note. Though there may be covenants, the amount borrowed is generally fixed and not tied to a formula. Debt may be convertible to equity or carry warrants, which are essentially

Banks typically are less likely to lend against inventory, as the likelihood of recovering fair value in case of default is substantially less.

options to purchase shares of stock. Repayment may resemble a mortgage, where each payment is a fixed amount and includes both interest and principal. Other payment structures, though, may only require interest payments plus fixed principal payments at specified points or at the end of the loan. Be sure your cash forecast includes these payments.

These are only a few features of financing. A complete evaluation of financing strategies is beyond the scope of this book. However, additional books are available from Entrepreneur Press, including *Financing Your Small Business*.

Crisis Management

Cash planning and management are not simply strategies for dealing with a cash crisis. They are tools for avoiding a crisis in the first place. In spite of the fact that a crisis can seem to come on with unexpected suddenness—the loss of a key customer, a lender or key supplier cutting off credit, or an unanticipated expenditure—most cash shortages are avoidable. As venture capitalist Stanley Rich has said, "There's no excuse for running out of money."[4]

Cash planning and management are not simply strategies for dealing with a cash crisis. They are tools for avoiding a crisis in the first place.

If a crisis arises, the role of cash is magnified and you shift to a cash mentality. How much cash is coming in? What customers can be called to speed payments? How much money is available to meet payroll and pay vendors? Who can wait and who must be paid?

One of the hardest adjustments in a cash crisis, particularly for a controller, is to understand how irrelevant typical financial statements and accounting valuations can become. The focus becomes very short-term, as assets and operations are evaluated based on their ability to generate immediate cash, rather than long-term profit. Bankers, who are nervous about their collateral, may stop looking at book values and start to assess assets at liquidation values.

One key to resolving a cash crisis is to generate cash by speeding collections and slowing payments, even if it means taking a book loss. Strategies you can implement include the following:

▶ Reduce inventory, especially obsolete or excess items, even if they are liquidated below cost.

▶ Settle disputed accounts receivable.

▶ Sell excess fixed assets.

▶ Finance purchases wherever possible, even at high interest rates.

▶ Prioritize all payables and pay only the most essential items and vendors.

Clearly, no business can operate long term under these conditions. But your job is to first survive the crisis and then turn the practices of tight cash management into an ongoing habit to prevent a relapse.

Lenders and Investors in a Crisis

Lenders and outside investors can play a key role in rescuing a company from an impending crisis. Sometimes, however, they are the ones that precipitate the crisis. Venture capitalists often try to limit their exposure and keep entrepreneurs hungry for cash by keeping each round of investment as small as possible. Although entrepreneurs who anticipate upcoming cash needs and meet their operating targets can usually get additional funds, others may be surprised when investors are unwilling to put in additional funds or seek onerous terms. Failure to realistically manage their cash needs can leave those entrepreneurs scrambling.

> Like many ventures swept up in the dotcom boom of the late 1990s and early 2000s, a software company raised $14 million in venture money. Its investors seemed comfortable with projected losses and willing to make future investments. As a result, the company expanded rapidly, spread itself thin by tackling multiple projects, and reached a spending rate that was projected to burn through the initial investment in less than a year. When the time came to raise additional financing, lack of progress and the end of the boom period led investors to pull the plug. More cautious planning that put survival ahead of growth and ensured sufficient progress before seeking new financing could have saved the company.

A banker is said to be someone who will lend you an umbrella when it is sunny out and wants it back when it starts to rain.

Dealing with banks is not much easier. A banker is said to be someone who will lend you an umbrella when it is sunny out and wants it back when it starts to rain. Bankers are extremely risk-averse and cannot be expected to step up with more money during a crisis. In fact, they are more likely to react to a crisis by restricting credit. Here again, good cash management is needed. A forecast will help you communicate your plans and needs with the bank. If you achieve your targets and can demonstrate control over the situation, your bank is more likely to keep supporting you. Reducing your cash needs is the best plan, since you will reduce borrowing and minimize exposure to any actions by the bank.

185

Cash Keys

Ultimately, the keys to cash management are to understand the sources and uses of cash and to anticipate potential problems. The feedback you get from cash flow is timely and objective. Persistently poor cash flow is usually a symptom of operating problems. For growing companies, though, poor cash flow may be quite normal. Regardless of the cause, running out of cash is almost always avoidable and the consequences range from costly to catastrophic.

Careful planning and aggressive management are the keys to maximizing cash flow, starting with inventory and accounts receivable. A large part of a controller's job should be to keep these exposures under control. The next chapter looks at managing credit and collections.

Notes

1. Shelly Branch, "Go with the Flow—or Else," *Black Enterprise*, November 1991, p. 77.

2. Ibid.

3. William McGowan, quoted in *The Manager's Book of Quotations*, p. 6.

4. Edmund L. Andrews and Stanley R. Rich, quoted in "Running Out of Money," *Venture*, January 1986, p. 33.

Cash Flow Forecast—Sample

	Jan	Feb	Mar	Apr	May	Jun
Beginning Cash Balance	30,500	9,590	28,760	20,930	71,270	86,601
Cash In						
Cash sales	20,400	21,290	19,230	21,290	20,600	21,290
Collections on receivables	270,200	279,500	252,600	279,900	271,200	280,400
Sales of fixed assets			15,000			
New borrowing						
Total Cash In	290,600	300,790	286,830	351,190	291,800	301,690
Net Cash Available	321,100	310,380	315,590	372,190	363,070	388,300
Cash Disbursements						
Operating Expenditures						
Inventory purchases	150,400	135,900	150,600	145,900	150,800	155,800
Payroll	77,500	70,000	77,500	75,000	77,500	78,500
Benefits	25,300	22,500	24,300	23,000	23,300	23,600
Rent	10,000	10,000	10,000	10,000	10,000	10,000
Utilities	4,710	5,120	4,060	2,350	1,060	1,060
Repairs & maintenance	500	500	500	500	500	500
Travel	3,000	2,000	8,500	3,000	2,000	3,000
Leases	1,300	1,300	1,300	1,300	1,300	1,300
Insurance	27,000	0	0	27,000	0	0
Phone/postage	2,000	2,000	2,000	2,000	2,000	2,000
Other	9,800	7,300	7,800	10,800	8,000	8,600
Subtotal	331,510	256,620	286,560	300,850	276,460	284,360
Interest			8,100			8,100
Principal on Loans						50,000
Fixed Asset Purchases		25,000				
New Disbursements	331,510	281,620	294,660	300,850	276,460	342,460
Net Cash Flow	−20,910	19,170	−7,830	50,340	15,340	−40,770
Ending Cash	9,590	28,760	20,930	71,270	86,610	45,840

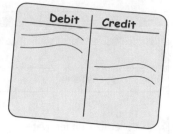

Chapter 10

Credit and Collections

Creditors have better memories than debtors.

—Ben Franklin[1]

The Check Isn't in the Mail

GOOD CASH MANAGEMENT DEPENDS ON A STRONG CREDIT AND collections program. Together with inventory, receivables often are the greatest drain on cash, tying up funds that could be used to fuel other aspects of a business. Growth and protection from cash crunches also require a predictable cash flow, something that can come only from an effective collections strategy.

Collections often get inadequate attention because bill collecting is one of the least favorite activities of managers and controllers. The work is mundane, disputes with customers can be emotionally charged, and, in the words of one CEO, "I always told myself that accounts receivable didn't create sales, so they weren't worth paying attention to."[2] However, no sale is complete until payment is received. And few businesses can prosper when squeezed between demands for payment by creditors and slow receipts from customers.

Collecting receivables is not simply a matter of chasing after customers with phone calls and letters. It results from having a total credit strategy. To implement an effective credit strategy, you must do the following:

▶ Decide on payment terms.

▶ Perform credit checks.

▶ Choose which personnel to involve.

▶ Monitor receivables.

▶ Follow up on problem accounts.

▶ Identify when to look outside your company for assistance.

The following sections of this chapter cover each of the above-listed topics, so that you can put into effect your own strategy for handling credit and collections.

Extending Credit

The first step in your credit strategy is deter- mining whether to extend credit.

The first step in your credit strategy is determining whether to extend credit. Consider the following example:

> One company claimed to have no receivables problems. Few accounts were past due and someone always followed up with phone calls as soon as accounts went even a few days beyond terms. "The accounts we have written off," the office manager said, "are all customers we can't do anything about. They are in bankruptcy or have shut down." On closer examination, it turned out these write-offs had totaled several hundred thousand dollars the year before on sales of about $10 million. The issue was not how the company collected past due bills, but to whom they extended credit.

The key to making good credit decisions is gathering pertinent information up front. Nationally published credit reports, the best known of which is Dun & Bradstreet (D&B), are popular sources. Subscribers can obtain information about a firm's management, products, number of employees, credit history, financial relationships, debts, and records of payments from these published credit reports.

There are limits to the reports' value. The financial information can be quite old and nearly all of it is unaudited. Bureaus such as D&B verify little of the information on credit histories and you have no way of determining who supplied that information. Bad news about a company may never show up on its credit report, because most of the information comes either from the company itself or from vendors that may be reluctant to damage the reputation of a customer.[3]

Rather than rely solely on these national services, your company should develop its own sources of information. When setting up a new account, ask for bank and credit references and call them promptly, so that problem customers can be spotted before credit is issued.

If financial statements are desired, get them directly from the customer. Up-to-date credit information, similar to what is available from D&B, may also be available from local credit bureaus or through exchanges of information with suppliers.

Though finan-cial data on private companies generally won't be available on the Internet, most companies have Web sites that will provide basic information about management, products, and locations.

The Internet can be a fast and easy way to locate information. Though financial data on private companies generally won't be available on the Internet, most companies have Web sites that will provide basic information about management, products, and locations. Other Web sites may contain articles about the company, press releases, and other background information.

Involving the Sales Force

One of the best sources of information can be your company's own sales force. A single visit to a customer's plant or conversations with its employees may provide more insight than reports and phone calls. Use salespeople for this task with caution, since there is a risk that their selling relationship with the client may be affected if the credit process becomes adversarial.

Also, limit the role of salespeople in the final credit decision. Depending on the commission structure, salespeople may have a built-in incentive to ship merchandise to marginal accounts. Consider the example below:

> A company experienced nearly half its bad debt losses in a sales territory that contributed just 10% of sales. The salesperson, through bad judgment or self-interest, convinced the home office to continue shipping to several delinquent accounts in that territory. The salesperson racked up commissions and the company ended up writing off several hundred thousand dollars.

If possible, pay all or a part of commissions only after customer payments have been received. Salespeople can be helpful following up on delinquent accounts, since they may have a rapport with customer personnel responsible for approving an invoice for payment or may be in a better position than a receivables clerk to work out any issues. However, salespeople are generally incentive-driven, so if commissions aren't contingent on collections, they are likely to push aside the concern of collecting on their accounts.

For the most part, expect some resistance to these measures. Many salespeople see their job as just selling and view bad debt losses as an administrative cost. In addition, they will likely not react well if their commissions are delayed because of collections. They may also fear losing future sales if their relationship with customers is damaged by collections efforts.

Not every sale is a good one. Unfortunately, selling to troubled accounts is often easier than selling to sound ones, because your company may be the only one willing to extend credit. It is hard to walk away from a sale, particularly in tough times, but sometimes you have to do it.

Unfortunately, selling to troubled accounts is often easier than selling to sound ones, because your company may be the only one willing to extend credit.

Credit Limits and Terms

Once you have reached the decision to extend credit, set a credit limit and stick to it. Review the limit periodically or as events demand. If a customer has reached the credit limit and an increase in the limit is not justified, do not ship additional product without payment of at least part of the oldest outstanding invoices. Even though putting a customer on hold may threaten a sale, this action is also your greatest source of leverage.

Payment terms should fit your overall credit strategy and vary by customer. For new or high-risk customers, you may want to make terms tight, such as net 10 days or even cash on delivery (COD). As you gain experience with a customer, you can gradually loosen the terms.

Early payment discounts are effective in encouraging rapid payment, but can be very costly. For example, a 2% discount for payments within 10 days, when normal terms are 30 days, is a 36% annualized interest rate. (On the flip side, when paying bills, try taking advantage of such discounts if cash flow allows.) In addition, many companies will take offered discounts, but continue to pay in 30 or 45 days as usual. Because of this, offering cash discounts usually makes sense only when early payment by customers is critical.

One exception may be in dealing with government agencies. Consider what one manufacturer discovered.

The manufacturer was selling to the federal government and its typical invoices were close to $100,000. Though the agencies were notoriously slow payers, they were required to take advantage of any offered discount, even if fairly small. By offering a 0.5% discount for paying in 15 days, the manufacturer greatly improved cash flow at a low cost.

At the other end of the spectrum, what if a customer pays late? Should you assess interest or late fees? How much should you charge? How late is the payment before you assess a charge? These charges are very much a judgment call.

Additional charges can add some leverage when negotiating with a troubled account and do represent an attempt to recoup a very real cost. However, many companies simply ignore these charges and other customers may be annoyed by the charges. The best strategy is to reserve the right to add finance charges and then add them only in extreme circumstances. Then, put effort into collecting on time to avoid the need for tacking on late fees.

No matter what your payment terms, they can best be met only if you issue invoices promptly and your customers understand the terms.

No matter what your payment terms, they can best be met only if you issue invoices promptly and your customers understand the terms. Communicate terms up front when the order is placed or an account is set up. Make sure your invoice is intelligible and the due date is clear. Observe how unclear terms can affect payment in the example below.

One company stated its terms as "3%/10 Net 30." The intention was that customers invoiced by May 25 could deduct 3% if paying by June 10; otherwise, the net amount was owed on the June 25, 30 days after the date of the invoice.

While nearly all customers understood the deadline for taking a discount, there was great confusion, even among employees of the company, on when balances were due for customers not taking a discount. Many thought the balances weren't due until 30 days after the discount period, or July 10. As a result, many customers routinely paid 60-75 days from the invoice date.

Even when you make sound decisions about extending credit and have clearly communicated your credit terms, you will probably have some customer accounts that become delinquent. The next step in your credit strategy is to learn how to manage those delinquent accounts.

The Check Is in the Mail

Nothing is more pleasant and courteous than a customer who pays bills promptly and in full. Unfortunately, payments slide all too commonly. Whether due to cash flow problems or simply an effort to improve float, some customers simply pay late. They can also tell many different stories why, such as:

- ▶ We do not have a copy of your invoice.
- ▶ We pay everyone in [45, 60, or 75] days.
- ▶ We do not pay partial shipments.
- ▶ There was an error on the original. We are waiting for a correction or credit.
- ▶ We do not start the payment clock until the invoice is in our system.
- ▶ We cannot pay you until we get paid.
- ▶ I think it is scheduled for next week.

Effective Responses

How do you effectively respond to these delinquent accounts? The first rule is to take an active approach, not passive. Don't wait to take action. The odds of collecting an account diminish greatly as time passes. In addition, companies with revolving lines of credit will find that banks generally will not lend against invoices older than 90 days. Call as soon as an account becomes past due. For large invoices, you may want to call before payment is due, just to be sure all paperwork is in order and that payment will be processed on time.

Call or e-mail as a first approach; don't depend on letters or statements. Since letters are expensive, are easily ignored, and avoid confronting the issue, make your first approach to the problem effective. Many companies send dunning letters to customers and yet continue to have conversations totally unrelated to the collection effort, effectively dodging the issue.[4]

A cordial, but firm approach usually works best. Do not threaten or browbeat customers. Politely explain why it is important that they adhere to terms and then listen carefully to why your customers are not paying. If a problem exists with the product, the customers may provide valuable feedback on your operation. In many cases, the problem is with the invoice itself. It may have been sent to the wrong person, not match terms in the purchase order or contract, or be unclear. This is yet another reason to contact customers early in the collection cycle and not escalate the tone of collection efforts before talking with customers.

Conversations should be carefully documented. Documentation helps to avoid future misunderstandings and will record any promises made. If a cus-

Do not threaten or browbeat customers. Politely explain why it is important that they adhere to terms and then listen carefully to why your customers are not paying.

tomer acknowledges a debt and does not dispute the amount owed or raise a problem with goods or services provided, confirm the conversation in writing. This confirmation will strengthen your position in the event of future litigation.

If a customer will not or cannot pay the entire debt, try to get a commitment to pay at least a portion of the bill. Be willing to spread payments out over time. This flexibility may make payment manageable for the customer as well as reduce your overall exposure. You can also clearly establish agreement that the amounts are indeed owed by getting a commitment to pay.

Troubled Accounts

In spite of extending every effort to work with your late payment accounts, you will undoubtedly end up with a few very troubled accounts. When you sense that a customer with a past due balance is at risk of defaulting, the most important thing is not to wait. Maintain a sense of urgency and don't be afraid to be the "squeaky wheel." Consider the case below.

> A company that had filed for Chapter 11 bankruptcy still got letters a year later from creditors asking for payment to "avoid the embarrassment of legal action." These letters were both futile and costly. They also demonstrated how lax and out of touch some creditors are with their accounts. By contrast, another creditor had successfully attached the company's bank accounts six months before the filing and received payment in full for an $8,000 debt.

Letters, e-mails, and calls are most effective when the content and style of the message are varied.

Letters, e-mails, and calls are most effective when the content and style of the message are varied. If calls and e-mails do not get a response, various letters, such as legal or registered, are possible. Numerous types of action give alternate media a chance to work and also keep the debtor's attention.

Collection agencies and lawyers are costly options. Troubled accounts should not be turned over to them as a first response. Do consider these options—discussed in more detail later in this chapter—but only after failing to collect with calls and letters.

Try some creative techniques. You may be able to minimize your risk by getting a lien against assets of the customer, especially the product you shipped. Accept postdated checks or negotiate more favorable terms on pending orders. One possibility is to work down an outstanding receivable balance by insisting that future sales be COD plus an additional percentage to be applied to old invoices.

At some point, you may need to cut your losses. While no one likes to take a loss, persistently chasing an undesirable credit risk may not be worth your time and expense. However, you may be able to negotiate a settlement of the account that would allow you to salvage something.

Bankruptcy

Particularly in tough times, a working knowledge about bankruptcy laws can pay off. If you have many troubled accounts, you can expect that some of those may choose bankruptcy to solve their debt problems. In recent years, the number of Americans and American businesses filing annually for bankruptcy has grown steadily, reaching over 1.5 million in 2002. Of these, over 38,000 were for businesses.[5] Usually coming on the tail of a string of broken promises, bankruptcies can leave a creditor feeling betrayed and angry. However, an understanding of the law and the particulars of each case can help you deal with a customer's bankruptcy.

In all cases, companies filing for bankruptcy have an automatic stay on any debt incurred before the filing. Creditors are not allowed to pursue collection of the old debt or offset subsequent payments against it. Any pending lawsuits are also stopped and the bankrupt company has the option of accepting or rejecting contractual agreements, including leases. As a creditor, if you wish to protest any aspect of the bankruptcy or have the automatic stay lifted, you must go through the bankruptcy court. However, contesting a bankruptcy is a costly process and usually not worth the effort.

A bankruptcy does not necessarily mean you will not be paid—although that may happen. But you will have to wait in line with the other creditors.

A bankruptcy does not necessarily mean you will not be paid—although that may happen. But you will have to wait in line with the other creditors. Here is the pecking order for payment:

- ▶ **Secured debts**—those tied to specific assets or collateral.
- ▶ **Priority debts**—unsecured debt, usually amounts owed to taxing authorities like the IRS.
- ▶ **Unsecured debt**—not tied to any assets or collateral.

Most trade debt is unsecured. Clearly, if you can secure your receivable before the bankruptcy filing, which is unlikely unless you have substantial negotiating leverage, you greatly improve your odds of payment.

Three main classes of bankruptcy can be filed. Chapter 13 is for individuals and involves setting up a payment plan over three to five years to satisfy the debt. Chapter 7 is for both individuals and businesses. In Chapter 7, the trustee simply sells the assets of the debtor—certain property is exempt—and distributes the proceeds. Chapter 11 is a business bankruptcy that allows the debtor to continue to operate. The company must submit monthly reports to the court and file a plan for paying the creditors.

Emotionally, you may want to stop doing business with companies that file for Chapter 11, but they can still be excellent customers. Often, you can extract favorable credit terms and a customer who defaults on a debt in Chapter 11 risks being shut down involuntarily. Plus, what better way to get even with a company that stiffed you by filing for bankruptcy than to continue to sell to them and make a healthy profit?

A customer on the verge of bankruptcy may approach creditors and propose a settlement of debt at a discount in lieu of filing for bankruptcy. This is often referred to as an "out-of-11" settlement. Taking a loss may be hard to swallow, but generally is preferable to waiting in line for an uncertain payment during a bankruptcy.

Alternatives to Internal Collections

The risk and effort of collections can be transferred to outsiders in several ways.

The risk and effort of collections can be transferred to outsiders in several ways. One possibility is to turn to a *factoring* company—often simply called *factors*. Factors essentially buy from you receivables for approved customers. You submit invoices to the factor as soon as possible after issue and, once the factor has verified that the goods have been delivered or services completed, the factor immediately pays 70%-80% of the invoice amount. Then, the customers remit payments directly to the factor. Once payments are received, the factor forwards the 20%-30% held back, less any fees.

The fees can be substantial. There are upfront charges that run roughly 1%-3% plus interest charges well over prime, perhaps 1% for every 10 days an invoice is outstanding.

The major benefits are that factors generally assume the risk of nonpayment, may lend in situations where bank financing is not possible, and pay you up front so your cash flow is accelerated. Factors may also reduce some administrative costs by processing customer payments. However, due to the extremely high costs, factoring is generally not a preferred option, especially over the long term.

Another possibility is to buy credit insurance. This insurance is structured like most other forms of insurance: for a premium the insurer assumes the risk of loss from default on receivables. The cost is roughly 0.2%-0.4% of sales, although the exact premium will depend on a company's risk profile. Generally, deductibles and liability limits are included in the policy. Sometimes coinsurance provisions are included, as well. Credit insurance works best for companies at risk of catastrophic loss. This category includes companies that sell to a few, very large accounts or are at risk in case of a general industry slump.

Both factoring companies and insurance companies are interested in healthy receivables. In contrast, collection agencies specialize in tracking down bad debt accounts. Most agencies are paid on a contingent basis, which limits your out-of-pocket cost if their efforts are unsuccessful. But their fees generally range from 20%-35% of what is collected. Most will also insist that you turn the account over to them exclusively. The high fees and loss of control over how the collection is handled make agencies desirable only after internal options have been exhausted.

Lawyers can be used at several stages. If phone calls have been ineffective, a letter on legal letterhead may provoke a response. Attorneys can help in obtaining a security interest in a debtor's property. In the case of default, the attorney may seek a writ of attachment, placing a lien on a debtor's assets, or a writ of possession, taking possession of assets in which your company has a security interest. Many lawyers also provide the same services as collection agencies. If needed, legal action should be taken quickly, because other creditors may try the same remedies. Legal action is also a very expensive option, of course, and may not make sense with smaller accounts.

By keeping poor records, many companies become their own worst enemy when it comes to collections.

Collections Made Easier

If you decide to keep collections in house, you can make the process easier and more effective by establishing some foundations in your accounting procedures. Keeping good records is the key. Your controller must ensure that records are accurate, timely, and complete to avoid hindering the collections efforts. By keeping poor records, many companies become their own worst enemy when it comes to collections.

> A law firm discovered that for every billable hour worked, only 75%-80% was being collected. The problem had several root sources. There was no structured procedure for people to track and submit their time sheets, a

problem made worse because attorneys were paid on salary rather than according to their billing. In addition, bills weren't going out on time and no one was pursuing collection.

The firm fixed the problem by tying compensation to billing, instituting strict deadlines for submitting time sheets, and calling all accounts after 45 days. Furthermore, the firm instituted a one-time amnesty program with its past due accounts that succeeded in getting payments on 50% of the outstanding accounts. Overall, cash flow at this $10 million firm improved by more than $2 million per year.

On your invoices, use the date the product ships or the services are performed, rather than the date the invoice is cut.

To get paid in time, invoices should go out on time. If you ship products, get bills out by the next day. If you bill professional services, consider billing weekly rather than monthly. On your invoices, use the date the product ships or the services are performed, rather than the date the invoice is cut. This starts the payment clock sooner. For very large invoices, consider using overnight mail or electronic forms to send invoices or receive payment.

Eliminate any excuses a customer may have for not processing invoices immediately. Make sure that quantities, prices, and extensions are correct and that terms have been agreed on and are clearly stated. Follow up by phone before payment is due, to make sure the customer has found the invoice in order and has it "in the system."

A solid accounting system is a valuable asset. The system provides current account agings, alerts clerks to credit limit problems, and assists in tracking changes in payment patterns—often the first indicator of problems with an account. The system can also ensure a good audit trail, needed for tracing the history of orders, invoices, and payments.

Accurate posting of transactions to the receivables system is also essential. Most accounts have a stream of invoices, partial payments, credits, and adjustments that complicate recordkeeping. Taking the time to keep account changes straight and up-to-date is worthwhile, especially to ease the resolution of discrepancies. Here is an example:

A company with a complicated billing structure, including third-party payments and several layers of discounts, often had difficulty matching payments and invoices. As a result, the company became frustrated tracking receivables and started simply applying all payments to the oldest open invoices. Resolving payment disputes with customers quickly became nearly impossible, because their records disagreed on which invoices had been paid and which were open. It took six months to restore order, during which time customers expressed frustration at having to repeatedly explain the history of their accounts. Many disputed balances were written off for lack of supporting detail.

Finally, to repeat, document all conversations with debtors. Documentation provides a record of promises made and makes it easy to track the history of an account.

Involve the Right People

Collections often end up in the hands of a lowly clerk, overburdened with other daily chores and untrained in credit procedures and collection techniques. This situation can happen when collecting is not given high priority or is considered such an unpleasant task that it keeps getting handed down until it can go no further. That approach is a recipe for failure.

Sales without collections are meaningless and collections should be given as high a priority as sales. A starting point is to hire or train a qualified credit professional and give that person the resources and support needed to make credit decisions. Like sales, collections are a total company effort. The effort starts with the salesperson who decides to approach an account and continues with the customer service employees who take an order, explain terms, and get references. The credit manager must check the references, approve terms, and monitor payment history. The accounting department is responsible for issuing invoices on a timely basis and providing accurate records. The effort then continues, if an account becomes past due, with follow-up calls and mail from appropriate personnel including sales and management, if necessary.

Sales without collections are meaningless and collections should be given as high a priority as sales.

Slow, Steady, and Persistent

While collections may never be the highlight of your day, they do not need to become emotionally charged. You should not need to issue threats or hire muscle-bound henchmen to collect funds. A persistent, professional approach will usually convince customers that you are serious about collections and bring results. And if customers are not willing to pay, be willing to enforce your claim and walk away from future sales. After all, who needs a customer who doesn't pay?

Now that you know the essentials of managing your assets and you understand the basic accounting functions involved, you are ready to really take charge. The next few chapters will show you how to look forward by using planning and forecasting and how to stay on target with techniques in budgeting and project evaluation. You will also find out how to best use computers and software to achieve your goals. Finally, you will see how to pull all of your financial information together to make comprehensive decisions and maintain a firm grasp on your finances.

Notes

1. Quoted in Bohle, *Apollo Book of American Quotations*, p. 66.
2. Jill Andresky Fraser, "Getting Paid: How to Make Collecting Bills as Much a Part of Daily Business as Making Sales," *Inc.*, June 1990, p. 58.
3. Ibid., pp. 68-69.
4. John W. Seder, *Credit and Collections* (New York: David McKay, 1977), p. 82.
5. American Bankruptcy Institute, *ABI World*, "Annual U.S. Bankruptcy Filings by State 2000-2002," www.abiworld.org/stats/2000stateannual.html.

Part Four

Taking Control

Chapter 11

Planning and Forecasting

Men don't plan to fail, they fail to plan.

—Anonymous

It is hard to forecast, especially the future.
If you have to forecast, forecast often.

—Paul Samuelson[1]

JUST ABOUT EVERYONE KNOWS THAT IF YOU WANT TO RAISE OR BORROW money, a formal plan that includes financial projections is a necessity. Venture capitalists, bankers, and the U.S. Small Business Administration (SBA) will all require projections when reviewing a loan or investment. But how useful are projections the rest of the time or for internal use?

Smaller business owners and CEOs alike often become too immersed in daily operating issues to look at long-range issues. Or they may perceive budgets and projections as mere financial exercises that don't reflect reality or that quickly go stale.

Stories abound of very successful companies that never followed their business plan. "Nobody ever volunteers to give you a copy of their business plan, even when they're successful, because nine out of ten times that plan didn't come true," says Joseph R. Mancuso, who has authored several books on preparing business plans.[2]

Ben Cohen and Jerry Greenfield of Ben & Jerry's Homemade, Inc. knew they needed a forecast for the SBA to consider their loan proposal. They projected first-year sales of $90,000, a figure Cohen thought was impossible. Said Cohen, "I remember sitting around trying to figure out how many cones per hour we'd have to sell in order to get that $90,000 . . . we had absolutely no way of gauging what our sales were going to be. But we had to put in numbers to play the guessing game."[3]

In Ben & Jerry's first year, they did $200,000 in sales and in just a few years they went from operating out of a garage to being a public company with sales of more than $10 million. "It occurred to me," said Cohen, "that that's how all these major businesses get millions of dollars, doing this crazy little exercise that probably has as much bearing on reality as the one we did."[4] And at the headquarters of Newman's Own, Inc., a sign hung with the following quote from founder Paul Newman: "If we ever have a plan, we're screwed."[5]

Why Plan?

If so many companies succeed without following a business plan, why should you do financial projections? Note first that the companies discussed above were start-ups with short operating histories and products having little market exposure. They were forced to project sales based on not much more than unbridled optimism or were graced with explosive sales growth that quickly rendered sales targets obsolete. Established companies, on the other hand, have a base level of performance from which they usually can make reasonable assumptions of future results. A survey of 1,650 business owners revealed that 69% had a strategic plan. Of those with a plan, 89% said the plan had been effective.[6]

A survey by AT&T of 500 businesses with less than $20 million in sales provides even further concrete evidence of the importance of planning. In that survey, 59% of the companies with growing sales used formal business plans, while just 38% of those with declining sales did.[7]

Even if your sales projections are difficult or prove off the mark, you can and should revisit the planning process as often as needed. The purpose of planning is not to produce a document carved in stone. If your company's plan no longer reflects reality, update it—don't toss it aside.

The formal plan and projections are often less important than the process itself. If nothing else, strategic planning allows you to "come up for air" from the daily problems of running the company, take stock of where your company is, and establish a clear course to follow.

Regular planning also helps your company deal with change, both inside and outside the company. By constantly reevaluating your company's strengths, markets, and competition, you are better able to recognize problems and opportunities. You can react to new developments, rather than simply plugging along.

By constantly reevaluating your company's strengths, markets, and competition, you are better able to recognize problems and opportunities.

For some top managers, planning can be a response to vague feelings that profits should be better. Take the case of the small business owner who complained about business:[8]

"I feel that my store should be doing better. I guess I should be glad we're making a profit at all." But when asked what the store's sales and profit should be, possible ways to meet those goals, or how other retailers in the community were doing, the owner confessed to not knowing the answers. Unease about the company's performance resulted from not knowing where the company was headed or how to get there.

For other entrepreneurs, getting down into specific financial benchmarks and targets allows them to understand the ramifications of operating decisions. For example:

The owner of a small furniture manufacturing and retailing company had experienced five years of losses. Unwilling to finance the business any further, the owner wanted to know if the business was worth keeping alive. By putting together a pro forma projection and breakeven analysis, the owner and the controller determined what level of sales were needed from a new retail location, together with cuts in operating expenses, to become profitable. Encouraged that the goals were attainable, the owner succeeded in both increasing sales and cutting expenses, returning to modest profitability within six months. Furthermore, knowing the company's breakeven point enabled the owner to quickly gauge performance by tracking monthly sales and to gain a gut feel for the proper level of operating expenses.

Projections and planning can be a rather tortuous exercise, especially the first time through. Translating headcount to dollars, digging up the running rate of everyday expenses such as telephone and electricity, adding up the full cost of an hour of direct labor, and determining a breakeven level can be painstaking efforts. For example:

> One small company president dreaded every minute that went into putting his first set of projections together, complaining that it was a grinding process that caused a constant search for numbers. But the finished product was invaluable for understanding the business and evaluating strategies, not to mention essential for working with the bank and obtaining SBA funding.

Not Just Number Crunching

What if you feel your company's strategic goals and direction are clearly established and you do not need a formal plan to raise financing? What is accomplished by preparing projections and budgets? What keeps it from just being a number-crunching exercise?

- ▶ First, the financial plan translates your company's goals into specific targets. It clearly defines what a successful outcome entails. The plan is not merely a prediction; it implies a commitment to making the targeted results happen and establishes milestones for gauging progress.

- ▶ Second, the plan provides you with a vital feedback-and-control tool. Variances from projections provide early warning of problems. And when variances occur, the plan can provide a framework for determining the financial impact and the effects of various corrective actions.

- ▶ Third, the plan can anticipate problems. If rapid growth creates a cash shortage due to investment in receivables and inventory, the forecast should show this. If next year's projections depend on certain milestones this year, the assumptions should spell this out.

In the example of the furniture manufacturer, an annual three-week shutdown during the summer and payment of Christmas bonuses, combined with a seasonal slowdown, strained cash at specific points during the year. The projections anticipated the cash needs and how much needed to be set aside ahead of time.

Communication Tool

As already mentioned, plans are a vital communication tool. If your company is dealing with outside investors or lenders, you need to convey how investments will be paid back plus the timetable and milestones for sales and profitability.

Not only is this true at the time the funds are sought, but ongoing communication of progress against projections, explanations of variances, and any revised projections are critical. In loan workout situations, lack of communication between the bank and company is often a key reason for the bank calling or threatening to call a loan. Updated projections, followed by monthly updates of performance versus plan, are key tools for keeping bankers and other key creditors updated.

Your plan not only communicates with outside investors, but also reveals your goals and expectations to people within the company. It educates employees about planned actions, guides them in what is to be done, and provides a basis for ongoing communication.

Your plan not only communicates with outside investors, but also reveals your goals and expectations to people within the company.

Crunching the numbers will also help ensure coordination and consistency among the various stated goals of your company. Commonly, companies will adopt a number of objectives—perhaps for sales growth, ROI, R&D spending, or debt-to-equity ratio—only to find that, while each goal is admirable, together they are impossible to reach.

Consider the following example of a company with an outstanding planning process that recognizes the need for coordinating financial goals.

> Analog Devices, Inc. has grown steadily from a start-up in the mid-1960s to a company with more than a $2 billion in sales in 2003. Analog built much of its early long-range planning around its "fundable growth rate," which combined a goal of self-funded growth and a target profitability level. These, plus other inputs, helped define an achievable target for long-term sales growth.

Just the exercise of planning is a valuable learning process. The planning process may be the first time you think about how objectives translate to financial results, study past and present performance, investigate what drives expenses, and determine what some key indicators of success are. Understanding the dynamics of your company—financial and nonfinancial—is a key benefit of the planning process.

Planning Process Outputs

Depending on your company's situation and objectives, you will need to develop several types of projections and budgets.

▶ *A model that projects either the current year or a rolling 12-month period by month.* This type of forecast should be updated at least monthly and become the main planning and monitoring vehicle. Information in this model can be the springboard for preparing the other types of plans discussed below. A sample model is presented at the end of this chapter.

▶ *A long-range, strategic plan looking out three to five years.* While the 12-month forecast often reflects short-term expectations and tactical plans, the long-range projection incorporates the strategic goals of the company. For start-up companies, the initial business plan should include a month-by-month projection for the first year, followed by annual projections going out a minimum of three years. Some investors may prefer to see the second year broken out by quarters. It is fine to append the projections for years two and beyond to the 12-month forecast, but the numbers should be more than just a simple extrapolation of the current year. A strategic planning process should accompany development of the "out year" projections.

▶ *Budgets, typically covering one year.* Budgets translate goals into detailed actions and interim targets. Budgets should provide detail, such as specific staffing plans and line-item expenditures. Given the detail required, the size of a company may determine whether the same model used to prepare the 12-month forecast can be appropriate for budgeting. In any case, unlike the 12-month forecast, budgets should generally be frozen at the time they are approved. They should also be consistent with the goals of the long-range plan. Budgets are discussed in detail in the next chapter.

▶ *Cash forecasts, as discussed in Chapter 9, if needed.* These break down the budget and 12-month forecast into even further detail. The focus is on cash flow, rather than accounting profit, and periods may be as short as a week in order to capture fluctuations within a month.

▶ *Formal project tracking,* another form of planning and control that should be used, such as for software development or construction projects.

Mechanics of Projections

As noted above, a solid 12-month forecasting model is the key vehicle for monitoring your business. What follows below is a discussion of how to construct and maintain such a model.

A sample set of projections is included at the end of this chapter. Projections should be broken out by months for at least one year. If you choose to include additional years, they generally do not need to be any more detailed than by quarters for another year and then annually after that.

A solid 12-month forecasting model is the key vehicle for monitoring your business.

The projections should include an income statement and a balance sheet. Expenses can be summarized by department or major expense category; you can hold line-item detail for the budget. Cash needs should be clearly identified, possibly by adding a separate statement of cash flows. If your financial statements usually report financial ratios or expenses as a percent of sales, calculate and report these as part of the projections, too.

Projections are an ideal spreadsheet application. The projections can incorporate many different factors and, if programmed properly, can handle multiple scenarios or "what-if" analysis. However, this should not be taken as an opportunity to dazzle your readers with brilliant programming or baffle them with pages of printouts. Communication is an important goal of the projections and, therefore, you need a clear, professional presentation. Good presentation is particularly necessary for business plans, where your audience consists of potential investors and bankers.

Many accounting packages include the ability to do very basic budgeting and forecasting. Capabilities, though, are generally limited to simple extrapolations of prior budgets or actuals. This functionality is much too limited to be useful. Some business planning software exists for preparing assumption-driven forecasts. In general, these packages are very rigid and will be appropriate only for either simple forecasts or for people without the spreadsheet skills to build a basic model.

Lay Out Assumptions

As in the sample projections at the end of the chapter, all assumptions should be laid out very clearly. Rather than simply showing that annual sales will be $5 million, show how you reached that figure. Did you take last year's sales and assume a certain percent growth? Is it based on a customer-by-customer sales forecast? Maybe it includes factors for seasonality, price changes, or changes in market size and share. Spelling these assumptions out has several advantages.

- ▶ First, printouts can look very impressive, but important logic and assumptions are too often buried in formulas and hidden from the reader. To make an informed judgment about the validity and consistency of the projections, the reader must know not just the final result but also what went into the figures.

- ▶ Second, clearly spelling out the assumptions can make it easier to track variances. Sales may be a function of variables such as product mix, the number of days in a month, and prices. If these assumptions aren't known, there is no basis for evaluating future differences.

- ▶ Finally, laying out the assumptions makes it much easier to play with multiple scenarios. For example, referring to the sample projections at the end of this chapter, if you quickly change the average selling price per unit by 10%, you can see the impact immediately.

Modeling Tips

Because wages are often the largest expense, it pays to model these in detail. Line items like supplies, postage, and telephone might be unlikely to vary more than 10%-20% from period to period, with a relatively limited dollar impact. However, just a one-month delay in hiring a new manager at a salary of $60,000 equals a $5,000 saving. The timing of a raise could have a similar impact. Multiplied by the number of employees in a company and the swings from headcount changes or the timing of raises can become very large. The sample projections at the end of this chapter provide an example of a basic payroll model.

Another tip is to let cash "fall out" of the projections. What this means is not trying to derive cash balances directly by adding together collections, sales, borrowing, and other sources and deducting expenses, reductions of payables, loan payments, and other uses of cash. Instead, determine the other elements of your balance sheet first. For example, equity will be the beginning balance plus earnings, plus new investments. Receivables may be based on a percentage of revenue in recent months and payables similarly derived from expenses. When all other elements of the balance sheet have been entered, the surplus of equity plus liabilities less all noncash assets will be your cash balance. One exception: if your company requires financing, such as a bank line of credit, you would set cash equal to a minimum working capital balance and back into the borrowing need instead of the cash balance. Start-ups and other companies that need to determine how much funding to raise can use this method.

Be careful of assumptions in the first and last months of a forecast, as these may require formulas different from the rest of the model. For example, if inventory purchases are a function of future months' sales, when you reach the last month of your model, there may be no place to pick up an assumption for future sales. Even worse, if the next column includes a total for the year, your formula could pick up a number that's much too high. Conversely, your projected receivables balance will generally be a function of current and prior months' sales. In the first month of the forecast, there may not be any historical sales figures to reference. You may need to either add that data in specifically for this purpose or alter the formula.

Be careful of assumptions in the first and last months of a forecast, as these may require formulas different from the rest of the model.

Employ consistent assumptions about the economy and the industry in all your calculations. If inflation is built into your sales assumption, it must be part of your costs as well, including interest rates.

Although it seems an obvious suggestion, if you have written your own spreadsheet, be sure to double-check the calculations. Because spreadsheets easily handle so many complex formulas and look impressive, you may have an impulse to assume they are accurate. However, if you don't check the numbers, you can be sure readers of the plan will. At the very least, it's an embarrassment when someone else quickly spots an obvious error. Though it's impossible to list all the things that can go wrong, these are some checks for common errors:

▶ Ensure that the balance sheets balance. Note that if you use the method recommended above for computing cash, this should bring your balance sheet into balance automatically.

▶ Make sure that numbers foot down and across. For example, net income for the year should be the same whether you add up net income for each month or take annual revenue and deduct annual expenses.

▶ Look for negative numbers or big swings in numbers from month to month. Either may indicate formula problems; at the least, they need to be understood.

▶ Compare key numbers, such as gross margin, profit margins, or return on assets against benchmarks to determine reasonableness.

Updating

One complaint about formal plans is that they quickly become obsolete. When this happens, either the plan gets ignored, as in the start-ups discussed at the beginning of the chapter, or there is a risk it will restrict managers' ability to react to change, simply because it is not in the plan.

If you have a long-range plan, rather than let it go stale, review it and, if needed, revise it at regular intervals. This is particularly true in small, fast-changing companies. How often you need to revise your plan will depend on your company and its environment.

12-month models should be updated no less frequently than monthly. As monthly financial statements become available, overwrite past months' projected figures with the actuals. When you do this, take the time to compare actual results with budgeted figures. Then update assumptions for the remaining months, so your full-year forecast remains current. For example, if you have a calendar fiscal year and have just closed the month of June, the model would now have six months of actuals (January through June) plus six months of forecast (July to December). If you prefer, you can keep a model that always looks out 12 months rather than just the current fiscal year. In this example, your model would be changed to project from July through the following June.

While updating your model regularly ensures that you work with the most current data, you should not lose track of prior plans. While the main use of your plan may be to set the direction of your company, don't forget to monitor actual performance against targets. Failure to reach key objectives may jeopardize other goals, as well as indicate possible operating problems. Successfully meeting your targets can be the basis for rewarding managers.

Variances from your plan should be investigated quickly and corrective action should be taken. These are some questions to ask:

▶ How large is the variance and is it significant?

▶ Was the variance caused by actions within the company or by factors beyond its control?

▶ What corrective action is needed?

▶ What feedback should be given to managers?

If you have a long-range plan, rather than let it go stale, review it and, if needed, revise it at regular intervals.

- ▶ Should assumptions about the market or operating environment be changed?

- ▶ What are the implications for the company's strategy and operating plan?

Though you'll want to keep your plan current while raising financing, be careful to advise potential investors of any changes and to throw away outdated copies. They also will likely want to see how you've performed against earlier plans, so provide comparisons. Constantly putting new projections in front of them can erode confidence, especially if key milestones keep slipping.

To clearly distinguish among the different plan versions you are producing, adopt terminology such as "benchmark plan" or "budget" to identify the original plan for the year. "Rolling forecast" or simply "forecast" can be used to refer to your current model.

As you approach a new fiscal year, a fresh model should be created. This should be done early enough to allow timely completion of the budgets. For a smaller company, one to two months prior to the start of the next budget year should be sufficient. In cases where the model has the account-level detail desired for budgeting, the model itself can be used to generate the budget. The next chapter discusses the budget process in more detail.

Long-Range Planning

Not only should the budget fit within the parameters of the model, but the model itself should also fit within the framework of a strategic plan. Though managers of smaller businesses may find it hard to break away from day-to-day issues to plan, a common approach is to take time once a year to lay out strategic objectives, which can, in turn, be translated into a three- to five-year financial plan. If a company does not do a full plan, it should at least consider adopting metrics to work toward, perhaps a targeted growth rate, profit margin, or return on assets.

Planning can seem like a distraction and doing the homework needed to produce a thorough plan may be arduous. But failure to plan can leave your company drifting and unprepared. In the words of business writer Ronaleen Roha, "The fact is poor management is the biggest cause of business failure. And the basis of poor management almost always comes down to lack of planning."9

Strategic planning is not just an exercise done to please investors or validate existing assumptions. The very process elicits new ideas and visions,

Planning can seem like a distraction and doing the homework needed to produce a thorough plan may be arduous.

213

anticipates problems, challenges and refines your perceptions of operations, and sets the course of your business.

Even if explosive growth is your goal, don't assume any plan will become obsolete. Consider the case of Stratus Computer.[10]

> A maker of fault-tolerant computers, Stratus started with a business plan that called for sales of $75 million in its fifth year—and it hit that total almost exactly. CEO William Foster said the next year, "That plan was something we took very seriously. I'm convinced that if the original plan had a lower goal, we would have achieved less."

If your sales explode and render your original plan obsolete, as with Ben & Jerry's, terrific! But use the opportunity to update your plan and set new targets. As a proverb says, "If you don't know where you're going, any path will get you there."

Uncertainty

As you project out several years, confidence in the figures will clearly decline the further they go into the future.

As you project out several years, confidence in the figures will clearly decline the further they go into the future. However, do not let this deter you from including them in the projections. Investors understand the uncertainty involved and will not hold you to those numbers. Just pick a reasonable basis for those future-year assumptions. Modest year-to-year growth rates are one possibility. Another method is to develop a model of where you would like to be in five to seven years and move slowly toward that target. Looking at the published financials of companies similar to yours will give you possible targets for the distribution of expenses among departments.

Because of the uncertainty inherent in long-range projections, try preparing several scenarios—such as best-case, worst-case, or best-guess scenarios, for example. Multiple scenarios should generally be for internal use only. When presenting to outsiders, it is usually better to go with just a single set of numbers.

Learning from the Planning Process

When it comes to projections, don't be discouraged if your first few efforts stray off the mark. Forecasting is partly art, partly science.

Forecasting sales, in particular, can be extremely difficult and the tendency is to be overly optimistic. In general, operating expenses are much easier to both project and control.

Planning is a repetitive process. Each time around, you will get a little bit better at it. A few planning cycles may be required before you can accurately predict the flow of receipts and expenses. But the very act of investigating variances and challenging or refining assumptions about your business can be more valuable than having an accurate forecast.

You cannot delegate responsibility for planning. True, the process is time-consuming and others may seem better qualified to put a plan together. You should seek the inputs of all key employees—not to mention as many outside sources as possible. Your finance staff will likely do most of the necessary spreadsheet work of building models and budgets; others may do a significant amount of writing needed. But the ideas and insights contained in any plan must come from the top. Furthermore, with the viability of the company at stake, why would you want to relinquish control over the plan?

The ideas and insights contained in any plan must come from the top.

Your controller should play a key role in the mechanics of planning. This might include compiling historical financial data; gathering information on margins, headcount, ownership, past performance, and market share; and preparing spreadsheets included in the plan. The controller, who is usually knowledgeable in all areas of a business, is also in a strong position to evaluate the nonfinancial aspects of a plan.

Even the projections must be the responsibility of top management, not the controller or other financial specialist. This does not mean you have to sit at the computer and bang out a spreadsheet. But the assumptions and goals you established in the other sections should drive the projections. And you should work with the controller on any additional assumptions that are needed. This way, the numbers and any written plan are consistent—plus you understand how the projections were derived and can answer questions posed by investors and key personnel.

Planning or Control?

With both long-range plans and operating budgets comes an important, but sometimes subtle trade-off between the planning and control aspects. You have the opportunity to use these plans to set the general direction of your company and establish guidelines for operating managers. Or you can use the plans to specify actions to take, set spending limits, and evaluate performance. Often, some combination is used.

The degree of emphasis you give to planning and control will vary depending on management style, company size, and the stability of the environment. For example, a small company, with a limited number of management layers and a need to react swiftly to changes in its environment, will place a higher emphasis on the planning aspect. The goal is assistance in allocating resources and anticipating operating problems, not restricting or measuring management decisions.

A larger company usually operates in a more stable environment and with many levels of management. There is a need to coordinate the actions of the managers to ensure achieving corporate goals. Larger companies often require more formal spending guidelines and performance evaluations. Here, the control aspect is paramount.

In a large organization, top management's only control over spending may be a budget. In a small company, the president may be personally involved in all spending decisions, minimizing the control issue.

Another trade-off comes when the operating environment changes. For example, if the economy improves and sales take off unexpectedly, should plans and budgets be revised or not? Revising will provide the most accurate guide for ongoing operations. But having moving targets makes it difficult to measure managers.

The degree of emphasis you give to planning and control will vary depending on management style, company size, and the stability of the environment.

Business Plans

Companies trying to attract financing will want to put together a formal business plan. Many excellent books and templates can guide entrepreneurs looking to write a business plan. One helpful product that may be of interest is *Entrepreneur Magazine*'s *Creating a Successful Business Plan.* (For ordering information, check in the Related Resources pages at the back of this book.)

Most business plans will have the following sections:

▶ Executive summary, providing a short synopsis or narrative of your business plan

▶ Description of the company, including the operating history, products, and competitive strengths

▶ Market analysis, describing the industry, target customers or markets, anticipated market share, test marketing results, and competition

- ▶ Sales and marketing strategy, including distribution and pricing, selling strategies, advertising and promotion, and customer service

- ▶ Products and services, covering present stage of development, specific benefits, any proprietary features, and future products planned

- ▶ Operations, encompassing production and service capabilities, work force, and suppliers

- ▶ Management and ownership, highlighting the experience and accomplishments of the key team members and describing the legal and financial structure

- ▶ Financial summary, covering historical performance, projected income statement, cash flow, balance sheet, and funding requirements (projections by month for the first year, by quarter or annually for the second year, and with annual numbers for an additional one to three years)

While investors need to know how much of an investment a company needs and what their return will be, they pay the closest attention to the nonfinancial sections. Investors like to invest in people and so they will look closely at the management team. They also need to understand why a company's products or services stand out. And the marketing sections are perhaps the most important. Is there demand for the product, how big is the potential market, what other companies are competing, and how will the customers be reached?

Investors like to invest in people and so they will look closely at the management team.

A business plan used for raising financing is not necessarily a lengthy document. In fact, most experts recommend a document between 10 and 25 pages, including the sections listed above, but not counting appendices such as copies of résumés, articles, or key contracts.

The typical business plan is usually a distillation of far more detailed information that can and should be used internally to manage a company. If, as some experts recommend, your company also prepares a formal internal operating plan, it may run several hundred pages, providing a detailed picture of all aspects of your business.

Tips for Business Plan Projections

Potential Investors and other outsiders are an audience different from company management. Here are some tips for sharing financials as part of a business plan or similar presentation:

- ▶ **How much data is right?** Show three to five years—the first year by month, the second year by quarters or an annual total, and subsequent years with annual figures. Include an income statement and balance sheet and either a full cash flow statement or an analysis of cash needs. Limit the amount of line-item detail. Do not drown the audience in pages of detail; less is generally more.
- ▶ **Present only one scenario.** Though projections are inherently uncertain and you may want to run multiple scenarios for yourself, present just one plan to investors.
- ▶ **Clearly show assumptions.** As important as the financials themselves is being able show how you got there.
- ▶ **It's OK to be optimistic, but don't be unrealistic.** Investors expect entrepreneurs to have high aspirations and aggressive goals. To attract venture funding, you may need to be able to demonstrate the potential for exceptional returns. In these cases, being optimistic is all right, especially since these investors instinctively discount most projections. However, don't be unrealistic. Common errors cited by venture capitalists are profit margins that exceed those of even the most successful companies or several years of exceptionally high sales growth.
- ▶ **Show how investors get their money out.** For lenders, be sure to include a reasonable interest rate and the timely repayment of principal. For equity investors, indicate what total financing is likely to be plus how and when they will be able to exit.

Conclusion

This chapter has focused on the planning process and developing a financial model that you can use on an ongoing basis to help steer your business. The next chapter focuses on budgeting, an annual process that translates strategic goals and financial targets into detailed actions and account-level spending.

Financial Projections, Sample Assumptions

	Jan	Feb	Mar	Apr	May	Jun	Jul	Aug	Sep	Oct	Nov	Dec	Total Year
# of Working Days	22	20	21	22	22	20	22	22	20	23	20	20	
Average Unit Sales/Day	210	250	240	270	275	280	240	250	270	270	260	220	
Sales Mix													
Regular – NY	20%	20%	20%	20%	20%	20%	20%	20%	20%	20%	20%	20%	
Contract – NY	32%	32%	32%	32%	32%	32%	32%	32%	32%	32%	32%	32%	
Regular – PA	17%	17%	17%	17%	17%	17%	17%	17%	17%	17%	17%	17%	
Contract – PA	26%	26%	26%	26%	26%	26%	26%	26%	26%	26%	26%	26%	
Overstock	5%	5%	5%	5%	5%	5%	5%	5%	5%	5%	5%	5%	
Average Selling Price													
Regular Sales	$115	$115	$115	$115	$115	$115	$115	$115	$115	$115	$115	$115	
Contract Sales	$87	$87	$87	$87	$87	$87	$87	$87	$87	$87	$87	$87	
Overstock	$60	$60	$60	$60	$60	$60	$60	$60	$60	$60	$60	$60	
Net Average	$96	$96	$96	$96	$96	$96	$96	$96	$96	$96	$96	$96	
Cost of Materials													
Regular Sales	52%	52%	52%	52%	52%	52%	52%	52%	52%	52%	52%	52%	
Contract Sales	46%	46%	46%	46%	46%	46%	46%	46%	46%	46%	46%	46%	
Overstock	70%	70%	70%	70%	70%	70%	70%	70%	70%	70%	70%	70%	
Sales Impact on Inventory													
Regular Sales	0%	0%	0%	0%	0%	0%	0%	0%	0%	0%	0%	0%	
Contract Sales	2%	2%	2%	2%	2%	2%	2%	2%	2%	2%	2%	2%	
Overstock	-22%	-22%	-22%	-22%	-22%	-22%	-22%	-22%	-22%	-22%	-22%	-22%	
Indirect Labor Pay/Month	20,500	20,500	20,500	20,500	20,500	20,500	20,500	20,500	20,500	20,500	20,500	20,500	
Direct Labor Wages/Day	2,000	2,000	2,000	2,000	2,000	2,000	2,000	2,000	2,000	2,000	2,000	2,000	
Payroll Tax and Fringes	24%	24%	24%	24%	24%	24%	24%	24%	24%	24%	24%	24%	
Freight/Unit – NY	$6.90	$6.90	$6.90	$6.90	$6.90	$6.90	$6.90	$6.90	$6.90	$6.90	$6.90	$6.90	
Freight Unit – PA	$3.45	$3.45	$3.45	$3.45	$3.45	$3.45	$3.45	$3.45	$3.45	$3.45	$3.45	$3.45	
Commissions													
Contract Sales	4%	4%	4%	4%	4%	4%	4%	4%	4%	4%	4%	4%	
All Others	5%	5%	5%	5%	5%	5%	5%	5%	5%	5%	5%	5%	
Co-op Advertising – Reg. Sales	4%	4%	4%	4%	4%	4%	4%	4%	4%	4%	4%	4%	
Fixed Assets - Avg. Months Life	48	48	48	48	48	48	48	48	48	48	48	48	
Fixed Asset Purchases		20,000	20,000				40,000			40,000			120,000
Average Days AIP Outstanding	32	32	32	35	35	35	36	36	36	36	36	36	
Average Days AIR Outstanding	52	52	52	50	50	50	50	50	48	48	48	48	
Average Tax Rate	38%	38%	38%	38%	38%	38%	38%	38%	38%	38%	38%	38%	
Interest Rate	6.0%	6.0%	6.0%	6.0%	6.0%	6.0%	6.0%	6.0%	6.0%	6.0%	6.0%	6.0%	
Debt Principal Payments		25,000			25,000			25,000			25,000		100,000

Financial Projections, Sample P&L

	Jan	Feb	Mar	Apr	May	Jun	Jul	Aug	Sep	Oct	Nov	Dec	Total Year
Sales													
Regular and Contract - NY	230,630	249,600	251,597	296,525	302,016	279,552	263,578	274,560	269,568	310,003	259,584	219,648	3,208,861
Regular and Contract - PA	190,714	206,400	208,051	245,203	249,744	231,168	217,958	227,040	222,912	256,349	214,656	181,632	2,651,827
Overstock	22,176	24,000	24,192	28,512	29,040	26,880	25,344	26,400	25,920	29,808	24,960	21,120	308,352
Total Sales	443,520	480,000	483,840	570,240	580,800	537,600	506,880	528,000	518,400	596,160	499,200	422,400	6,167,040
Cost of Sales													
Materials	219,188	237,216	239,114	281,813	287,031	265,682	250,500	260,938	256,193	294,622	246,705	208,750	3,047,752
Direct Labor Wages	44,000	40,000	42,000	44,000	44,000	40,000	44,000	44,000	40,000	46,000	40,000	40,000	508,000
Indirect Labor Wages	20,500	20,500	20,500	20,500	20,500	20,500	20,500	20,500	20,500	20,500	20,500	20,500	246,000
Payroll Tax and Fringes	15,480	14,520	15,000	15,480	15,480	14,520	15,480	15,480	14,520	15,960	14,520	14,520	180,960
Rent	10,000	10,000	10,000	10,000	10,000	10,000	10,000	10,000	10,000	10,000	10,000	10,000	120,000
Utilities	4,700	5,120	4,060	2,350	1,060	1,060	1,180	1,180	1,350	2,800	3,800	4,250	32,910
Depreciation	2,700	2,700	2,800	3,000	3,000	3,000	3,000	3,300	3,300	3,300	3,700	3,700	37,500
Other Overhead	900	900	900	900	900	900	900	900	900	900	900	900	10,800
Total Cost of Sales	317,468	330,956	334,374	378,043	381,971	355,662	345,560	356,298	346,763	394,082	340,125	302,620	4,183,922
Gross Profit	126,052	149,044	149,466	192,197	198,829	181,938	161,320	171,702	171,637	202,078	159,075	119,780	1,983,118
Gross Profit %	28.4%	31.1%	30.9%	33.7%	34.2%	33.8%	31.8%	32.5%	33.1%	33.9%	31.9%	28.4%	32.2%
Operating Expenses													
Salaries	30,000	30,000	30,000	30,000	30,000	30,000	30,000	30,000	30,000	30,000	30,000	30,000	360,000
Commissions	19,604	21,216	21,386	25,205	25,671	23,762	22,404	23,338	22,913	26,350	22,065	18,670	272,584
Payroll Tax and Fringes	11,905	12,292	12,333	13,249	13,361	12,903	12,577	12,801	12,699	13,524	12,496	11,681	151,821
Leases	1,300	1,300	1,300	1,300	1,300	1,300	1,300	1,300	1,300	1,300	1,300	1,300	15,600
Insurance	6,000	6,000	6,000	6,000	6,000	6,000	6,000	6,000	6,000	6,000	6,000	6,000	72,000
Travel and Entertainment	2,500	2,500	2,500	2,500	2,500	2,500	2,500	2,500	2,500	2,500	2,500	2,500	30,000
Phone/Postage/Internet	2,000	2,000	2,000	2,000	2,000	2,000	2,000	2,000	2,000	2,000	2,000	2,000	24,000
Depreciation	4,000	4,000	4,200	4,500	4,500	4,500	4,500	5,000	5,000	5,000	5,500	5,500	56,200
Trucking	23,430	25,358	25,560	30,125	30,683	28,400	26,778	27,893	27,386	31,494	26,372	22,315	325,794
Co-op Advertising	6,564	7,104	7,161	8,440	8,596	7,956	7,502	7,814	7,672	8,823	7,388	6,252	91,272
Warehousing	2,500	2,500	2,500	2,500	2,500	2,500	2,500	2,500	2,500	2,500	2,500	2,500	30,000
Other Office	1,700	1,700	1,700	1,700	1,700	1,700	1,700	1,700	1,700	1,700	1,700	1,700	20,400
Total Operating Expenses	111,503	115,970	116,640	127,519	128,811	123,521	119,761	122,846	121,670	131,191	119,821	110,418	1,449,671
Operating Income/EBIT	14,549	33,074	32,826	64,678	70,018	58,417	41,559	48,856	49,967	70,887	39,254	9,362	533,447
Interest Expense	3,500	3,500	3,375	3,375	3,375	3,250	3,250	3,250	3,125	3,125	3,125	3,000	39,250
Taxes	4,199	11,238	11,191	23,295	25,324	20,963	14,557	17,330	17,800	25,750	13,729	2,418	187,794
Net Income	6,850	18,336	18,260	38,008	41,319	34,204	23,752	28,276	29,042	42,012	22,400	3,944	306,403
Net Income %	1.5%	3.8%	3.8%	6.7%	7.1%	6.4%	4.7%	5.4%	5.6%	7.0%	4.5%	0.9%	5.0%

Financial Projections, Sample Balance Sheet

	Beginning Balance	Jan	Feb	Mar	Apr	May	Jun	Jul	Aug	Sep	Oct	Nov	Dec
Assets													
Cash and Equivalents	110,463	78,953	50,687	23,341	107,603	94,526	102,213	159,482	198,558	226,660	234,482	249,411	360,153
Accounts Receivable	699,872	768,770	805,250	835,840	892,800	960,960	924,800	865,280	865,920	835,200	907,200	856,900	721,920
Inventory	535,773	536,040	536,330	536,620	536,960	537,310	537,630	537,930	538,250	538,560	538,920	539,220	539,470
Less: Reserves	-45,000	-45,000	-45,000	-45,000	-45,000	-45,000	-45,000	-45,000	-45,000	-45,000	-45,000	-45,000	-45,000
Prepaids/Other	72,200	71,700	71,200	70,700	70,200	69,700	75,700	75,200	74,700	74,200	73,700	73,200	72,700
Fixed Assets	318,900	318,900	338,900	358,900	358,900	358,900	358,900	398,900	398,900	398,900	438,900	438,900	438,900
Less Accum Depreciation	-62,200	-68,900	-75,600	-82,600	-90,100	-97,600	-105,100	-112,600	-120,900	-129,200	-137,500	-146,700	-155,900
Total Assets	1,630,008	1,660,463	1,681,767	1,697,801	1,831,363	1,878,796	1,849,143	1,879,192	1,910,428	1,899,320	2,010,702	1,965,931	1,932,243
Liabilities and Equity													
Trade Payables	201,405	233,800	253,030	255,050	328,780	334,870	309,960	300,600	313,130	307,430	353,550	296,050	250,500
Accrued Wages	24,690	24,500	22,000	22,000	18,500	18,200	18,100	19,200	17,300	17,900	15,400	17,000	22,500
Accrued Liabilities	102,000	93,400	104,638	100,392	125,716	151,040	112,193	126,750	144,080	109,030	134,780	148,509	150,927
Long-Term Debt	700,000	700,000	675,000	675,000	675,000	650,000	650,000	650,000	625,000	625,000	625,000	600,000	600,000
Invested Capital	220,000	220,000	220,000	220,000	220,000	220,000	220,000	220,000	220,000	220,000	220,000	220,000	220,000
Retained Earnings	381,913	388,763	407,099	425,359	463,367	504,686	538,890	562,642	590,918	619,960	661,972	684,372	638,316
Total Liabilities and Equity	1,630,008	1,660,463	1,681,767	1,697,801	1,831,363	1,878,796	1,849,143	1,879,192	1,910,428	1,899,320	2,010,702	1,965,931	1,932,243

Notes

1. From a lecture at Sloan School of Management, 19 October 1991.

2. Quoted in Erik Larson, "The Best-Laid Plans," *Inc.*, February 1987, p. 60.

3. Ibid., p. 61.

4. Ibid.

5. Ibid., p. 62.

6. BDO Seidman, "Pulse of the Middle Market 1990," a survey reprinted in *Small Business Reports*, July 1991, p. 55.

7. William D. Bygrave, "Small Business Has Key to Success," *Boston Business Journal*, 6-12 August 1993, p. 15.

8. Ibid., p. 53.

9. Ronaleen R. Roha, "10 Ways to Scuttle Your New Business," *Changing Times*, July 1990, p. 63.

10. Larson, p. 62.

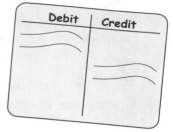

Chapter 12

Budgeting

The budget should be a door open to more satisfying and profitable work—not an instrument of torture. Then it will be known that what you can do without a budget you can do better with one.

—James L. Peirce[1]

WHILE THE LONG-RANGE, STRATEGIC PLAN IDENTIFIES THE goals of a company over several years, the budget process identifies the actions and milestones needed over a shorter time span—usually one year—to carry out the long-term strategy. Where the long-term plan lays out fairly general guidelines outlining the big picture, the budget provides a specific and detailed allocation of resources.

Budgets, particularly in smaller companies, have a tarnished reputation. These are some common complaints and perceptions:

▶ Budgets unnecessarily restrict managers' actions. Who wants an inspired idea zapped because "it is not in the budget"?

▶ Budgets quickly become obsolete and either hold managers to unrealistic targets or get ignored.

▶ Managers play "budget games." To make their numbers, they may shift expenses between accounting periods, play with accounting practices, or unwisely freeze or cut vital spending.

▶ Budgets are simply a number-crunching exercise.

▶ Budgets are unrealistic because top management dictates the targets rather than encourage input from managers.

These problems are real, but usually result from poor implementation. Done properly, budgets are vital for coordinating the company's activities, anticipating possible problems, gaining the commitment of managers, and providing control and motivation. As was argued for long-term planning, the consequences of not having a budget are often worse than the drudgery of pulling it together.

Planning and Control

Preparation of the budget gets you and your managers involved in identifying and choosing among operating strategies.

You can use budgets for both planning and control. Preparation of the budget gets you and your managers involved in identifying and choosing among operating strategies. The budget also lays down specific targets and milestones. This planning aspect sets the direction of your company and provides a basis for predicting financial performance.

Budgets are also powerful tools for coordinating, motivating, and evaluating the performance of managers. Many companies base some portion of compensation on performance vs. budget. Just the act of setting targets and providing regular feedback motivates many managers. The budget also can define spending limits and communicate expectations so that top management can harness the actions of line managers.

Many budget decisions involve some degree of trade-off between planning and control. Should sales goals be set aggressively to motivate performance or at lower levels that more realistically predict expected performance? Should budgets be revised during the year to improve their accuracy or should managers be held to their original targets?

How you prepare and use a budget will depend on your company's structure and your management style. In general, though, smaller companies are more likely to use budgets as planning instruments. Larger companies, with more complex operations and layers of management, tend to use budgets for control.

Regardless of how the budget is used, it is more than simply a forecast. A forecast is a prediction of future results. Budgeting asks for a commitment from management and provides a blueprint to make the results happen.

Size and Complexity

Developing a budget does not need to be a complex procedure. Smaller companies with few, if any, layers of management and one very focused line of business might be able to draw up a budget in one meeting between the president and the controller. But even a simple budget is valuable, if for no other reason than to ensure that cash out doesn't exceed cash in.

Take the example of a family household. The typical family determines how much income it expects and identifies goals, such as saving for college and retirement, taking a vacation, and improving the house. The family then translates these goals into dollars and then adds in necessary expenses, such as food, clothing, and paying off the mortgage. The numbers are then compiled, and massaged as necessary, to see if the household budget balances or leaves a little extra money for a rainy day or emergencies.

In most companies, past spending is the best clue to future expenditures.

For small companies, whose operation is expected to continue largely as is, the budget might be little more than an extrapolation of previous years' spending. In most companies, past spending is the best clue to future expenditures. Once the sales target is set, determining how expenses should change is a fairly straightforward exercise.

Before putting the budget to rest, take a critical look at whether the projected profit is really in line with long-term goals. If possible, compare key assumptions, such as gross margin or G&A spending, with those of other companies or even past performance. If savings are needed, challenge current spending and try to identify sufficient savings to bring the budget in line with the new targets.

Budget Cycle

Larger companies will have a more formal budget cycle that involves key managers. Starting with the completion of a long-range plan, the cycle would include preparation of an operating budget, some form of feedback and control, plus possible updates. These are some of the questions to answer:

▶ Who prepares the budget?

▶ Should the process be top-down, driven by upper management, or bottom-up, driven by department needs?

▶ What time period should the budget cover?

▶ How will the budget be linked to the long-range plan?

▶ When should the budget be prepared?

▶ Should the budget be fixed or updated regularly?

▶ What is the balance between planning and control?

▶ Will compensation or performance reviews be tied to the budget?

▶ How will intangibles be measured?

Top-Down or Bottom-Up?

A budget can be prepared "top-down" or "bottom-up."

A top-down budget is dictated by upper managers .... Bottom-up budget processes are initiated by department managers.

A top-down budget is dictated by upper managers, based on their vision of the company and knowledge of its goals and resources. Department managers may budget specific line items, but their overall budget is set from above.

Bottom-up budget processes are initiated by department managers, taking advantage of their detailed knowledge of the operation or marketplace. Starting with only broad guidelines from top management, the line managers identify and request projects and staffing they feel are needed. The department budgets are then added together to form the company budget.

The advantages of top-down budgets are that they enhance coordination of department budgets and can be implemented quickly. Also, if department managers lack the training or support staff to effectively participate in planning, a top-down budget may be needed. On the other hand, because line managers are closer to the market and day-to-day operations, bottom-up budgets may be better at recognizing opportunities for innovation. In addition, the higher degree of participation helps win the commitment of managers to the budget goals.

In practice, a combination of these approaches is usually used. Projections, prepared in conjunction with the long-range plan, are created at the top and incorporate the vision and objectives of the owner or top management. The basic assumptions of the plan, such as sales, inflation rate, and capital investment, are given to the department managers, who are asked to prepare their budgets consistent with these assumptions. These budgets are totaled and compared to the targeted spending of the long-range plan. Any inconsistencies are then resolved by revising the budget or the long-term plan or both.

A Nonaccounting Function

No matter which process is used, you and your managers should own the budget process. These are the purposes of budgeting:

► Evaluate operating options,

► Set targets, and

► Provide a basis for monitoring performance.

These activities are management functions, not accounting. You will almost surely want your controller or other accounting personnel to help prepare projections and compile relevant figures. They will likely carry out the mechanics of the budget process, organizing and coordinating the collection and roll-up of numbers. During the year, they should also track actual and budgeted performance, providing essential feedback.

But while these functions keep the budget process moving, ultimately they make up only a supporting role, not the leading role. The accounting department lacks the clout and leadership needed to implement the budget. Gaining the commitment of line managers, allocating resources, and controlling operations are management's job. If accounting owns the budget, management commitment may be limited.

Timing

For most companies, the budget cycle will start after the long-range plan is updated. A normal target for a smaller company to start the budget cycle is one to two months before the beginning of the period covered by the budget.

A typical budget covers a one-year period—more by convention and conformity with the fiscal year than by necessity—and is usually broken down further by month or quarter. A company with lengthy projects will probably want to budget each project separately over its expected life span. Another option, but uncommon, is a quarterly budget cycle in which only the upcoming quarter is budgeted by month and the remainder of the year is budgeted by quarter. Every three months, a new budget is prepared, looking out 12 months, even though the budget year does not correspond to the fiscal year.

Your first step in starting the budget cycle is to communicate to each manager the assumptions and targets contained in your long-term plan. Each manager must work from the same set of assumptions about factors such as sales,

A normal target for a smaller company to start the budget cycle is one to two months before the beginning of the period covered by the budget.

227

the economy, and target raises. If one manager budgets on the assumption that sales will be flat or ignores inflation while another predicts a sharp sales increase or assumes 5% inflation on all expenses, the combined budget will be seriously flawed.

As a starting point, the controller should provide the managers with historical financial information. As mentioned earlier, the best clue to what a particular expense will be is often the past run rate, especially for recurring expenses such as supplies, telephone, and postage. History is only a guide, though. Managers need to identify changes in trends. One error to avoid is having managers uncritically project the results of the old year onto the next or simply budget the same number year in, year out.

Your controller can also help to model certain expenses. As mentioned in the previous chapter, this should be done for salary expenses. A department head can supply headcount figures with projected raises; an accountant can extend that into dollars, including a proper allowance for benefit and payroll tax expenses. As salaries are often the largest departmental expense, a careful headcount projection contributes greatly to the accuracy of a budget.

Another calculation the controller can help with is figuring the impact of seasonal variations or a rapid growth in sales throughout the year. Few companies have flat expenses from month to month, so managers cannot simply take annual targets and divide by 12 to get monthly budgets. But the mechanics of figuring out how to spread the expenses is often a task better suited to an accountant than a line manager.

Through give and take, the budget is revised and projects agreed on until all parties agree and the budget is in line with the long-range plan.

Arriving at the final budget is an iterative process. The initial input from the line managers is totaled and compared with the targets set forth in the long-range plan. Top management reviews both the spending levels projected and the merits of any new projects proposed. Any disagreements with the proposed spending are then communicated to the line managers. Through give and take, the budget is revised and projects agreed on until all parties agree and the budget is in line with the long-range plan. The budget is continuously restated until all issues are resolved. Unless top-down control is essential, top management should not simply impose its will on subordinates. Instead, selling any proposed changes will help ensure commitment to the budget.

If the budget does not fit within the targets of the long-range plan, you may need to consider changing the projections. Often, doing a budget points out inconsistencies in the more general, long-term projections.

Most companies will find that two or three budget cycles will be needed for the process to be effective. Remember that the entire budget process is iterative, so don't be discouraged by early difficulties.

Controlling Spending

Once budgets are set, a few overriding guidelines on spending within the budget make sense for most smaller organizations:

- ▶ Managers should not feel they are automatically entitled to spend the dollars budgeted for their departments. That approach may work in very large companies, but smaller organizations can benefit from flexibility to move money from one area to another or to simply say "no" to any project that doesn't make sense or can no longer be afforded.
- ▶ Nonetheless, it should generally be easier to get approval for anything in the budget than something unplanned. This reinforces the need to take the planning process seriously.
- ▶ Neither encourage a "use it or lose it" mentality nor the other extreme of feeling entitlement to carry unspent funds over from one year to the next.
- ▶ Emphasize meeting total revenue and total spending targets and not individual line-item budgets. For example, having fewer employees may lower wage costs but require more spending on contractors. It's OK to spend more than budgeted on, say, travel, as long as the budget is met in total.
- ▶ Focus on the large items. Even a large variance in supplies is likely to be dwarfed by spending on headcount.

People and Budgets

So far, the discussion has focused on the planning role of budgets. The budget process is where ideas are generated, compared, and tested for financial soundness. Spending targets are set at the department and company level and form a guide for the upcoming period.

In planning, the budget is shaped by a company's managers. But once the budget is in place, the focus shifts to the control function. You ask your managers to achieve the targets that have been laid out and you monitor their progress. Often, their compensation or career advancement depends on how well they do compared with the budget.

Attainable Budgets

The budget can shape the behavior of managers, which, of course, is one of the reasons for doing a budget. If the targets are set and management is committed to them, the people responsible will look for ways to meet those targets. What gets measured gets done.

Note that you may have a gap between a target that is set to motivate a manager, particularly if it is a stretch, and the best prediction of what will actually happen. For example, a salesperson might be given a quota 25% above the prior year's figure and be compensated based on how well he or she meets this quota. But for planning purposes, you may want to use a more conservative growth figure.

> One manager for a company selling a high-priced product with long sales cycles set sales quotas 20% or so above what he counted on for his budget. He took that approach one step further when reviewing actual sales pipelines each quarter. He would ask each salesperson for both a list of deals they were working on and a sales number for the quarter they would "bet their life on." He then routinely halved the numbers they gave him, realizing from experience how salespeople's natural optimism and desire to look good would bias the forecast. Inevitably, that discounted projection would be close to the actual.

Though some conservatism is generally warranted, hedging can be taken too far.

> A *Fortune* 500 company that rolled up budgets from the unit level to groups to divisions and then finally to the corporate level discovered that controllers at each level were building hedges into their forecast. With hedges accumulated at numerous levels, things finally reached a point where the full company forecast was simply too conservative. A directive from the top was required to make the unit forecasts more realistic.

One prerequisite for motivating managers is ensuring that the person assigned a budget item believes the target is attainable.

One prerequisite for motivating managers is ensuring that the person assigned a budget item believes the target is attainable. Targets set too tight may discourage managers or, as discussed below, encourage accounting games. In addition, the more the budget is dictated from the top, the greater the risk of managers not buying into it.

Responsibility

Responsibility for budgeted expenses should be assigned to specific people whenever possible. Because they cut across all departments, you may be tempted to treat certain overhead expenses, such as workers' compensation insurance, facility maintenance, or utilities as uncontrollable or simply allocate them across departments. However, if each manager is allocated a small piece of the total cost, no one has much incentive to control these expenses, even though, in aggregate, they are often highly controllable. They probably won't be managed unless someone is held responsible.

Of course, you need to choose an appropriate person. Where possible, this should be an operating manager. Consider the following story:[2]

> A company thought the cleaning expense for its factory was exorbitant. The manufacturing employees claimed the expense could not be reduced, so responsibility was assigned to the controller. Sure enough, cleaning costs were quickly reduced—and the facility became a mess.

Incentives

While setting goals and monitoring progress are powerful motivation tools, tying a portion of compensation to achieving budget goals can provide a further incentive to managers. You can design a bonus system to reward meeting or exceeding department, division, or company goals.

While setting goals and monitoring progress are powerful motivation tools, tying a portion of compensation to achieving budget goals can provide a further incentive to managers.

Since the bonus is primarily a control tool, alignment with your goals for the company is important. Regular feedback to managers on their progress is also a key for motivating them.

One risk of compensating managers based on performance vs. budget is the possible introduction of budget games. To make their performance look better, some managers may do the following:

- ▶ Build padding into the budget.

- ▶ Attempt to shift expenses to other departments.

- ▶ Slash expenses, such as advertising, maintenance, or R&D, for short-term gain at the expense of long-term performance.

- ▶ Make deals with vendors or customers that accelerate sales or defer expenses.

To defuse these games, either you must set compensation to reward actions that work toward long-term, corporate goals or you must have enough understanding of possible games to be able to detect and counteract them.

Other Budget Structures

Budgets can be used to plan and control more than just expenses. Many managers control not only costs, but revenues, intangibles, or a combination, and their departments should be measured accordingly. In addition to the traditional cost center, which is measured strictly on the basis of expenses, some of the following structures are possible.

Standard cost centers. Standard cost centers are structures usually used for a production department where volume and, therefore, total cost cannot be controlled, but unit costs can be. Supervisors are evaluated based on performance vs. standard cost for direct costs and for staying within budget on overhead items.

Revenue centers. Revenue centers are structures typically used for a sales department. Managers are expected to spend no more than budget and maximize sales.

Discretionary expense centers. Discretionary expense centers are applicable to administrative departments where there may be no clear relation between the amount of money spent and the quality of work performed. Managers are asked to spend the budget and obtain the best-quality output.

Profit centers. Profit center structures are useful when departments or divisions control both revenues and expenses. Managers concentrate on achieving the best combination of activities for generating income.

Defining Profit

The definition of profit, if you are using a profit center structure, can range significantly, depending on the focus you encourage.

The definition of profit, if you are using a profit center structure, can range significantly, depending on the focus you encourage. Profit can be affected by the methods you choose to account for indirect costs. Here are some possibilities:

▶ Include only revenues and direct costs, to show what each department contributes toward overhead,

▶ Add in overhead costs a manager controls, at least in the long term, such as capital equipment and use of space and accounting resources, or

▶ Allocate a portion of company costs a manager has no control over, such as interest.

By including allocations, you risk passing on costs that are beyond a manager's control. If the allocations are based on inappropriate measures, they may distort both reporting and decision making. The benefit is that your managers can gain an appreciation for the total costs of the company.

Customize Your Budget

Because budgets rely on accounting information, they are often subject to the limitations of accounting discussed earlier. Perhaps the most important information to remember is that budgets measure only financial items. Budgets can track where the money was spent or motivate managers to control spending or headcount. But they say little about the quality of the spending.

With intangibles, such as quality or customer service, increasingly becoming a major part of strategic objectives, the budget process must include some measurement or feedback on nonfinancial measures.

Aligning the activities managers control with budget responsibility may require breaking up traditional account groupings. If a production unit contributes directly to expenditures for R&D or accounting, these costs can be included in the production department's budget, even though GAAP statements would place the expenses in different categories. In addition, where R&D or accounting costs can be directly attributed to several departments, you can break the costs up. Rather than assigning the entire R&D budget to one manager, give various pieces to the departments that actually control them.

Decisions on allocating expenses should be based on the planning and control objectives of top management, not accounting conventions. For example, GAAP requires that manufacturing costs be spread to inventory, but there is no need for budgets to allocate manufacturing overhead. If management chooses to assign a portion of corporate overhead to profit centers, that would also differ with GAAP presentation.

Because department managers can engage in some of the creative accounting described in Chapter 5, as well as other budget games, you may need to set up some alternative measures to monitor results. These might include targets such as bookings-to-shipments ratios, inventory levels, or customers served per employee.

Budgets can track where the money was spent or motivate managers to control spending or headcount. But they say little about the quality of the spending.

Flexible Budgets

Usually, the largest variable in budgeting is predicting sales levels. Not only do sales vary more than expenses, and less predictably, but also many expenses are related directly to sales mix and volume. Sales variances can cause large swings in departmental expenses that are beyond the control of the line managers.

In addition, as part of your planning process, your company will want to identify the potential impact of higher or lower sales. You can then prepare strategies to respond to different revenue volumes.

A common budget technique that adjusts for variations in sales is the *flexible budget*. One method of flexible budgeting is to construct several budgets for different sales levels. More commonly, the flexible budget figures are developed by expressing expenses as a function of sales or activity levels. With a straightforward calculation, you can arrive at the expense level for any level of activity.

The next illustration demonstrates the use of a flexible budget, assuming the following simple budget for a shipping department:

Budget Item	Original Budget	Actual	Flexible Budget
Units shipped	10,000	9,000	9,000
Boxes ($1/unit)	$10,000	$9,900	$9,000
Freight ($5/unit)	$50,000	$47,000	$45,000
Salaried labor	$30,000	$29,000	$30,000
Total	$90,000	$86,900	$84,000

At first glance, the department seems to have spent less than budgeted: $86,900 versus $90,000. However, both box and freight expenses vary directly with sales—and sales were 1,000 units less than planned. Using the flexible budget, you can see that at the lower volume, total spending should have been only $84,000. Thus, total spending actually exceeded the budget.

By having the flexible budget and comparing it with the actual figures, you become aware of any important variances that occur within your business.

Budgets as Working Documents

Managers get beaten on both sides by budgets. CEOs hit the managers over the head about performance, while accountants paddle them from behind about expenses.

Although large companies may use budgets to restrict the actions of managers, smaller companies should seek to use budgets to enhance managers' performance. Budgets aren't written in blood and should not deter managers from pursuing unexpected opportunities. Budget busting may need to be encouraged if new opportunities or challenges arise.

To ensure that budgets are effective motivation and feedback tools, timely reporting and adequate follow-up of results are needed. Soon after the end of each accounting period, the controller should provide each manager with reports showing actual results compared with the original plan with the variance calculated. It's also useful to have actual monthly results for the current year laid out side-by-side to easily spot changes in trends.

To ensure that budgets are effective motivation and feedback tools, timely reporting and adequate follow-up of results are needed.

As a first step in investigating a variance, have your controller identify all transactions posted to the account during the period. Your controller can then make a first attempt to explain the difference. The controller will usually be able to isolate causes of variances related to:

- ▶ Timing of transactions, including a bill being posted late or an annual bill arriving a month earlier than in prior years
- ▶ Errors such as transactions being posted to the wrong account
- ▶ One-time expenses
- ▶ Significant price changes by vendors
- ▶ Increases in the overall level of activity for a department or company

In these cases, no corrective action is generally needed. The controller may just want to summarize the findings in brief comments to the appropriate people.

You or your operating manager should investigate unexplained variances. While the controller may be able to identify which transactions to investigate, the line manager is in the best position to determine the underlying cause. The problem may well be poor assumptions in the original budget. But if an operating problem exists, the budget and interim results will have provided an early warning.

Your controller should also be prepared to explain the results to outsiders. Investors and bankers, in particular, will want to understand how a company is performing against its business plan. In turnarounds and start-ups, for example, early losses are often expected, so progress against the business plan is usually more important than the actual bottom line. By breaking down the financial results and explaining the source of any variances, your controller can greatly enhance relations with outsiders.

Rolling Budgets

For many companies, budgeting is only an annual exercise. Of course, as the end of the year approaches, the budget no longer looks out many months ahead. In addition, the original budget may be hopelessly outdated because of changes in operations or assumptions.

Rather than toss the budget aside, you can update it. One option is a rolling budget—similar to the way you use a rolling plan, as discussed in the previous chapter in the section on timing and budgets. In an annual rolling budget, as one quarter ends, another quarter is added to the end of the budget. This way, a company is always looking forward nine to 12 months. While a rolling budget can be prepared without revising the existing budget, the entire budget is usually redone.

Clearly, a business can also choose to simply change the original budget without extending it. But revisions raise another important planning-vs.-control trade-off. A revised budget will probably be more accurate, which is important for forecasting. It also provides some flexibility for managers who might have been constrained by the original budget. However, constant revisions may make it difficult to judge managers against earlier targets.

If benchmarks constantly shift, using the budget as a tool for control becomes difficult.

If benchmarks constantly shift, using the budget as a tool for control becomes difficult. Even though you risk some confusion, one solution may be to monitor performance against both the original and the current budget. This way, original goals are not forgotten but managers are not held to unrealistic targets or outdated objectives.

Capital Budgets

Annual budgets typically cover operating expenses for a company. However, planning also requires investment decisions: what equipment to buy, whether to open a new plant, or which division to close. Because accounting conventions capitalize these costs and expense only depreciation, conventional budget exercises may overlook these investment decisions unless a separate process is in place.

The process of making these decisions is called capital budgeting. Much as individuals compare the costs of buying a new car with the expense of maintaining their old vehicle plus the risk of major repairs, department managers must decide on the best long-term investment strategy.

A capital budget for basic equipment costs may be little more than a list of anticipated purchases for the coming year. Having such a list will allow you to update your cash needs, prioritize spending, and identify potential duplicate requests from different departments.

Evaluating major capital investment projects involves calculating the risk and estimated return of investments and choosing among competing strategies. The tools used for evaluation—including discounted cash flow, payback, and internal rate of return—are discussed in the next chapter.

Note that depreciation expense may be a poor proxy for capital spending needs. Capital equipment needs may not be smooth from one year to the next. A heavy investment in one year will drive up depreciation expense in future years, perhaps to levels exceeding new purchases. Alternatively, a growing company or a company with a lot of outdated equipment may have new equipment needs that far outpace depreciation expense.

Budget Dynamics

The strategic plan and budget work together to express the goals of a company clearly and objectively. The plan expresses the long-term vision while the budget identifies the specific steps and resources needed in the near term. Budgets and planning are more than just number-crunching exercises. They provide a framework for clearly expressing where your company is, where it wants to get to, and the basis for measuring its interim progress against those goals.

Depending on the structure and style of your company, the budget may be used for planning, for control, or for a combination of both. Either way, both you and your top managers must be committed to the goals set forth in the budget. Lack of top management commitment or the failure of line managers to buy into the budget will almost surely make the budget process ineffective.

Budgeting can be time-consuming and your managers may complain that they have no time to plan, but the time is well invested. The next chapter discusses another area of planning on which spending time is also well invested—project evaluation. Many times you will need to choose between or among projects. How do you tell which one is best? Chapter 13 deals with making investment decisions.

Budgets provide a framework for clearly expressing where your company is, where it wants to get to, and the basis for measuring its interim progress against those goals.

Notes

1. James L. Peirce, "The Budget Comes of Age," *Harvard Business Review*, May-June 1954, p. 66.

2. Jerry A. Viscione, "Small Company Budgets: Targets Are Key," *Harvard Business Review*, May-June 1984, p. 48.

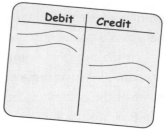

Chapter 13

Evaluating Projects

> One accurate measurement is worth a thousand expert opinions.
> —Grace Murray Hopper, Rear Admiral, U.S. Navy[1]

I N CAPITAL BUDGETING, AND THROUGHOUT EVERY YEAR, YOUR COMPANY will make a number of important investment decisions. These might include whether to open a new store, start a new business line, buy a piece of equipment, or go from outsourcing to doing work in-house. An investment decision may require a comparison of several alternatives, including the option of doing nothing at all. How do you sort out the alternatives?

The good news is that the techniques for evaluating projects are very straightforward and can be applied to a broad range of investment decisions. What is usually difficult is gathering good projected figures and dealing with the uncertainty inherent in them.

Whatever the project, "running the numbers" is important. Do not rely on gut feelings. Valuing projects provides a clear-cut basis for choosing among alternatives. Doing the analysis may turn up unexpected problems and help avoid costly mistakes.

In making this point, one manager described his company's "computer museum." "Any rudimentary analysis," he said, "would have shown that most of the computer equipment we bought was uneconomical." Instead, the equipment sat idle, a constant reminder of wasteful spending.

Like budgets, project evaluation also provides concrete financial targets and clearly communicates expectations. Unlike budgets, however, evaluation and tracking of projects extends over their entire lifetime, which may cover several accounting periods.

As with budgeting, the controller can assist you with the mechanics of valuing projects. However, developing reasonable cost and revenue assumptions requires the active involvement of the managers closest to the project. Each investment decision you make merits an individual appraisal. Although project evaluation may seem like a time-consuming task, this chapter can help you with techniques for evaluating projects and investments, and includes tips and pitfalls. At the end of the chapter is a worksheet that you can use to evaluate projects.

Net Present Value

The first step in valuing a project is to estimate all the associated costs and revenues—or cost savings.

The first step in valuing a project is to estimate all the associated costs and revenues—or cost savings. These should be calculated for the entire life of the project, though there may be a practical limit to how far out these can be projected.

Only actual cash outlays, savings, and revenues should be included. If a new machine is housed in an existing building, no cash outlay is needed for the space. Even if your accountants allocate a portion of facilities expense to the project, that expense should not be included in your valuation of the project. Similarly, if you depreciate your investment over several years, show the cash outlay in the period in which it occurs, not when you record the expense for book purposes.

Clearly, you are interested in projects that return more cash than you pay out. However, for a project to simply bring in more revenue than it costs or to reduce expenses may not be enough. You may not find it worthwhile to spend a dollar to save two dollars if the return comes only in the far distant future.

Some recognition has to be given to the fact that a dollar today is worth more than a dollar in the future.

The technique for recognizing this time value of money is called *present value* (PV). If you can invest money in a sure thing, like treasury bills at 5%, you will be indifferent about having a dollar today or $1.05 a year from now—$1.00 plus 5% interest. Restated, the $1.05 you will receive one year from now has a PV of $1.00. The equation below expresses this algebraically.

Equation: Present Value—Basic

$$PV = \$1.05 / (1+5\%)$$

Translated into words, the mathematical equation states that the present value of a payment received one year from today is equal to the future value divided by one plus the interest rate.

If you will not receive the $1.05 payment until two years from now, the formula below is applied.

Equation: Present Value—Two Years

$$PV = \$1.05 / (1+5\%)^2$$

In the equation above, the present value equals $0.95, so having $1.00 today would be preferable to $1.05 two years from now.

Formulas for additional years are computed in the same way by changing the exponent to reflect the number of years. Since alternative investments are assumed to earn a continuous and compounding return, the more into the future the payouts are, the less they are worth today. For example, if interest rates are 10%, $2.00 received seven years from now would only have a present value of about $1.00.

Most projects involve a stream of cash flow. If you invest in a piece of equipment or open a new store, you will have an initial outlay of cash, fol-

---

Rule of 72

The Rule of 72 is a quick way to figure out approximately how long it takes money to double in value without having to use a calculator. Simply divide 72 by the interest rate. For example, if an investment returns 6% per year, you divide 72 by 6. The result, 12, is the number of years it would take to double your money. At 10%, it would take 7 years.

Note that in the example above this same rule was stated slightly differently as a present value. At a 10% discount rate, $2.00 received seven years from now has a PV of $1.00, or half as much.

lowed by several years of increased cash flow. Here is an example of how to use the net present value method for determining the worth of a project.

Net Present Value Method			
Time Period	Cash Flow ($)	Discount Factor @ 10%	Present Value ($)
Day 1	−1,000	1	−1,000
Year 1	+300	$(1 + 10\%)$	+273
Year 2	+300	$(1 + 10\%)^2$	+248
Year 3	+250	$(1 + 10\%)^3$	+188
Year 4	+250	$(1 + 10\%)^4$	+171
Year 5	+200	$(1 + 10\%)^5$	+124
Sale of Equipt	+100	$(1 + 10\%)^5$	+62
Total Cash Flow	+400		+66

Although this project returns $400 more than it costs, due to the time value of money the *net present value* (NPV) is only slightly positive. But the fact that it is positive means the project is better than the alternative of investing at 10%.

The golden rule is that a negative NPV indicates that other investments are more attractive and a project should not be undertaken. A positive NPV means a project is attractive.

Sometimes, two or more projects are mutually exclusive. You may not have enough money to invest in all the projects or several projects may be directed toward solving the same problem, so that adopting one project eliminates the need for others. In these cases, you want to choose the combination of projects that provides the highest total NPV. To determine the net present value for one of your projects, use the Net Present Value Project Evaluation worksheet at the end of this chapter. Follow the instructions to determine what numbers you will need.

Technical Issues

Though the math described above is fairly straightforward, coming up with the cash flows and deciding on an appropriate discount rate are rarely simple.

As in any forecast, determining future revenues and expenses for a project can also require time-consuming analysis and there will likely be considerable uncertainty about the results.

As was briefly mentioned earlier, only incremental cash flows directly associated with the project should be included in the NPV calculation. This implies three things:

- Sunk costs should be ignored. If you are considering making a new investment in a struggling store or product line, you must ignore any previous investments. You are interested only in whether you make money on this additional investment. Frequently, human nature makes you want to recoup earlier money or cautions you about throwing good money after bad, but only the incremental investment and return are relevant.

- What matters is when cash is spent or received, not when the money shows up on the income statement. If you buy equipment with installment payments, the cash flow is different than when you pay up front. Also, noncash entries, such as depreciation or accruals, are not included.

- Only spending and revenue directly associated with the project are included. If you invest in an advertising campaign, only the incremental sales generated are included, not total sales. By the same token, include any incidental effects of the project. If the advertising spurs sales of other products, allow for this in your investment decision.

You need to have consistent assumptions about inflation in determining cash flows and the discount rate. When you project revenues and expenses, you can either assume that prices are stable or apply a factor for inflation. For example, if your expenses include payroll, you can either use salaries in effect today throughout the life of the project or assume you will make cost of living adjustments.

Either approach is acceptable as long as your choices for all cash flows and for discount rates reflect the same assumption. If the quoted or *nominal* interest rate on a mortgage or bond is 7%, roughly 3%-4% of that may be attributed to inflation. The remaining portion is the *real* return, what you will earn after adjusting for the effects of inflation. When you build inflation into your projections of cash flows, you should discount the cash flows at nominal interest rates. If current price levels are used, then use a real discount rate. For example:[2]

> The types of errors that can occur when real and nominal figures are mixed occurred in Ireland in 1974. The government created a furor when it purchased a stake in Bula Mines for 40 million pounds when some consultants valued it as low as eight million pounds and others as high as 104 million. A large part of the difference in valuations was attributed to confusion between real and nominal rates.

Finally, be sure to factor taxes into the cash flows. Taxes are a very real cost, plus the tax treatment of investment options may vary greatly. Some investments qualify for tax credits, others for capital gains treatment or accelerated write-offs.

Risk and the Discount Rate

Another issue is how to incorporate risk into the calculation. The higher the risk, the higher the required return needs to be.

Another issue is how to incorporate risk into the calculation. The higher the risk, the higher the required return needs to be. A high-quality bond is a safer bet and carries a lower expected return than starting a new product line. If two investment choices offer the same cash flows, you would clearly choose the less risky option. How do you incorporate this into the NPV?

The answer is to adjust the discount rate according to the risk of the venture. Basically, the discount rate of a project should be what you could expect to earn investing in a competing project with the same risk.

The discount rate for the bond might be compared with returns available on other government-issued or -insured investments; the new product line's discount rate could be set equal to the stock market returns of companies in the same industry. Venture capitalists often talk about needing to earn 30%-40% compounded returns on their investments. To compute present value through their eyes, you would need a discount rate in that range.

In the end, though, the choice of an appropriate discount rate is rarely this easy. One cannot usually assume that a project has the same risk profile as bonds, public stocks, or even other projects. It may be necessary, as with the example of venture capitalists above, to rely on rules of thumb or try a range of rates.

Choice of a discount rate can have an enormous impact on the result. Note that the higher the risk, the higher the discount rate and, therefore, the lower the NPV. In the example earlier in this chapter, there was a five-year projection for the purchase of a piece of equipment. Using a 10% discount rate, the NPV came out to $66. Had a 20% discount rate been used, the NPV would have been −$84 and at 30% −$202. The higher discount rates would have led to a different conclusion about the value of the equipment.

What if there is great uncertainty over just what the future cash flows will be? If you are launching a new venture, you face the possibilities the project will be a bust, a moderate success, or a home run. Rather than compromise on one possible outcome, prepare discounted cash flows for several scenarios and then assign probabilities to each case. The weighted average then becomes your expected outcome, as illustrated below.

Determining Weighted Average			
Case	NPV ($)	Probability %	Weighted Average ($)
Bust	−1,000	15%	−150
Breakeven	0	20%	0
Most Likely	+200	60%	+120
Home Run	+2,000	5%	+100
Total Weighted Average			+70

Alternative Methods

Two popular methods of evaluating projects that use similar inputs as NPV are the *payback* method and the *internal rate of return* (IRR) method. Both, though, have technical flaws that make them inferior to NPV.

The payback method measures how long it takes for a company to recoup its investment. In the earlier equipment purchase example, this occurs approximately halfway through the fourth year—or a payback of three and one-half years. Companies may insist that projects meet a maximum payback period, such as two to three years.

This method fails to take into account the time value of money. To adjust for this, some companies use a *discounted payback*, where the cash flows are discounted using the present value method. Under this measure, the project would have a payback of five years.

The payback method has several weaknesses. It fails to take into account cash flows beyond the point where payback is achieved. If the project above returned an additional $1,000 in years six through 10, the payback method would not pick it up. The payback method also fails to reflect the magnitude of the returns, reflecting only the timing, not the size of the cash flow.

The IRR is closer to the NPV in theory. In the example, the discount rate was assumed to be 10%. Because the NPV is positive, you know that the rate of return on the project is better than 10%, but not how much better. That is what the IRR calculates. Put another way, the IRR is the interest—or discount—rate that makes the NPV exactly equal to zero. In the example above, the IRR works out to about 12.6%.

Firms may set a target IRR, sometimes called a *hurdle rate*. Projects with a rate of return that exceeds the target rate are accepted. This is the same as saying the project has a positive NPV.

The weakness in using IRR instead of NPV is that, like payback, IRR does not reflect the magnitude of a project. This can be a problem when you have to choose between two mutually exclusive projects, like the following:

IRR vs. NPV Comparison		
Evaluation Technique	Project A	Project B
Internal Rate of Return (IRR)	25%	20%
Net Present Value (NPV)	$100	$5,000

Even though Project A has a higher IRR, the company is worse off than if it chooses Project B, because the net return is $4,900 less.

Valuing a Business

NPV can be used to value a business as well as a project. Instead of projecting cash flows for an isolated investment, use the cash flows for the entire business. The total discounted value of the cash flows equals the current value of the business.

When valuing businesses using NPV, a few special problems exist. As with any forecast, it can be hard to develop reliable estimates of future cash flows, and buyer and seller may have very different ideas about what those will be.

In addition, unlike projects that may have finite lives, businesses generally are expected to endure far into the future. It's unrealistic, though, to expect projections to be reliable beyond several years. To account for a business's worth after, say, five years, the projections will use a "terminal value." If the business is expected to reach a position where the level and growth of future earnings are relatively stable, this terminal value may be a multiple of earnings or sales based on what similar businesses sell for. This terminal value is discounted in the same way as the sale of equipment in the earlier NPV example. The main difference is that, in the earlier example, the equipment was assumed to have limited value after being in use for five years and the sale value had only a small impact on the project's value. However, the terminal value when valuing a business may be more significant than the cash flows for the first three to five years and become the largest variable in the NPV calculation.

The discount rate also becomes a major factor. The risks of smaller, privately held companies are generally greater than larger companies. Returns are more volatile, rates of failure are higher, the investments are less liquid, and diversification is harder when a large portion of a business owner's wealth is tied up in his or her company. This requires use of a higher discount rate, which drives business valuations down.

Though NPV is theoretically sound and a preferred way to value companies, because of the variability introduced by the factors above, other valuation techniques are often used in practice. These include multiples of earnings, sales, or book value. Finding sale values for comparable companies can help establish what these multipliers should be. Though this type of data may be hard to find for some companies, for common types of businesses there often are published rules of thumb. Businesses should also appraise the fair market value of their assets. Businesses generating limited earnings may have low or negative NPVs. In these cases, valuation may be based on the net value of a company's assets less any liabilities.

Your choice of a valuation technique may depend on your background. A survey showed that accountants and financial consultants prefer present value for valuing a business. Techniques that use a multiple of expected earnings or cash flow ranked second. Business owners and brokers, on the other hand, overwhelmingly relied on appraisals of tangible assets, such as customer lists, fixed assets, and inventory.

These findings may indicate that business owners are most comfortable with more tangible, less abstract measures of value. In addition, the survey concluded that "Business owners may envision a worth for their business that turns out to be quite different" from what is established by a consultant.[3] To avoid a surprise, or inadvertently establishing too low a value, you should apply several valuations, including the present value technique, in valuing your company.

Opportunity Cost

Even if no cash actually changes hands, the cost of a resource may be relevant. Consider in your calculations some of the types of opportunity costs that may apply to a project. For example:

> One manufacturer was evaluating the option of opening outlet stores. The business had a lot of excess merchandise that had been returned, was out of season, or was slightly imperfect. Selling through outlet stores could generate enough cash to cover the operating costs of the store. Since the merchandise was already paid for, the stores would generate cash and the company went ahead with the project. What had not been considered was that the merchandise could have been sold to wholesale discount stores or liquidators with little out-of-pocket expense. So, even though no cash was needed to move the merchandise from storage to the outlet stores, the opportunity to sell to discounters was lost.

This type of lost revenue is called an *opportunity cost*. This cost is very real and you must always consider it whenever you choose one option that excludes another. Put another way, instead of asking whether cash flow would be better after opening the stores, the right question for the manufacturer in the above example would have been "Do the stores generate more cash than selling the excess merchandise to discounters?"

For smaller companies that can focus on only a few projects at a time, the opportunity cost of a time- or resource-consuming project can be enormous.

For smaller companies that can focus on only a few projects at a time, the opportunity cost of a time- or resource-consuming project can be enormous.

> The founder of a specialty book publisher told the story of the consulting work the business accepted from a *Fortune* 500 company. Though the money seemed good, the work required different skills than the core business and new people had to be hired. Cash was also tied up as the new employees were paid promptly, but the *Fortune* 500 company stretched its payments out. When the dust settled about a year later, the project had broken even, but the publisher had missed a year's opportunity by focusing on consulting rather than books.

Cash is clearly a scarce resource in many companies and can also carry a high opportunity cost.

> A software developer with a modest 10% market share in a primary market spent $100,000 to develop an unrelated product, a touch-screen system for executive information retrieval. Not only was the money lost, but

so was the return that could have been earned building market share for the core product.

Another type of opportunity cost not normally picked up by accounting systems is lost time in getting products to market. For high-tech companies where product life cycles are relatively short, lost time can be critical, and missing a window of opportunity can be very costly. The NPV calculation can reflect this cost, provided market opportunities lost due to slow product development can be measured.[4]

Buying and Selling Products

Evaluating projects applies to all types of purchases and sales. If you sell a product or a service that represents a major outlay for a customer, you can expect that the customer will run some type of evaluation. You can improve your chances of closing the sale by understanding your customer's costs, benefits, and alternative solutions. Ensuring a quick payback or fully demonstrating the value proposition you offer will help close business.

Use a discount or hurdle rate that ensures an adequate return and properly rewards you for risk.

Similarly, before entering into a contract, ensure that you earn an adequate return. Use a discount or hurdle rate that ensures an adequate return and properly rewards you for risk. Be prepared to turn down deals where the numbers don't work.

> A company that contracted with major developers to place laundry machines in apartment buildings carefully analyzed each deal over what was generally a 10-year contract life. Resisting the lure to take on less profitable business in order to grow revenues, the managers made it a policy to walk away from deals that didn't offer at least a 20% IRR. They discovered through experience that revenue growth did not add as much efficiency as they first thought. On rare occasions, they accepted business that offered intangible benefits such as a key reference account. By sticking to a disciplined approach and making sure each building block was profitable, they were able to steadily grow the business.
>
> By contrast, a school busing contractor, in order to win business, consistently submitted bids that left each individual deal unprofitable. The owner pursued growth in hopes that size would eventually translate into success. Forced to chase profitability, the business eventually folded.

Breakeven Analysis

A simple, but effective tool for evaluating risk in your projects is the breakeven analysis. This analysis usually assumes a very simple relationship between sales and expenses and shows the profit a company or project will earn across a range of sales volumes.

In the classic breakeven analysis, expenses are classified as either fixed or variable. As sales increase, it is assumed that fixed expenses don't change, but both revenue and variable expenses increase in proportion to volume. At low volumes, fixed costs exceed the total contribution margin (revenue less variable costs) earned on sales and the business is unprofitable. At some level of volume, however, the contribution margin will exactly offset fixed expense. This volume is called the *breakeven point*. At volumes above this, the business is profitable. The breakeven analysis is commonly shown in graph form, like the one shown below, with dollars plotted along the Y-axis and volume on the X-axis.

The figure on the next page shows the breakeven point for a project in which each unit brings in $10 (revenue) and has expenses as indicated.

First, the expenses are classified as either fixed or variable. The fixed expenses, expressed as a dollar amount per month, are those that do not change as volume changes—such as administrative salaries, rent, and equipment leases. The fixed costs in this project add up to $1,000 and are represented by the horizontal line drawn at $1,000 on the Y-axis. The fixed cost line remains the same for any level of volume that is shown on the X-axis, since fixed costs will not change.

The variable expenses, expressed as costs in dollars per unit, change in proportion to volume. Expenses, such as direct labor, raw materials, commissions, and shipping, are typical variable expenses. Total variable costs in this project add up to $6 per unit. Since each unit sells for $10, the contribution margin per unit (revenue less variable cost) is $4.

The breakeven point is reached when the total contribution margin is equal to the fixed costs ($1,000).

To draw the diagonal cumulative contribution margin line, select any level of sales volume, for example, 100 units, and multiply it by the contribution margin per unit ($4) to get the total contribution margin ($400). This point is plotted on the graph by locating 100 units on the X-axis and $400 on the Y-axis. Draw a diagonal line, starting at the origin—when volume equals zero

Breakeven analysis usually assumes a very simple relationship between sales and expenses and shows the profit a company or project will earn across a range of sales volumes.

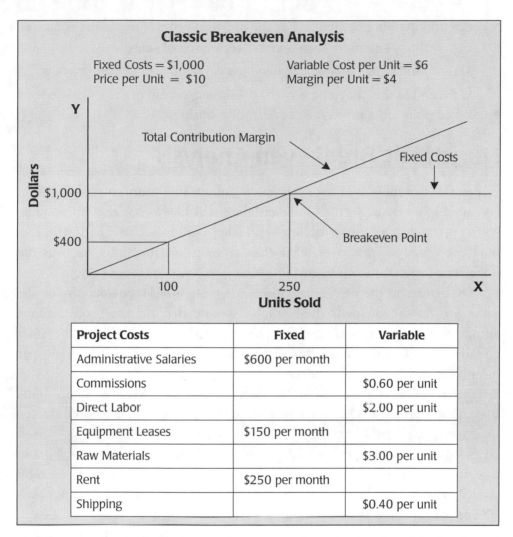

Classic Breakeven Analysis

Fixed Costs = $1,000   Variable Cost per Unit = $6
Price per Unit = $10   Margin per Unit = $4

Total Contribution Margin

Fixed Costs

$1,000

$400

Breakeven Point

Dollars

100   250

Units Sold

Project Costs	Fixed	Variable
Administrative Salaries	$600 per month	
Commissions		$0.60 per unit
Direct Labor		$2.00 per unit
Equipment Leases	$150 per month	
Raw Materials		$3.00 per unit
Rent	$250 per month	
Shipping		$0.40 per unit

and the contribution margin equals zero—and continuing through the plotted point and beyond. This line shows the total contribution margin for all levels of volume. Where this line crosses the fixed costs line is the breakeven point, since fixed costs and the contribution margin are equal at that intersection.

To compute the breakeven point directly, divide your total fixed costs by the contribution margin per unit. In the example above this is the equation:

Equation: Breakeven—Cost per Unit

$1,000 fixed costs / $4 contribution margin per unit = 250 units

If the contribution margin is expressed as a percentage of sales, breakeven volume in dollars can be calculated by dividing your total fixed costs by the contribution margin percentage. For the previous project, this is the equation:

Equation: Breakeven—Percentage of Sales

$1,000 fixed costs / 40% contribution margin per unit = $2,500 revenue

At the end of this chapter are two worksheets you can use to calculate your breakeven point on a project, a product, or a business.

Nonclassic Breakeven Analysis

In practice, revenues and expenses rarely follow this simplistic relationship. So-called fixed costs, such as indirect labor, will likely change with volume, while per-unit costs may decline at higher volumes. You can devise a breakeven analysis that uses other than straight-line functions, such as the nonclassic analysis shown below, in which fixed costs increase in steps.

The figure on the next page depicts a simple nonclassic analysis for the same project shown in the first graph. Assume that for the project above administrative salaries were not truly fixed, but that, in addition to the $600 already being spent, one additional person is needed at a cost of $166 per month for each 100 units produced.

The difficulty in evaluating projects generally is not in finding the proper analysis tool, but in developing reasonable estimates of revenues and expenses and trying to quantify factors such as opportunity costs.

Instead of fixed costs staying flat, they would start at $1,000 when volume was zero, increase to $1,166 when volume reached 100, and continue to increase in a stepwise manner. On the nonclassic breakeven graph, "fixed costs" are no longer represented by a horizontal line, but a line that shifts in discrete steps. The breakeven point is still where this line is met by the total contribution margin line, but at a different volume than before. In the nonclassic analysis, the new breakeven point is at 375 units.

Conclusion

Investment analysis techniques are quite simple and straightforward. The difficulty in evaluating projects generally is not in finding the proper analysis tool, but in developing reasonable estimates of revenues and expenses and trying to quantify factors such as opportunity costs. This problem can be more acute in smaller companies, which do not have the same access to in-house expertise or historical data as larger firms.

To deal with this risk, use more than one tool or evaluate several scenarios of the same project. Even though NPV is theoretically sound, you can gain

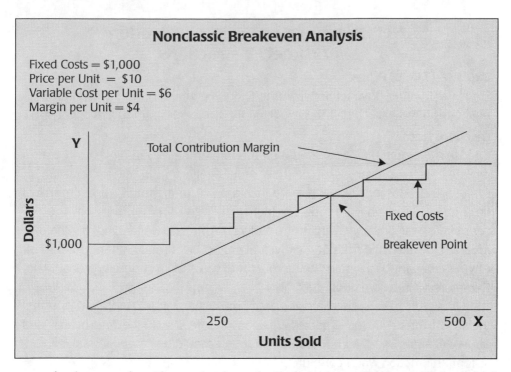

Nonclassic Breakeven Analysis

Fixed Costs = $1,000
Price per Unit = $10
Variable Cost per Unit = $6
Margin per Unit = $4

Y

Total Contribution Margin

Dollars

$1,000

Fixed Costs

Breakeven Point

250

500 X

Units Sold

some further comfort if a payback analysis shows a swift return of the initial investment or a pessimistic case indicates the downside is limited. As a starting point, use the worksheets at the end of this chapter to calculate NPV on your projects and determine your breakeven point.

As with long-term projections and budgets, there likely will be a large degree of uncertainty in the calculations. Forecasting is always more art than science. But just the act of running the numbers will improve the decision-making process both by introducing some structure and by asking managers to take a hard look at the assumptions behind their investment proposals. A little homework up front can prevent you from accumulating your own computer museum.

Net Present Value Project Evaluation
Worksheet—Instructions

Expected Life of Project

Enter the number of years between the first expenditure on the project and the final cash flows expected. If the expected life is greater than 10 years, enter 10.

Discount Rate

Choose a discount rate. This should be the rate of return you expect to earn on investments of similar risk. The rate should reflect both the time value of money—a dollar today is worth more than a dollar in the future—and the risk of the project. The higher the risk, the higher the rate of return must be. The discount rate will probably vary from project to project, depending on the risk involved. Because the risk of an individual project will usually differ from the risk of your company as a whole, the discount rate you should choose is probably not the interest rate you pay on debt.

Once you have chosen a rate, check off whether it is a nominal rate that includes a premium for expected inflation or a real rate—the return over and above inflation. You can choose either, but you should be careful to make a consistent assumption when computing your expected cash flows.

Incremental Cash Flows

What will the net cash inflows and outflows be over the life of the project? Start by computing your upfront costs and enter those on the first line as a minus. Then, for each year in the life of the project, enter the incremental cash flows expected, plus or minus. In your calculation:

▶ Ignore sunk costs—which are costs for past investments. Include only new spending.
▶ Include only the cash that will be received and paid out directly on this project. Ignore any allocated costs.
▶ Be consistent about using real or nominal cash flows.
▶ Include the impact of taxes.

At the end of the project, there may be a residual value. Perhaps you are starting an operation that can be sold to an outside investor or purchasing equipment that can be sold for a salvage value. Or perhaps the project will continue to operate beyond 10 years and you want to place a value on the continuing cash flows. Whatever you estimate that value to be, if any, enter it on the last line in the Incremental Cash Flows column for the residual value.

Discount Factor

Enter the discount rate you chose above on each line in the Discount Factor column—for example, 1 + 10%. For residual value, enter the number of years in the expected life of the project from above in the exponent field.

Compute each period's discount factor.

Present Value

Divide the cash flows by each discount factor and enter the result in the Present Value column.

Total

Add the numbers in the Present Value column to get the net present value. If this number is greater than zero, the project is worthwhile. Less than zero, the project should not be undertaken. Other statistics you might wish to compute:

► Internal Rate of Return. The discount rate at which the net present value exactly equals zero.

► Payback. To calculate, add the figures in the Incremental Cash Flows column until the cumulative total reaches zero. The number of years where this occurs is your payback period.

► Discounted Payback. To calculate, add the figures in the Present Value column until the cumulative total reaches zero. The number of years where this occurs is your payback period.

Net Present Value Project Evaluation Worksheet

Project:

Expected life of project: _____ years:

Discount rate: _____ %

Check one: ❏ Nominal   ❏ Real

Brief description of project:

Time Period	Incremental Cash Flows	Discount Factor		Present Value
Initial start-up	$_____	÷ 1	=	$_____
Year one	$_____	÷ 1 + _____%	=	$_____
Year two	$_____	÷ $1 + \_\_\_\%^2$	=	$_____
Year three	$_____	÷ $1 + \_\_\_\%^3$	=	$_____
Year four	$_____	÷ $1 + \_\_\_\%^4$	=	$_____
Year five	$_____	÷ $1 + \_\_\_\%^5$	=	$_____

Time Period	Incremental Cash Flows	Discount Factor	Present Value
Year six	$_____	$\div\ 1 + \_\_\_\%^6\ =$	$_____
Year seven	$_____	$\div\ 1 + \_\_\_\%^7\ =$	$_____
Year eight	$_____	$\div\ 1 + \_\_\_\%^8\ =$	$_____
Year nine	$_____	$\div\ 1 + \_\_\_\%^9\ =$	$_____
Year ten	$_____	$\div\ 1 + \_\_\_\%^{10}\ =$	$_____
Residual value	$_____	$\div\ 1 + \_\_\_\%^-\ =$	$_____

Total Cash Flow: $_____   **Net Present Value:** $_____

Payback: _____ years

Discounted Payback: _____ years

Breakeven Analysis Worksheet—Cost-per-Unit Basis

Depending on the types of numbers you have for your business or project, use either this worksheet or the one on the next page to calculate your breakeven point. If the numbers and projects you work with are based on per-unit costs, use this worksheet. If your figures are expressed as a percentage of sales, use the worksheet on the next page.

❏ Classify all expenses for your business or project as either fixed or variable. Fixed expenses are items you expect to basically stay constant as sales volume changes. Typically, these include expenses such as rent, administrative salaries, and insurance. Classify as variable any expenses that change in proportion to volume, such as raw materials, direct labor, and commissions. Recognize that these divisions are highly simplified, since in practice expenses are rarely totally fixed or variable.

❏ Enter your expenses in the correct columns below. Fixed expenses are entered as the total expense for the month or any other period of time you are using. Variable expenses are listed as cost per unit.

Fixed Expense	Amount	Variable Expense	Cost per Unit
_____	$_____	_____	$_____
_____	$_____	_____	$_____
_____	$_____	_____	$_____

Fixed Expense	Amount	Variable Expense	Cost per Unit
_____	$_____	_____	$_____
_____	$_____	_____	$_____
_____	$_____	_____	$_____
_____	$_____	_____	$_____
_____	$_____	_____	$_____
_____	$_____	_____	$_____

Total Fixed Expenses: $_____   Total Variable Expenses: $_____

Total both columns.

Enter your sales price per unit here: $_____

Then, subtract your total variable expenses per unit (calculated in the column above) from the total price per unit to determine the contribution margin. Enter the contribution margin here: $_____

Divide your total fixed expenses by the contribution margin to determine the number of units needed to break even.

Unit sales needed to break even: _____ units

Breakeven Analysis Worksheet— Percentage-of-Sales Basis

You can use either the worksheet on this page or the worksheet on the previous page to figure out your breakeven point for your business or a particular project. This worksheet is for businesses or projects that generally encompass a variety of activities, where costs are expressed as a percentage of sales.

❏ Classify all the expenses for your business or project as either fixed or variable. Fixed expenses, such as rent, administrative salaries, and insurance, are expenses that do not vary as sales volume changes. Variable expenses, such as raw materials, direct labor, and commissions, vary in proportion to volume.

❏ List your expenses in the appropriate columns below. For fixed expenses, enter the anticipated total expense for the period of time you are using. For variable expenses, enter a percentage of sales volume.

Fixed Expense	Amount	Variable Expense	% of Sales
_____	$_____	_____	_____%
_____	$_____	_____	_____%
_____	$_____	_____	_____%
_____	$_____	_____	_____%
_____	$_____	_____	_____%
_____	$_____	_____	_____%
_____	$_____	_____	_____%
_____	$_____	_____	_____%
_____	$_____	_____	_____%

Total Fixed Expenses: $_____   Total Variable Percent: _____%

Total both columns.

To calculate your breakeven volume, use the following equation:

breakeven volume = (total fixed expenses) ÷ (1 − total variable expenses)

Breakeven volume: $_____

Enter your price per unit: $_____

To figure your breakeven volume in units, divide your breakeven volume (calculated in the step above) by your average price per unit to determine the unit sales needed to break even.

Unit sales needed to break even: _____ units

Notes

1. Quoted in *The Manager's Book of Quotations*, p. 390.

2. Richard Brealey and Stewart Myers, *Principles of Corporate Finance* (New York: McGraw-Hill, 1981), p. 88.

3. "Is Value in the Eyes of the Beholder?" *Small Business Reports*, July 1992, p. 7.

4. Preston G. Smith and Donald G. Reinertsen, "Developing Products in Half the Time," *Small Business Reports*, January 1992, p. 65.

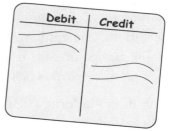

Chapter 14

Computers, Software and the Internet

If accountants don't understand that all double-entry bookkeeping today is computer driven, they don't understand the accounting environment.
—Anthony M. Santomero[1]

COMPUTERS AND ACCOUNTING ARE INEXTRICABLY LINKED. Accounting is repetitive and transaction-based, making it an ideal computer application. Starting in the 1960s, most companies bought their first computers to handle accounting functions. In the 1980s, it was Lotus 1-2-3—a financial spreadsheet software program—that created the boom for IBM personal computers.

Despite the proliferation of computers, smaller businesses were slow in truly embracing them. Well into the 1990s, many companies had minimal setups, ran on outdated equipment, or used manual systems. However, a number of factors have made accounting software and related computer applications more prevalent and essential than ever.

Omnipresence of Computers. Computers and software are now integrated into every facet of business, including Web sites, e-mail, word processing, presentations, and customer relationship management. Computerizing accounting no longer requires the technological leap it once did. In addition, a whole generation of employees has grown up with computers, so less resistance exists.

Common Platform. High-caliber accounting software runs on the same networks and PCs as other applications, so little need exists to invest in expensive and quickly obsolete mini-computer systems.

Ease of Use. The latest generation of accounting software is easier to use, more flexible, and more feature-rich than its predecessors.

Over time, the question has gone from whether a business should computerize to which technologies it should embrace. How do you select and implement accounting software? How far can you push low-end software before needing an upgrade? Will the Internet change the way we transact business? How does one integrate spreadsheets, third-party add-ons, and specialized software packages within a company? This chapter will examine these and other basic technology questions impacting accounting and finance. It will help you make the right software decisions and avoid mistakes that are costly in the long run.

PC Accounting Software

An excellent selection of PC accounting software is available to you. Although the divisions are somewhat blurred, the classes basically break down as follows.

Checkbook: At the lowest end are programs such as Quicken™ and Microsoft Money™ that provide basic checkbook functions, such as writing checks, recording deposits, and reconciling bank statements. In general, these programs cannot do basic business functions such as invoicing and accounts payable. As a result, though useful for managing personal finances, they are not appropriate for most businesses.

Low-End: This group includes a number of well-supported, integrated accounting packages that sell for under $1,000, including QuickBooks™, Peachtree™, and M.Y.O.B.™ . These packages usually include:

▶ General ledger
▶ Accounts payable

- ▶ Accounts receivable
- ▶ Billing
- ▶ Inventory
- ▶ Purchasing

Some have modules that do payroll and point-of-sale. Most can be integrated with other business applications, such as Web sites, merchant accounts, spreadsheets, and contact management software. They may, however, contain only rudimentary order entry features and little manufacturing support. They may also have limits on the number of users or transactions, such that companies may outgrow them.

Nonetheless, programs in this class offer tremendous value and are a great fit for smaller businesses. They are generally easier to install and use than the more complex mid- and high-end packages and are designed for use by nonaccountants. They often hide some accounting complexity by replacing debit-and-credit bookkeeping with more intuitive interfaces and eliminating steps such as maintenance of accounting period ends or the need to post transactions in batches.

Because of the software's power, cost-effectiveness, and ease of use, it's not unusual to see businesses sticking with their low-end packages as they grow beyond the size generally considered appropriate. In turn, the low-end packages are expanding their reach by offering added features and capacity. But if a business does outgrow its original package, upgrade paths exist, such as QuickBooks Enterprise Solutions or a path from PeachTree to MAS90™.

Low-end packages are generally easy to install and come with sample charts of account to get you started. Though you can easily "do it yourself," some expertise is needed to get the most of your system, such as customizing accounts, designing forms, reconciling balances, and designing processes.

Midrange Level: Companies needing more capacity, flexibility, or features, such as manufacturers needing inventory and production control, will want to step up to mid-range software offerings. These include Great Plains, MAS90, Solomon, ACCPAC, and Navision. These packages bear tremendous similarity to the mini-computer software of the 1980s and 1990s, with good reason—many packages are directly adapted from minicomputer applications. Though they have been updated to use familiar interfaces and rewritten to take advantage of new database tools, they are more complex and less user-

Because of the software's power, cost-effectiveness, and ease of use, it's not unusual to see businesses sticking with their low-end packages as they grow beyond the size generally considered appropriate.

friendly than their low-end counterparts. They generally retain a modular format and, because they contain more features and options, also require more decisions and work to set up and use.

Midrange software typically sells in modules rather than an all-in-one package. In addition to the basic modules available in low-end software, midrange packages often offer consolidations, costing, multi-currency, and e-commerce. They may also have integrated modules for general business functions such as human resources, project management, document management, and sales force management. Midrange software targets companies between $10 million and $250 million and, depending on the modules chosen and number of users, can typically range in cost from $10,000 to $250,000 for software alone.

In general, midrange packages are sold through value-added resellers (VARs) and are too complex to be installed without assistance.

In general, midrange packages are sold through value-added resellers (VARs) and are too complex to be installed without assistance. In many cases, users' experiences with their software will depend more on the quality of the VAR or other software consultant than on the software itself. As a result, it makes sense to shop as carefully for a VAR as for the software itself.

High-End Level: Most packages in this category, such as SAP, PeopleSoft, and Oracle, are beyond the reach of small to medium-sized businesses. However, they bear mentioning because they demonstrate the extent to which software can pull together all aspects of business processes. In addition, some manufacturers are attempting to extend their reach down into smaller companies. High-end software is sometimes offered via application service providers (ASPs), discussed more below. Though this model has yet to take off, it offers promise for bringing high-powered software within the budget of smaller companies that would typically be unable to purchase the software outright.

High-end software is extremely complex and highly integrated and it often requires business process reengineering. Implementations are lengthy and costly, with a high rate of dissatisfaction or failure. Targeted buyers are companies over $250 million in sales and costs typically run from several hundred thousand to over $100 million.

Custom and Vertical Software: Many companies and industries have specialized needs that even fairly sophisticated off-the-shelf software cannot handle. For example, a men's dress shirt manufacturer would require styles broken down by fabric, color, collar style, collar size, and sleeve size without creating a new part number for each combination. Most generic packages would handle one or two combinations, such as size and color. However, industry-specific software would generally be needed to handle all the possible combinations. Construction, healthcare, and nonprofits are other markets for which generic packages are often not well suited.

In many of these markets, vendors exist with software customized to the industry and able to handle its special needs. These may be stand-alone packages or add-on modules to off-the-shelf software. A manufacturer or VAR should be able to locate third-party add-ons and industry contacts may be the best source of industry-specific packages.

In general, it's best to avoid developing a customized, in-house package. Custom programs add additional expense and will likely be more prone to bugs, lack proper documentation, and be hard to maintain. Consider the following examples:

> At one company, which modified an existing package, the programmer moved away. The only way to modify the system was to have the programmer connect remotely at night—if available and at a hefty hourly rate.
>
> Another company was stunned to learn it had spent $60,000 per year just for maintenance on its custom system. Even minor adjustments, like changing a report heading, required a costly programming change and, since the company had never been given documentation, switching to a new programmer would have entailed a struggle deciphering the code.

If an off-the-shelf product can give you 90% of what you need, you are usually better off to go with it rather than custom software. You will also find that many packages allow a large degree of customization by letting users choose and change numerous options. These options might include report and entry screen layouts, whether to track history, and allowing some user-defined fields. If necessary, some of these packages allow modification of the underlying software. Be aware, however, that software companies are constantly enhancing their programs and custom features you add may not be compatible with the upgrades. In addition, over time upgrades may deliver features that bring the standard software closer to your company's needs without the need for customization.

If an off-the-shelf product can give you 90% of what you need, you are usually better off to go with it rather than custom software.

Overextending Office Software

A related problem is trying to do too many accounting tasks in database, spreadsheet, or word processing programs. For example:

One entrepreneur, like many others, started out entering a price list and printing invoices in a database program. Because this approach worked, the owner became comfortable using the program and additional accounting features were programmed in as the business's needs grew. The system was awkward and had the occasional glitch, but the entrepreneur was getting by with it. Eventually, though, when the owner had to produce financial statements to attract financing, the programming effort became too much work.

Others have repeated this approach, writing complex routines in spreadsheets or finding tricks to use checkbook accounting software for payables, receivables, and more. As discussed later, sometimes this is necessary to do calculations, like complex commissions, that accounting software can't handle or to avoid a costly change in software. More frequently, though, this type of effort is unnecessary and just reinvents the wheel. Even worse, these hybrid programs usually lack important controls, have only very basic features, and may be nearly impossible for all but the developer to use or modify.

Sorting Your Options

Canned demos will illustrate what the vendor wants to show you and a salesperson, perhaps unwittingly, could promise you functionality that does not exist.

While the number of quality, PC-based packages available is good news, it can make the selection process confusing. In sorting through the options, you will discover that all the major packages can handle the basic accounting and reporting functions very well. Concentrate on features that may be unique to your company or industry and see how each package handles these. Rather than focusing on general ledger, receivables, and payables, which are usually very straightforward, zero in on inventory, order entry, project costing, and similar modules, if appropriate for your type of business. Stick with the leading packages, if at all possible, as they are the most likely to be stable, stay around for the long term, get upgraded regularly, offer a wide range of third-party add-ons, and be supported by a wide selection of consultants.

Try to see a software demo illustrating your issues and your processes. Canned demos will illustrate what the vendor wants to show you and a salesperson, perhaps unwittingly, could promise you functionality that does not exist. Beware also of features promised for future releases, as no guarantees exist that those features will make it into the released product. In addition, as important as a VAR is to a successful implementation, avoid depending on a reseller to assess your needs. Even if they do so for free, they are unlikely to provide an unbiased opinion.

Features vs. Ease of Use

A common trade-off is between the number and sophistication of features built into accounting software and the ease of installation and use. No one program seems to combine the best of both.

Larger packages provide impressive functionality, but can overwhelm you with the number of reports, data fields, or options. Low-end programs are easier to set up and navigate, but may lack key features or be quickly outgrown. Older, more mature programs often have built up an impressive list of features but may have a proprietary data format or an outdated interface. Newer programs may take advantage of new technology to provide better navigation, reporting, and Web access, but may not have built up a full library of modules or third-party add-ons. Software from a new company also adds the risk the developer will not achieve a large enough installed base to ensure survival. Over time, the two options may converge as more mature suppliers upgrade their software and newer packages add features.

The trade-off between features and ease of use can pit users without significant accounting or computer experience against more sophisticated users or outside consultants. Outside accountants and consultants in particular may lean toward mature, more complex products. These provide the most features and build in the tightest controls. In addition, these professionals have usually used the products for a long time and understand how to make them work. By contrast, less experienced users are willing to trade off some features to ensure that the system can be up and running and operated without constant handholding.

Test-drive the system you are considering and do not buy on features alone.

The final choice is individual. Try to achieve a good balance between features and ease of use. Test-drive the system you are considering and do not buy on features alone. But make sure the system you choose has the functionality you need and room to grow.

Total Costs

The upfront cost of software and hardware is only a fraction of your total cost. Training, installation, data conversion, and forms will account for most of your cost. Allow 20% of the upfront license costs for annual maintenance including support and upgrades. In some cases, these maintenance fees may be mandatory for as long as you use your software, so be sure to understand the vendor's terms. The wrong system will also cost you in aggravation, fixes, and

265

workarounds—procedures that get the job done but don't correct the root problem. Be sure to figure all these costs into your budget.

When software is cheap, as so many low-end packages are, you may be tempted to say, "If I don't like it, I can just toss it out and try something else." But when you factor in the time and hidden expense of converting, the cost of even a cheap package can get high. In addition, don't lock yourself into a system that is less than you need because it costs less initially. If you need to start small, look for a package that provides an easy upgrade path.

Do you have to become an accountant to use or set up a system? Not entirely, but a basic understanding of accounting is important. Though low-end programs have simplified the initial setup, you should still take an active role in designing the chart of accounts, establishing procedures for accurate and timely data entry, and reviewing reports. You should do the same even if your company is large enough to require midrange software or above. However, at that stage you probably have financial managers who can handle many of the technical aspects of the system.

Do you have to become an accountant to use or set up a system? Not entirely, but a basic understanding of accounting is important.

Conversion

Converting to a new accounting system is a significant undertaking. Here are a few things to keep in mind:

▶ Allow plenty of time and allocate a sufficient budget. There are bound to be surprises.

▶ Data conversion, either from your old system or from third-party software being integrated with your accounting package, may present your biggest headaches. Though vendors are quick to claim conversion won't be an issue, stay on top of it and be sure to test carefully.

▶ Even if the new software can convert the data in your current software, you will still have setup issues. The new software will have additional features, preferences, and forms. The only time you will not have these issues is when simply upgrading to a new version of the same software.

▶ New software, no matter how well designed, cannot make up for poor manual systems or unresolved errors in your current software. Be sure your data is clean and processes are tight before converting.

▶ It may not be necessary to parallel your old system and new one. Running in parallel requires duplicate effort and you may lose many hours trying to resolve discrepancies without knowing if the error exists in the new system or old one. It is often easy to verify whether transactions are posting properly in a new system without having to compare with output from the old system.

▶ Time your conversion properly. The start of a fiscal year may be the best time to convert your general ledger, but have everything ready to go on Day One or you will overlap with year-end closing work. To phase the conversion in and avoid a crunch, you can convert subsystems such as payables and receivables earlier.

The Internet

The internet introduced a number of technologies capable of changing financial processes, including these:

▶ Electronic presentation and settlement of invoices

▶ E-commerce with sales and purchases through web sites

▶ Electronic banking

▶ The ability to run software hosted on remote servers

For accounting applications, the change so far has been evolutionary rather than revolutionary. Though electronic payments, e-commerce, and remote access to data speed many processes, they basically replace existing processes such as wire transfers, faxes, and dial-up access. Most accounting software continues to run on in-house networks rather than web-based systems and paper transactions such as checks and invoices still dominate. Although most software now comes with features that allow remote access, design of Web sites capable of accepting orders and payments, e-mailing of documents, and interfaces to electronic banking, the changes have been incremental. Change will undoubtedly continue, but accounting applications will likely trail the technology adoption curve this time around.

Application service providers (ASPs) illustrate this point. In the ASP model, financial software is hosted on the vendor's hardware and accessed by users over a network or the web. Benefits to the client include not having to make large, upfront investments to purchase and install the software, ensuring the people running the software have the proper technical skills, faster implementations, regular upgrades, and buying only what is needed. Despite these apparent benefits and the fact that a number of vendors offer ASP services, few clients have signed up. The cost savings have yet to be proven, especially as early ASP pricing was closer in price to a financed purchase rather than a low-cost rental. Companies also frequently have concerns about data security, risk that the ASP provider cannot deliver the promised service, and loss of control and in-house expertise. The ASP model also fails to eliminate the work involved in converting data and processes and the savings on in-house technology to host accounting software is offset in part by the costs of technology to handle data communications.

Other Software

Financial managers have other software tools at their disposal. Spreadsheets have become ubiquitous, but specialized tools also exist for fixed asset management, budgeting, consolidations, sales taxes, time tracking, and payroll. These tools can provide functionality either unavailable in off-the-shelf accounting software or more sophisticated. As a result, they are an important part of an overall solution.

Spreadsheets

A spreadsheet's main advantage has always been the ability to create, and then replicate, fairly sophisticated formulas.

Made popular by the 1982 release of Lotus 1-2-3, spreadsheets are the favorite tool of financial managers. Their main advantage has always been the ability to create, and then replicate, fairly sophisticated formulas. However, they also have powerful database functions, graphics, macro languages that allow user-defined formulas and routines, and the ability to exchange data with other programs. Though, for example, accounting software often comes with the ability to do very simple commission calculations, cash flow forecasts, and budgeting, spreadsheets can handle these tasks far better.

The danger of spreadsheets is that their complexity and slickness can mask underlying problems or legitimize weak logic. Spreadsheets give any user the ability to build impressive-looking models, but don't ensure that valid assumptions or checks and balances have been used. Digital Equipment Corporation's founder Ken Olsen, a strong proponent of understanding accounting statements, warns that many spreadsheet users "take garbage and reprocess it, contributing nothing but confusion.... If you say, 'Lord bless my spreadsheet,' I guarantee you He won't."[2]

Spreadsheet data security can be a troubling issue. Spreadsheets often contain confidential data that can be hard to hide or formulas that can be unwittingly broken by less skilled users. Passwords can keep unauthorized users from opening spreadsheets, but other controls—such as protecting individual cells from changes or hiding certain cells or sheets—are less effective. Users must remember to reset any controls they've temporarily disabled and there are often ways to discover what's contained in hidden fields. All in all, these make any shared data files quite vulnerable.

Spreadsheets often contain confidential data that can be hard to hide or the formulas that can be unwittingly broken by less skilled users.

The key is to use spreadsheets as a tool, not a crutch. Users should be able to see the source of any inputs and follow the flow of the worksheet. Make sure that assumptions are laid out clearly and drive the calculations, so changes to the assumptions can ripple through the spreadsheet, making updating quick and easy. This way the logic behind the calculations becomes evident and people other than the developer can understand the spreadsheet and make modifications themselves, if needed. Test all conclusions to see if they are consistent with external data and past experience.

Payroll

Though most accounting software packages offer payroll modules, it makes sense for most companies, even very small ones, to outsource this function. Because of the hassles of regular filings, keeping up with rate changes, and potential penalties, it is not worth it to do payroll yourself. Use reports from your accounting software or time-tracking software to generate time and sales reports for inputs to payroll. Then use spreadsheets to summarize the payroll outputs for entry into your ledger.

Time Tracking

Time tracking has two main uses: to tally and bill professional service hours chargeable to clients and to manage projects and allocate costs in-house. Time and billing software does not need to be expensive or complicated. For example, QuickBooks has a built-in feature for doing basic tracking of both time and expenses, while programs such as Timeslips™ can do invoicing and integrate with accounting software.

Getting employees to complete their timesheets fully and on time often presents a bigger challenge. Recalling the example presented in Chapter 10 of the law firm collecting only 75%-80% of the hours worked, strict procedures and tying compensation to time billed were needed to ensure timely submission of timesheets. Employees often wait until the end of the week to fill in their time; having to recreate their efforts may diminish accuracy. When using time tracking to evaluate productivity or allocate costs, a number of decisions also need to be made about how to account for hours in excess of 40/week or absences such as vacations or sick days.

Since many employees tracking time may be working remotely or not have access to the main accounting system, some type of remote access is needed. Programs like QuickBooks and Timeslips solve this by spinning off time and expense sub-modules for individual use, which are then collected and consolidated. Web-based time packages may offer advantages, since remote users can access the time-tracking program without being connected to the company's network.

Data Collection

Studies show that error rates for bar codes are about one per one million characters, compared with one per every 300 characters entered manually.

New technology continues to change the way data can get entered into accounting and control systems. Actions such as supermarket checkouts, package delivery, medical records, and manufacturing inventory control have been greatly improved by bar codes. Studies show that error rates for bar codes are about one per one million characters, compared with one per every 300 characters entered manually.[3] Another showed that automated inventory systems averaged a 98% accuracy rate versus 73% for nonautomated ones.[4] More recently, companies have experimented with new technology for embedding tiny radio frequency I.D. sensors (RFIDs) into product labels, which could allow the same data-collection abilities as bar codes without scanning. Wherever the need for highly accurate, repetitive data collection exists, investment in technology is likely to pay off.

Conclusion

In the early days of computers, mistakes and mix-ups were commonly blamed on computer errors. That, of course, is a misnomer. While there are rare hardware glitches, computers do as they are told and problems can invariably be traced to human error and poor processes. One joke says that computer errors almost invariably involve two errors, the first of which is blaming it on the computer.

Software errors do occur. Even the best-selling software can contain bugs, especially new releases. Avoid the first release of new software versions; wait until updates are released. Internally developed applications and spreadsheets are even riskier. Be sure to test all software thoroughly, even minor updates. Back up data regularly to protect against errors and other problems, such as system crashes and viruses.

However, most errors in transaction processing have more to do with incorrect inputs and weak controls. As discussed in the next chapter, computers can enhance and automate certain control processes, but they cannot atone for weak manual controls. Inaccurate data entry, failure to establish checks and balances, and an inappropriate reporting structure will carry over to any automated system. As programmers say, "Garbage in, garbage out" (GIGO). Computerized applications provide great financial management tools, but the backbone of any system is strong internal controls.

Notes

1. Anthony M. Santomero, quoted in *The Manager's Book of Quotations*, p. 8.
2. Ken Olsen, quoted in Ronald Rosenberg, "A Little Moralistic Curmudgeonry from the Master Himself," *The Boston Globe*, 1 August 1993, p. 80.
3. Automatic Data Capture Association, *Data Capture Suppliers Guide 2003-2004*, www.adca.com.au/buyers_guide/2003-2004_Buyers_Guide/Barcoding_Basics.pdf.
4. Jacquelyn Denalli, "Bellying up to the High-Tech Bar," *Small Business Reports*, May 1991, p. 64.

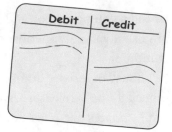

Chapter 15

Internal Controls

EFFECTIVE CHECKS AND BALANCES ARE THE BEDROCK OF ANY accounting and control system. Employees make mistakes, theft is a concern, and the perpetual question of managers seems to be "The numbers look good but are they right?" Strong internal controls—systematic procedures for verifying information, detecting errors, and ensuring proper authorization for all transactions—provide the needed level of confidence in the accuracy of financial systems.

Internal controls should also be efficient. At many companies, accuracy and control are achieved only by constantly recounting inventory, double-checking data entry, or having the owner or CEO personally approve almost all expenditures. These are signs that something is almost certainly wrong and resources are being wasted. Tight control does not mean constant oversight and redundant processing. Instead, control can be achieved with fairly simple, routine procedures and the discipline to enforce them.

The thrust of internal controls should be to ensure accuracy in everyday processing. Though theft and fraud are clearly of concern, the cost of errors in routine data collection and entry is insidious and usually far greater. Duplicate payments, billing errors, and lost paperwork are more common than dishonesty and routinely cost companies significant amounts of time, money, and goodwill.

Strong controls are also needed to ensure timely information. A system that fails to provide current balances, such as for stock on hand or cash in the bank, results in costly "workarounds"—employees developing personal files or procedures to override information in the system. That's at best. At worst, these systems simply get ignored.

These problems apply to both manual and automated processes. While computers have altered the look of accounting systems and greatly expanded what can be accomplished, basic internal control procedures are little changed. In fact, strong manual controls are a prerequisite for an effective computerized system. The computer will only magnify weaknesses in manual controls, not compensate for them.

The core of any accounting system is strong controls. This chapter explains the role of controls and describes some basic procedures to implement and enforce controls. You can use the Internal Control Questionnaire for Cash Disbursements at the end of this chapter to check some of your basic procedures for cash disbursements.

The thrust of internal controls should be to ensure accuracy in everyday processing.

Comparison to a Personal Checkbook

You, like most people, probably apply basic controls to the handling of your personal checkbook. You start by keeping tight physical control over your checks, storing them in a safe place or carrying them securely in your pocket or purse. Even if a check were to fall into the wrong hands, certain procedures help prevent losses. The checks cannot be used at most stores without also presenting proper ID and the bank will compare the signature to a card on file.

Checks are numbered so that if each check written is recorded in the checkbook, you can quickly see from the register whether every number in a sequence is accounted for. Recording each check and deposit also enables you to keep a running balance of money in your bank account, so you can budget spending and avoid overdrafts. At the end of every month, reconciling the checkbook with the bank statement can detect any errors. When the statement is reconciled, you can be secure in knowing exactly how money was spent and how much money remains in the account.

Of course, many people keep their checkbooks a bit less rigorously than this. Whether they fail to reconcile their statements, forget to record every check, or don't keep running totals of cash in the account, they pay a price. Here are some of the consequences:

▶ Uncertainty about cash on hand, perhaps incurring overdraft or other bank charges

▶ Lost information, such as "Where did all the money go?"

▶ Poor tax records

▶ Inability to spot bank errors

▶ Extra effort needed to "catch up" or to reconcile statements months later

▶ Difficulty finding canceled checks if a proof of payment is needed

▶ Lost interest if extra funds are kept in noninterest-bearing checking accounts, rather than invested

▶ Disorganized or unprofessional appearance

At the same time, some people make effective use of checkbook software programs to pay bills and do budgeting. The use of a computer requires an up-front investment in buying software and forms and learning the programs, but these costs are offset by advantages, which include:

▶ Calculations that are automatic and correct

▶ Time savings for repetitive transactions

▶ Information that can be broken down to the desired level of detail and is easily summarized

▶ Credit cards, investments, and other assets that can be tracked in the same program

▶ Excellent tax records and historical information

The issues that face businesses are much the same. But they involve not only cash, but payables, receivables, inventory, and other subsystems. A combination of strong physical controls, clearly defined authorization levels, transaction logs, timely recordkeeping, and reconciliations work together to ensure control over assets and accurate information. Properly done, the transactions and procedures are routine and unobtrusive. Conversely, lack of discipline and controls is costly in terms of lost information, duplication of effort, errors, and unprofessional appearance.

Businesses must deal with an additional problem—having more than one person entering information and controlling the movement of assets. Individuals and sole proprietors have no problem keeping their best interests at heart and ensuring accurate communication. But once a business includes even two people, the protection provided by internal controls becomes an even greater necessity.

*O*nce a business includes even two people, the protection provided by internal controls becomes an even greater necessity.

Basic Concepts

A few basic underlying concepts and techniques are all you need to set up an internal control system.

Separation of Duties

The first concept is to maintain distinct separations of duties. Loss of an asset, whether from theft, unauthorized expenditure, or error, requires both physical access to the asset—including the authority to approve expenditures—and a failure to detect or stop the loss. Writing a check does not appropriate funds; it must also be signed and it is scrutinized during the reconciliation process. Inventory shortages in a warehouse or stockroom require removal by authorized personnel, but can be detected by comparing on-hand quantities with perpetual accounting records.

If you give a person access to an asset and, at the same time, control of the relevant recordkeeping, you are inviting trouble. However, simply splitting the duties, so that different people control access to the asset and review of the transaction, can provide adequate control.

Some examples include:

▶ The person preparing checks should not have authority to sign them or reconcile the bank statement.

▶ Different people should authorize purchases, place orders, and issue payment for goods and services.

▶ Customer payments received by mail should either go directly to a bank lockbox or be opened and totaled by someone who doesn't post the payments in the accounting system.

Another simple example can be seen the next time you go to an entertainment event where tickets are sold, such as a movie theater or a club. One person takes the money and hands out the tickets and another person takes the tickets. The tickets collected provide an independent check on the number sold and, therefore, the cash that was collected. If just one person sold and collected tickets or if there were no tickets and one person collected the money, that person would have sole control over both the money and any recordkeeping. Proper payment to the owner would depend entirely on the cashier's diligence and honesty.

Physical Controls

The second concept you do not want to overlook is physically restricting access to assets. Sample physical controls include the following:

The second concept you do not want to overlook is physically restricting access to assets.

- ▶ Keep checks and possibly other important forms and documents locked.
- ▶ Put inventory into stockrooms and restrict access.
- ▶ Affix permanent labels to or etch identifying marks on all equipment.

These types of controls are especially important for inventory, since parts and finished products may be easy to remove and detection of small losses is unlikely. In many companies, inventory is not subject to precise recordkeeping, or shrinkage is almost expected, so loss of a few items is shrugged off. Fixed assets, in contrast, may be so large or easy to identify that they are hard to remove without someone noticing. Cash can be reconciled to the penny, so loss from theft of cash or a check can be detected quickly.

The records of your company must also be physically controlled to maintain both confidentiality and prevent unauthorized changes. Lost records can also be damaging if needed to research a payment, tax, or legal dispute. For computer systems, restricted physical access to servers and any networked computers needs to be combined with firewalls, passwords, and other electronic means. Passwords should be changed regularly, kept confidential, and not shared by users. Regular backups, including keeping copies offsite, provide protection over data loss or corruption.

Reconciliations

The third concept for establishing internal controls is maintaining timely reconciliations of general ledger account balances. When your ledger balances can be compared with an objective, independently determined balance, a reconciliation can and should be performed. Tying cash to a bank statement—as for a personal checkbook—is the most common type of reconciliation. The bank statement provides an opportunity to verify that all checks and deposits have been recorded and for the right amount. These are errors that routine processing may not detect.

The third concept for establishing internal controls is maintaining timely reconciliations of general ledger account balances.

Other important reconciliations you should perform include:

▶ Ensure that ledger balances for payables and receivables agree with detailed agings.

▶ Maintain a fixed asset register that foots (adds up) to the book balance. You can use the same register to compute depreciation. Periodically, fixed assets should be inventoried.

▶ Periodically, match vendor payable balances to any statements received. Resolve discrepancies promptly.

▶ Ask for a listing of what is contained in prepaid, other assets, and accrued liabilities accounts, as these can accumulate long-forgotten balances.

Ledger account balances are interconnected, so reconciling one account may clear up problems in another. For example, if your receivables records differ from a customer's because a payment was not recorded, the bank reconciliation will catch this error. The bank statement will show a deposit not reflected on the internal records and the reconciliation will not balance until this discrepancy is resolved.

In practice, because so many transactions involve cash, the bank reconciliation is perhaps the best control for ensuring that all revenues and expenses have been booked properly. Personally reconciling the bank statement can be an excellent way for a controller or a business owner who is not routinely involved in handling the checkbook to gain insight into how cash flows and how well the accounting is being controlled. Doing so also helps achieve separation of duties.

Smaller business owners should also insist that bank statements be sent directly to their homes to gain added physical control over these records.

Once accounts have been reconciled, or a month has been closed and reports have been run, make sure your system prevents retroactive entries. In most systems, running a routine to close the accounting period or updating a setting does this. Keeping copies of key reports also allows you track down changes made at a later date, if necessary.

Self-Interest

When a business or a merchant makes an error in a customer's favor, like failing to bill for a purchase, the customer is likely to keep quiet and pocket the windfall.

When a business or a merchant makes an error in a customer's favor, like failing to bill for a purchase, the customer is likely to keep quiet and pocket the windfall. Of course, if a customer is billed twice, the customer will demand a credit or ignore the second bill. Simply put, people can be expected to act in their own best interest. And this expectation is a powerful influence on the effectiveness of controls and should be considered in shaping any system.

If you have to choose between a procedure that prevents double-billing and one that ensures that all shipments get billed, the latter will more tightly close the control loop. Though neither type of error is desirable, the protection against double-billing is somewhat redundant, since the customer is almost sure to notice. However, no such built-in safeguard exists for failing to bill.

The same logic applies to internal transactions. If a stockroom clerk is responsible for shortages, he or she will have an incentive to properly count incoming shipments or insist on having proper paperwork before releasing goods out of stock. Similarly, if a salesperson is not reimbursed for expense reports if receipts are missing, he or she has a strong incentive to collect the documentation.

Control Numbers and Logs

Finally, the concept of using control numbers and logs can be an important control issue. While an incorrect transaction may be quickly spotted, you may not notice a missing one. You also need a way of identifying transactions so they can quickly be researched or followed up on later.

Using control numbers and logs—an extension of the concept of using check numbers and a checkbook—will enable you to solve problems quickly.

Suppose you need a control against failing to bill a customer. In addition, once the bill has been issued, you need a record for tracing payments owed and made. A way to do this is to assign numbers to sales orders and shipments and ensure they are recorded automatically by your accounting system or manually into a logbook.

When an invoice is issued, assign a number to it and cross-reference that with the order number. Orders not matched to invoices indicate items yet to be shipped—or items shipped and not billed. Similarly, any invoices without a payment against them are part of a list of open receivables.

This concept extends to a wide range of accounting documents. For example, many restaurants assign servers numbered pads and account for all meal checks at the end of the night; for a physical inventory, tag numbers issued are carefully logged and must all be accounted for at the end of the count.

Assigning and accounting for the transaction numbers ensures that items do not slip through the cracks and also provides a useful means of cross-referencing them. Most accounting software will do transaction numbering for you. You then need to run reports to find gaps in a sequence, open orders, and other double checks.

Delegating Authority

If you personally approve every expenditure, a high degree of control might exist, but little gets done. You will devote too much energy to minute details, while managers waste time interrupting their work for approvals and standing in line outside your office. At an early stage in any company's growth, authority to initiate or approve transactions must be passed down.

At an early stage in any company's growth, authority to initiate or approve transactions must be passed down.

To do this and maintain adequate control, give your line managers spending authority, but with specified dollar limits. Above those specified limits, transactions should require joint signatures or review at a higher level. For the checkbook, this might take the form of requiring two signatures above a certain amount.

Formal approvals are not required just for spending money. Many noncash transactions involve a commitment of resources. You may need formal approvals to provide a paper trail to establish accountability or to use as a systematic vehicle of communication within an organization. Here are some situations where you should require formal authorizations:

▶ **Sales orders**—Make sure to include credit checks and price verifications. Without controls, salespeople will often push through orders at unfavorable terms.

▶ **Purchase orders**—Many companies allow managers to order directly, leading to poor price negotiation and little control over the amount and timing of expenditures.

▶ **Return authorizations**—Specify terms under which products are accepted back. Customer complaints need special handling.

These authorizations should be obtained early in the processing cycle. For example, the time to do a credit check is before an order is processed, not after an invoice is cut. Dollar limits for approving transactions should apply even on noncash transactions—such as return authorizations.

Maintaining Control

Several prob-lems may occur within your system that require preventive mainte-nance to keep the system running smoothly.

Several problems may occur within your system that require preventive maintenance to keep the system running smoothly. The credibility of your system must be kept high. Once information is perceived as unreliable, people begin to work around systems.

Late information can have the same negative effect. Improper training can produce either discomfort with the system or a failure to understand the interdependency of each department and lead to a breakdown. Operators may adopt a technique that gets their job done, even though it forces adjustments downstream. Observe the following illustrations of these types of problems:

At one manufacturer, the purchasing manager routinely added 10% to certain raw material orders, because inaccurate bills of material distorted projected usage. The same manager would also physically count on-hand quantities before ordering, because of inaccuracies in the perpetual inventory. At other companies, salespeople request extra copies of invoices or clerks keep personal files or reference cards because they do not trust information they get from the computer system.

At another manufacturer, the production manager did scheduling manually because daily updates to the computer system were routinely processed first thing in the morning–which meant they were completed after the day's work had begun in the plant.

In a company where a new production system was installed, many orders came in that included new part numbers. When this happened, the order entry clerk found it quicker to type the sales orders by hand, using the old forms rather than adding the new parts to the system and then entering the order. This not only forced clerks from production through shipping and invoicing to adopt special manual steps to deal with these orders, but eventually caused the production control aspects of the system to be abandoned altogether.

Enforcing controls may seem to slow work down and tempt people to take shortcuts. However, time lost on the front end is invariably recouped later. Creating exceptions leads to confusion and errors.

Doing things right usually saves time, even if procedures that ensure control seem cumbersome. Ironically, what seems like more work can often take less time.

For example, if an invoice is created for the wrong amount, should you void the original and issue a new invoice or should you just print an invoice for the difference? While voiding and reissuing seems to add an extra step, these are very routine transactions. Issuing an adjustment may require stopping for an added calculation and perhaps attaching a note to the customer. Doing two routine steps is often faster than one special one. In addition, when the transaction is reviewed—perhaps when payment arrives—you can see what was involved more clearly with the two-step procedure.

Audit Trails

This last point leads to a vital internal control feature—the audit trail. Any accounting system must provide a way to easily trace transactions from the ledger or any summary back to supporting detail. Examples include:

Any accounting system must provide a way to easily trace transactions from the ledger or any summary back to supporting detail.

The balance in accounts payable should tie to an accounts payable aging, listing all open items by a reference number, such as invoice number. Summary information about the invoice should be retrievable online and the paper copy should be in an easily accessible file.

Salary expense for the month may be the total of several entries. Each entry should be traceable to a payroll register that shows pay for each individual together with a check number or reference to a direct deposit. Hours paid should be verifiable to a time card and the pay rate to a personnel file.

A breakdown in the audit trail makes assigning accountability for transactions and doing reconciliations extremely difficult. A breakdown can also prove costly when disputes arise over payments with vendors or customers. A company may show a vendor invoice as paid, but not be able to identify the check number—and therefore cannot provide a proof of payment. Similarly, a customer may claim to have paid an invoice and provide a canceled check—yet you show the invoice still open. If you cannot demonstrate where that check has been applied, perhaps to a different invoice, your customer's claim will stand.

To maintain an audit trail for general ledger entries, write up all transactions before they are entered, attach supporting documentation, and require sign-off by your controller. Most accounting systems will not allow a transaction to be altered once it has been posted. However, if this is optional in your system, either set your system to track all changes or ensure that any amendments to a written entry have clear documentation.

Make Controls Routine

A key factor to successful internal controls is to make the control measures you implement routine. This ensures proper procedures are followed without singling out employees or making them feel policed. For example:

A car dealership chain was having problems controlling cash down payments given to its sales managers. Rather than submitting them right away to the home office, the sales managers would wait until all paperwork for the sale was complete and submit the cash with it. At times, this meant the managers were carrying a large amount of cash. Occasionally, the company experienced a loss if the sales manager was fired. More frequently, the cash would get used as petty cash to pay miscellaneous expenses, making reconciliation of the paperwork for the sale and office expenses next to impossible.

A very simple check was devised, calling for accounting to randomly compare the sales managers' cash receipt books against cash turned in. This raised the ire of the sales managers who were selected; they objected to being treated like thieves.

The solution? The company instituted two random checks per month of every sales manager's cash receipt book. This allowed a needed control to be implemented without the overtones that came with singling out managers.

The job of your controller is to ensure that these proper checks and balances exist—not because the controller suspects people of being dishonest or incompetent, but because it is simply part of the job. Quite the opposite of being a burden, good checks and balances ensure accuracy and eliminate the need for constant policing and monitoring.

Controls must treat people with respect. An example is the monitoring of expense reports. If a manager with full responsibility for running a major department is missing a $20 receipt on an expense report, don't badger him or her over it. The information is not critical to your company and you have no reason to worry that the company is being ripped off—if there is, and that manager controls a large budget, you have a greater exposure than the $20.

If necessary, in order to gain employees' acceptance, consider blaming the need for controls on your outside auditor. CPAs are perceived as straight and narrow, so people are likely to accept their recommendations.

If necessary, in order to gain employees' acceptance, consider blaming the need for controls on your outside auditor.

Scaling Controls

As a business expands, the need to delegate work increases and ability to personally control things decreases. This problem can be particularly acute when a business expands from a single location to multiple sites. Consider the following examples:

Two friends opened up a small retail store. Because they sold numerous small items that were hard to inventory and label they implemented few controls. They felt that handwritten sales slips gave them more flexibility than a point-of-sale system with part numbers, tags, and fixed inventory storage locations,. When the store succeeded and a third party approached them about opening up and running additional stores, they realized there would be a number of control issues. The friends couldn't ensure that at least one of them would be physically present in the store at all times, so they needed controls to ensure that all sales were recorded and that cash was reconciled at the end of each day. Because they also would be stocking more than one store, they needed a way to monitor what was selling and when to reorder.

A firm bought up multiple golf driving ranges but made little investment in systems. It was a cash business with dispersed locations and the owners discovered that money was being stolen and employees were not working the hours they said they were. Unable to watch each store individually and no time to set up controls, the owners ended up divesting most of the locations.

Simply put, decentralized businesses will have greater oversight costs. It is also better to ensure that controls work in the first location before attempting to expand. Similarly, growing businesses should invest in proper checks and balances while possible problems are still manageable.

Computers and Controls

The computer has changed the way accounting is done and, therefore, impacted the structure of internal controls. Processing problems can be repeated or magnified more easily than they could on old manual systems. Users have the ability to rapidly access files to view or alter data, from remote or local sites. Though you still have the threat of theft or fraud, the most dangerous risk is of accidental error, such as data lost to disk crashes or operator error.

Though you still have the threat of theft or fraud, the most dangerous risk is of accidental error, such as data lost to disk crashes or operator error.

Basic Controls

Some basic controls should bring you peace of mind. As mentioned earlier, passwords should be used to tightly restrict access to PCs, accounting software, and key spreadsheets. Physical controls should be established, including limiting access to servers and any networked PCs with sensitive data on the hard drive or left connected to the network while unattended. Storage media, such as disks and CDs, should also be locked up. Daily backups can minimize data losses from disk crashes, corrupted files, or accidental file erasure.

Daily backups also provide the best protection from routine processing errors. Mistakes, such as prematurely closing an accounting period or using the wrong transaction date on a string of entries, can often be corrected by restoring the previous day's data from a backup and starting over. Proper storage and handling of computers and using devices such as surge suppressors can prevent equipment failures.

Commercial accounting software can be relied on to process data accurately and reliably. Software that is developed or modified in-house is prone to bugs and should be tested thoroughly before changing over your entire system. Keep a backup of earlier software versions and data so changes can be reversed.

Despite these risks, computers generally enhance overall control. Software can perform a wide range of checks and balances that otherwise would require tedious human review. Accounting programs routinely check to see that entries are in balance and they issue and track invoice and other control numbers. They can test payables invoice numbers to avoid duplicate entries, alert order entry clerks when customers have exceeded credit limits, and flag inventory reorder points to avoid stockouts. Most software also provides routines for reconciling bank statements and strong audit trails, including the ability to "drill down" to see a list of transactions making up an account balance.

The biggest control risk in a computerized system, as discussed earlier, is not the computer itself, but manual procedures and disciplines. The computer system will not solve problems due to poor manual controls. Those controls must be fixed before attempting to install a computerized system, or confusion and duplication of effort may grow out of hand.

To return to the analogy of the personal checkbook, the computer can open up a range of opportunities for more efficient recordkeeping, but only with the proper discipline. A person who fails to physically control checks, properly categorize expenses, or reconcile the bank statement will have problems using a manual or computerized checkbook.

The biggest control risk in a computerized system, as discussed earlier, is not the computer itself, but manual procedures and disciplines.

Audits

A review of internal controls is a standard part of a CPA's audit. In addition, the extent of transaction testing done in an audit depends in part on how reliable the CPA feels your internal controls are. At the end of the audit, the CPA should issue a management letter that discusses weaknesses in internal controls and recommends corrections. Management should carefully review these comments and either implement changes or justify current practices. Note that because the controller's work is being reviewed in the letter, the controller should be involved but not solely responsible for this review.

Examinations of internal controls are not to be confused with searching out fraud. As discussed in Chapter 2, typical audits are not designed or intended to detect fraud. In fact, cleverly disguised fraud, particularly if top management is involved, is nearly impossible to detect in a routine audit.

If fraud is suspected and has not been detected with basic controls as described in this chapter, you may want to call in a forensic accountant. These specialists, who generally work individually or in small accounting firms, dig deep into transactions. Where a routine audit may only send out confirmation letters to customers, a forensic accountant might examine all invoices and contracts, research the ownership of the outside firms, and search for signs of collusion.

Conclusion

Not all desirable internal control features will be cost-effective. Small companies with few clerical employees will find it more difficult to separate duties. Requiring multiple signatures on checks or purchase orders may delay and impede operations. In these cases, you must weigh the relative costs and benefits of controls in deciding which controls to implement.

Once in place, internal control procedures become routine, providing unobtrusive, but effective protection against loss and errors. While you may experience initial resistance to adding procedures or paperwork, the investment up front usually reduces work down the line—not to mention giving you added security that will let you sleep at night.

To help you evaluate your internal controls, ask your auditor or accountant for any literature or checklists he or she may have on the subject. In addition, you can use the Internal Control Questionnaire for Cash Disbursements below to check your internal control procedures for cash.

Internal Control Questionnaire for Cash Disbursements

Internal controls can provide protection from loss and errors. Use this questionnaire to determine if you have established effective internal controls in the area of cash disbursements.

Accessibility or Safeguarding

Physical controls and restricted access are important control tools. Review this section to see if your procedures can use improvement.

Yes	No	
❏	❏	Are all payments made by check or other negotiable instrument?
❏	❏	Are checks made payable to specific payees?
❏	❏	Are your checks prenumbered and used in sequence?
❏	❏	Are voided, special, or mutilated checks saved and filed?
❏	❏	Does someone check the sequence of checks periodically?
❏	❏	Do you store unused checks in a restricted area in the possession of a specified person?
❏	❏	Are checks made of protective paper?
❏	❏	Is a check protector used?
❏	❏	If you use facsimile plates or similar devices for check signatures, have you identified who is to have custody and use of the plates?

❏ ❏ Do you keep facsimile plates in a restricted, secure place apart from blank check stock? Are the plates used only in the presence of the person designated as responsible?

Separation of Duties

Maintaining a distinct separation of duties is one of the most important practices you can establish for controlling unauthorized expenditures, theft, and errors.

Yes No

❏ ❏ Are checks prepared by persons other than those with voucher approval authority?

❏ ❏ Is the person who prepares checks independent of purchasing and receiving functions?

❏ ❏ Are checks signed by persons other than those preparing or having approval authority?

❏ ❏ Are authorized signatures limited to employees having no access to accounting records, cash receipts, or petty cash funds?

❏ ❏ Is there a dollar limit at which all checks must be countersigned?

❏ ❏ Are bank reconciliations prepared monthly by an employee who does not sign checks, record cash transactions, or have access to cash?

❏ ❏ Does this person receive the bank statement unopened?

Processing and Recording

Review the questions below to check whether your processing and recording procedures provide enough checks and balances to detect incorrect transactions.

Yes No

❏ ❏ Are all regular disbursements that you make by checks prepared and based on adequate and approved documentation?

❏ ❏ Does the person who signs checks verify whether the amounts are approved and have adequate documentation?

❏ ❏ Do you pay only against original invoices and not against statements or photocopies?

❏ ❏ Do you mark invoices after payment and check for duplicate numbers to avoid paying twice?

❏ ❏ Are only complete checks—not blank—ever signed?

❏ ❏ After signing, are all checks recorded in a cash disbursement record that gives enough detail to allow accurate summarizing and posting?

❏ ❏ Are actual disbursements periodically compared with forecasted disbursements and large or unusual variances investigated and accounted for?

Answer Key

Ideally, you have answered all of the questions with a "Yes." However, a "No" to any of the questions does not necessarily indicate a problem. Not all internal controls are cost-effective or even possible for many companies. You will have to weigh the costs vs. the benefits of the controls you decide to use, as applied to your unique business situation. This questionnaire deals only with internal controls for cash disbursements. Don't forget to look at other internal controls, as well.

Chapter 16

Conclusion: A 10-Step Plan for Control

> Never ask of money spent
> Where the spender thinks it went.
> Nobody was ever meant
> To remember or invent
> What he did with every cent.
> —Robert Frost, "The Hardship of Accounting"

YOU HAVE COMPLETED YOUR SURVEY OF FINANCIAL CONTROL. THE concepts covered in this book are some of the nuts and bolts of business. Financial management is rarely exciting or the thing that sparks new ventures. As business consultant and author Tom Peters has written, "Inspiring visions rarely (I'm tempted to say never) include numbers."[1]

But a command of the numbers and a strong system of controls are critical for steering your company toward success. If you can measure the activities in your company, you can manage them. If you can quantify goals, you can evaluate your progress and determine if corrective action is needed. As former ITT Chairman Harold Geneen sums it up, "The professional's grasp of the numbers is a measure of the control he has over the events that the figures represent."[2]

To accomplish this, managers to do not need to become accountants. The controller or accounting manager is the chief numbers person. But this book has tried to provide a basis for nonfinancial managers and their accounting staff to work together. The goal has been to provide the nonfinancial managers with a working knowledge of finance, accounting, and control. In addition, it is hoped the accountants will gain a business perspective that enables them to apply their skills more broadly and effectively.

The goal of this book has been to provide the nonfinancial managers with a working knowledge of finance, accounting, and control.

Managing with the Numbers

You do need to find the right numbers. As discussed, too often the only numbers managers have to work with are those provided by the financial accounting system. This information is often too late, too aggregated, and too hard to interpret to be of the greatest use.

Return to the analogy of an owner being the pilot of a company. The controller has to provide more than financial accounting or it is like navigating with just a little black box—the flight recorders carried by commercial planes. As you travel along, accounting faithfully records everything that happens. However, since the information is historical and hard to access, it cannot be used to help navigate. Worse, no one might take the time to analyze the information unless something goes terribly wrong.

An effective control system is not a black box. Rather, it should function like the instrument panel on a plane. The feedback must be timely, accurate, and accessible. You should have tools for spotting problems and helping steer past them. You must be able to interpret the readings but also be free to exercise judgment in making the ultimate decisions that run the company.

What is often more important than a knowledge of accounting is developing an instinctive understanding, or ownership, of the numbers driving your business. What is your breakeven point? What should your target profit margins be? When do you add an employee? In addition, run the numbers to project cash or evaluate projects. The numbers can't replace judgment, but they do provide support.

The Payback

How much should you invest in a controller and, possibly, a staff or systems? How do you measure the payback? Sometimes, putting a dollar figure on a controller's work is easy. The savings can be directly measured, if:

▶ Your controller identifies places where costs can be cut.

▶ You are able to reduce the use of your outside CPA firm.

▶ Your systems that are put in place allow you to reduce headcount.

Other savings can be determined over time, including improvements in collections or reductions in inventory waste.

Many benefits, however, are intangible or hidden. It is hard to place a definitive value on having better, timelier information or avoiding errors in processing billings and payments. The cost of a cash crisis can be enormous, but if a controller's efforts prevent a crisis from occurring, the work may go unnoticed.

Maintaining good relationships with your banker and investors can largely depend on your controller's work.

Maintaining good relationships with your banker and investors can largely depend on your controller's work. Timely and informative financial reports, the ability to communicate your plans through projections and budgets, and the ability to demonstrate control over the business will earn the confidence of investors. Their confidence will help ensure their support during a downturn. Again, it may be hard to put a value on this.

Finally, consider the benefit to yourself of having a strong command over the numbers driving your business. Here is what one owner had to say after turning around his out-of-control, nearly bankrupt film production company with the help of a financial management consultant:[3]

> There are still things I can't do. I can't post information into the books, and I can't analyze four or five years of past P&Ls and such. What I can do, though, is on a daily basis see that only X dollars are being used in Y areas and know that I have only so many dollars to apply in so many different departments.
>
> Damn, I am running the company. I have a new controller who handles my finances. I have a sales manager who handles my sales. I have a production head, and I have a creative head. They all come to me with questions, and I know most of the answers. I am a CEO and I'm not ashamed of the title anymore. I deserve it. For the first time I get just as excited by doing business as I did before by producing films ....

I like the respect that I get now. I didn't enjoy being the head of a financially failing company. Furthermore, once I took away the fear caused by my own ignorance, I was able to relax and be more comfortable, even before all the problems got solved. Now I can sleep nights.

No single formula can determine what to spend on the controllership function. But the starting point is realizing that the job is much more than just accounting and, therefore, requires more than just a number cruncher. As one veteran financial manager wrote:[4]

The main blunder made by the owners I've worked for was sticking with a bookkeeping type for too long before hiring a capable financial manager. I think that's because they think of the number one finance person as the head bean counter. That is a huge mistake.

Much is at stake in the financial management of your company. The potential return is large, but also easy to underestimate. Add up both the possible tangible and intangible benefits of strong controllership. Look at successful competitors in your area and see what sort of reporting and systems they have. Then choose the areas that have the best payback and move forward.

Getting Started Now

On the next few pages, is a basic plan of attack that can get you started on taking control. These are 10 things you can do right now to improve cash flow, reduce costs, and give you a better understanding of the numbers driving your business.

Step One: Develop at Least a One-Year Projection

Include a profit-and-loss statement, a balance sheet, and a statement of cash flow. This does not need to be a full-blown business plan or budgeting exercise. Use a format like the sample projection at the end of Chapter 11 to develop a forecast. Monitor future results against a benchmark plan and update the forecast to stay on top of expectations. If cash is tight in the short term, also do a cash flow forecast on a weekly basis going out two to three months. Working with your controller or accountant, completing these projections for the first time should take about two days; future versions should go much faster.

The benefits of doing forecasts include:

- ▶ Preparing forecasts is an educational process. Having to review expense trends and what drives revenue, costs, and cash flow can provide insights you would not get from just reading financial statements. You are forced to get into the numbers and learn what is behind them. You also get the big picture, a summary of a year's operation and how the dollars flow from month to month.

- ▶ Forecasts clearly spell out milestones and expectations for your company. They are something you can monitor your progress against. Also use the projections to communicate with investors and employees.

- ▶ Forecasts will tell you in advance if you need to worry about a cash crunch or if your current path will generate sufficient profits. By anticipating problems or highlighting profit or margin weakness, forecasts give you time to take timely corrective action.

- ▶ Building a model allows you to play what-if games. For example, what happens if sales fall below expectations or if you can speed collections?

Step Two: Find the Key Indicators You Need

These numbers tell you how your business is doing. These can be financial or nonfinancial, such as the following:

- ▶ Daily sales and cash receipts
- ▶ Direct labor hours
- ▶ Bookings, backlog, and new sales leads
- ▶ Percent of capacity used or filled

Find the key numbers for whatever you need to develop a snapshot of events. Design a flash report that you can get every morning or every week that summarizes these numbers. This way you can see where you are and the direction you are going without waiting for financial statements.

Step Three: Speed up Your Monthly Closing Cycle

If you are not getting statements by the 10th business day each month, something is wrong. Aim for the sixth or seventh day, if possible. Close even sooner if faster turnaround is worth a slight loss in precision.

The slower the closing, the more stale the information. View slow monthly closings as a sign that your controller is spending time on financial statements that could be focused on management issues.

Step Four: Squeeze Cash out of Your Balance Sheet

Start by reviewing your accounts receivable again. Question each account that is past due and do follow-up. Develop a procedure for approving new customer accounts and steps to take during the collection process, including contacting customers before invoices are far past due. Try to clear up the oldest accounts, such as those over 90 days old. You may need to be flexible, accepting installment or partial payments. Make sure the person assigned to collections has the skills and time to be effective. In all cases, be persistent.

Reducing inventory levels will also generate cash; however, as discussed in Chapter 8, you may need to resolve operating problems before reducing stock. In the short term, review inventory for excess and obsolete items that can be sold off. You may also be able to change some buying patterns to reduce lead times or order quantities.

Other things you can try include looking at your accounts payable to see if payments can be stretched without hurting vendor relations. Consider leasing rather than buying assets or financing large expenditures, such as insurance. Use a lockbox to collect checks mailed by customers.

Step Five: Take a Walk-Through Tour of Your Inventory

Look for signs of underlying problems. How much do you have on hand? Is it balanced or do you have short supplies of some items and several months' worth of others? How long has it been sitting around? Are there items that are just gathering dust?

If you are a manufacturer, see if inventory is piled up in specific parts of your building. Are these areas bottlenecks? Are you overproducing certain finished goods or subassemblies? Make sure that valuable inventory is physically secured. Capture scrap as it is incurred and try to measure the cost of rework.

Step Six: Implement Basic Controls

Unless your business is very small, ensure that a separation of duties exists for transactions, especially cash disbursements. Make sure that cash accounts are reconciled monthly and that subsidiary ledgers for receivables, fixed assets, and payables are agreed to the general ledger balances. Ask for a listing of items in prepaid expenses, other assets, and accrued liabilities accounts.

Establish logs for sales orders, purchase orders, invoices, and shipments. Develop systems that don't allow transactions to slip through the cracks. For example, trace sales orders to shipments and shipments to invoices to make sure all orders are shipped and all shipments are billed.

Keeping logs will also allow you to summarize any open items, so you know your sales backlog and your exposure for outstanding purchase orders. If your accounting system tracks this information, periodically run reports on any open sales orders or purchase orders.

Add checks and balances or redundant processing in any place where errors can be costly. For most companies, errors are more costly than fraud. No matter how honest your employees, controls are still needed.

Step Seven: Audit Your Technology

If you are just starting out and haven't computerized your accounting, do so quickly with one of the leading low-end packages. If you are computerized, check for signs that you may not have the best fit, such as workarounds, custom programming, or unsatisfactory reporting. See if upgrades are available for your software and install as appropriate.

Where you use spreadsheets for key processing, insist on double-checks and clearly laid out assumptions. Make sure someone besides the person who built the sheet understands how it works. Don't worry if your company has not adopted the latest in technology, such as e-commerce or web-based accounting software. These areas continue to evolve. Consider outsourcing payroll rather than doing it yourself. Make sure all data files are backed up nightly.

Step Eight: Calculate Costs and Determine Target Profit Margins

Are you charging enough for your products and services? Your labor cost is much higher than wages alone. If you bill for services, understand your cost per hour after adding in benefits, down time, travel, and other direct expenditures. How much do you have to charge to cover overhead expenses such as space, support staff, and equipment?

If you sell goods, does your markup cover your handling, holding, and shrinkage costs? If you manufacture, can you trace production costs to units? Should other costs be added in, such as commissions, product development, and customer service? If so, what are your margins now?

Could you outsource the work more cheaply or, conversely, are there operations you could bring in house? If you can't calculate costs for all products, do it on a sample that includes your best-selling items.

If you have already calculated costs, but included allocations of overhead expenses, take a fresh look. Because the allocations can distort costs, looking at direct margins can give you a different perspective on the profitability of certain products.

Step Nine: Run the Numbers on New Projects

When new projects come along, run the numbers to see if they make sense. Ask managers to translate vague promises of cost savings or higher sales to hard figures. Make sure each project can be justified on its own and don't simply chase sales volume. Determine the net present value and set additional criteria, such as a hurdle rate or payback period, that investments must meet to be considered.

Running the numbers not only helps prevent costly mistakes, but also provides a basis for choosing among projects. As with projections, just running the numbers also helps clarify your thoughts about the project and may suggest improvements or alternatives.

Step 10: Clarify the Roles of Your Key Accounting and Finance People

Your key people could include a CFO, controller, accountant, bookkeeper, and outside CPA.

Start with your CPA firm. Ask yourself these questions:

▶ How do their fees compare with what other companies pay? Fees can range widely and are negotiable, so review them periodically.

▶ Is your CPA firm doing work that could be done more cheaply in house, like compiling monthly statements or processing payroll?

▶ Can you reduce their audit fees by doing more of the year-end work yourself? On the other hand, could the firm do more for you? CPAs are often very good sources of input on internal controls, systems, and—of course—taxes.

▶ What is the scope of the CPA's work? Make sure you are clear about whether you need an audit or a review and what work will be performed.

▶ Will you want your CPA to do work beyond taxes and auditing? This work might include evaluating internal controls, providing general consulting, or looking for fraud. Whatever you decide, make sure your engagement letter spells out the scope of work you agree on.

Next, evaluate your internal staff to see if their skills are well matched to what you need done. For example:

► Can they go beyond the mechanics of bookkeeping and accounting?

► Do you need to add someone with more management skills? If so, should that person be full-time or part-time?

Even more important, discuss with your employees the scope of their duties and how they should apportion their time. Your needs for support in cash management or budgeting may not match how they perceive their jobs. This is particularly true if they have primarily done just accounting. Let your controller know you would like to see less focus on financial statements and more on problems like planning or collections.

Final Words

The bottom line is that, whether you are a smaller business owner or a CEO of a large corporation, effective financial management is critical to the success, even survival of companies. A real payback comes with strong financial management when you move beyond doing just basic financial accounting. The payback comes from getting meaningful operating information, improving cash flow, doing planning, and having tight controls. Financial management, particularly in smaller companies, should be very hands-on and requires a strong working relationship between you and your financial managers.

Controllers and accountants who read this book may see how they can expand their roles and apply their financial know-how to operating issues. For nonfinancial business owners and managers, this book should provide the working knowledge needed to work with financial people and information. When you have succeeded at that, you have more than just a grasp of the numbers. You have control.

The bottom line is that, whether you are a smaller business owner or a CEO of a large corporation, effective financial management is critical to the success, even survival of companies.

Notes

1. Tom Peters, *Thriving on Chaos: A Management Revolution* (New York: Knopf, 1987), p. 402.

2. Tom Richman, "The Language of Business," *Inc.*. February 1990, p. 44.

3. Larry Crowley, "Look, Ma, I'm a Businessman," *Inc.*, July 1987, p. 97.

4. Robert Falconi (CFO, Planning Systems, McLean, VA), in a letter to the editor, *Inc.*, October 1993, pp. 25-26.

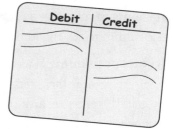

Appendix

Glossary

> He uses statistics as a drunken man uses lampposts for support
> rather than illumination.
>
> —Andrew Lang[1]

10K Annual financial statement required of publicly traded companies.

10Q Quarterly financial statement filing of publicly traded companies.

ABC classification Inventory management technique that ranks items as "A," "B," or "C" according to their relative importance. Each class of inventory is then controlled differently, with the greatest resources and effort being applied to the high-priority, A items.

Accelerated cost recovery system (ACRS) A method for depreciating assets. Permitted by the IRS, this method allows companies to record the greatest expense early in an asset's life.

Accounts payable Amounts owed for purchases made on credit.

Accounts receivable Amounts due from customers for merchandise or services delivered on credit.

---

[1] Quoted in *The Manager's Book of Quotations*, p. 390.

Accounts receivable/payable aging A listing of open (unpaid) invoices that also summarizes the items by how old (or past due) they are.

Accrual accounting Accounting method that records revenues and expenses when they are incurred, regardless of when cash is exchanged. The term "accrual" refers to any individual entry recording revenue or expense in the absence of a cash transaction.

Acquisition cost What was actually paid to purchase an asset. This is the basis of recording the value of an asset and includes all costs associated with the purchase, such as freight and sales tax.

ACRS See *Accelerated cost recovery system.*

Activity-based costing (ABC) A management accounting approach that attempts to trace all indirect costs, even those in so-called administrative departments, back to the products that generated them. ABC attempts to pinpoint actual cost drivers, rather than simply allocate costs.

Agings See *Accounts receivable / payable aging.*

AICPA American Institute of Certified Public Accountants.

Allocation Apportionment of expenses or revenues from one category to others, based on an estimate rather than direct measurement. A common example is allocating manufacturing overhead costs to departments or products, based on units produced or labor hours.

Amortization Similar to depreciation, involves assigning a portion of an intangible asset's cost to an accounting period. Items whose costs are amortized include capitalized software, start-up expenses, or a purchased patent.

APB Accounting Principles Board. A group that oversaw accounting standards from 1959 to 1973.

Application Service Provider (ASP) Vendor that hosts software on its own computers, which users access over a network or the Web. Users pay an annual or transactions-based fee rather than purchasing the software.

Asset An unexpired cost, something of future value to a business.

Audit Examination of a company's financial statements by an independent accountant. The result is a signed opinion of whether the statements fairly reflect the company's financial results and position. See also *Compilation* and *Review*.

Audit opinion Letter signed by an independent auditor and included with a published financial statement. The letter indicates the scope of work done, whether statements fairly present a company's financial position, and if the company has complied with GAAP.

Audit trail Cross-references that enable an accountant or auditor to trace accounting transactions back to source documents. A highly desirable internal control.

Bad debt reserve or write-off Losses on accounts receivable either estimated to become uncollectible (reserve) or specifically identified as such (write-off).

Balance sheet A financial statement that lists the assets, liabilities, and equity of a company at a specific point in time. A basic tenet of double-entry book-keeping is that total assets (what a business owns) must equal liabilities plus equity (how the assets are financed). In other words, the balance sheet must balance.

Bean counter Derogatory term for an accountant.

Big Four The four largest public accounting firms. These firms are international and significantly larger than the next tier of firms.

Bill of material (BOM) Listing of component parts and quantities that go into making a higher-level assembly.

Book value The value of an asset for accounting purposes. For assets for which depreciation is taken or reserves are booked, often expressed as a net book value (see *Contra accounts*). Book value of a company is the excess of assets over liabilities, which is equal to total owner's equity.

Bookkeeper An accountant, though the term generally refers to someone performing comprehensive yet basic tasks, such as recording transactions and simple statement preparation.

Bookkeeping Any form of basic accounting.

Bottom-up budget Process where managers propose spending for their departments and their inputs are added together to form the companywide budget. See *Top-down budget*.

Breakeven analysis A technique for analyzing how revenue, expenses, and profit vary with changes in sales volume. The classic form groups expenses as either variable with sales or fixed and frequently expresses the relationship in graphic form.

Breakeven point The sales level at which revenues equal fixed costs plus variable costs.

Budget A planned level of expenditures, usually at a fairly detailed level. A company may plan and maintain a budget on either an accrual or a cash basis.

Capital budget Spending plan for purchases of property, plant, and equipment. Usually budgeted separately from operating expenses.

Capital lease Long-term agreement that, because it most closely resembles the financing of an asset purchase, is treated as long-term debt rather than a rental.

Capital stock A balance sheet account that records the par value of shares sold. Amounts paid in excess of par are recorded to a separate account, such as paid-in capital.

Capitalization Recording of an expenditure as an asset.

Carrying costs Expenses, such as interest, maintenance and handling, incurred as a result of holding assets such as inventory and equipment.

Cash basis accounting An accounting method that does not record accruals; revenues and expenses are recorded when cash is exchanged.

Cash cow Mature, profitable business or product line that does not require substantial new investment. Not only are most of its earnings converted to cash, but the cash does not need to be put back into the business. The cash is available for payout to owners or reinvestment in growing ventures.

Cash flow The net receipt or disbursement of cash. Cash flow statements and projections express a business's results or plans in terms of cash in and out of the business, without adjusting for accrued revenues and expenses.

CEO Chief executive officer.

Certified management accountant (CMA) Accountant who has passed an exam sponsored by the Institute of Management Accountants and met experience and continuing education requirements. Emphasis is on management accounting.

Certified public accountant (CPA) Accountant who has met the criteria for certification, including passing an exam sponsored by the AICPA and meeting public accounting experience and continuing education requirements. Emphasis is on financial reporting, audits, and taxes.

CFO Chief financial officer. Generally distinct from a controller, due to responsibility for financing and treasury issues, not just accounting and control. Smaller companies may not employ a CFO or the CFO and controller may be the same person.

Chart of accounts Listing of accounts and account numbers to which transactions are posted.

Closing Most commonly, refers to monthly, quarterly, or annual procedures used to produce financial statements. Can also describe transferring the balance in one account to another.

CMA. See *Certified management accountant.*

COGS See *Cost of goods sold (COGS) or cost of sales (COS).*

Compilation Work performed, usually by a CPA, to assemble a company's prepared data into financial statements. No opinion is expressed about the accuracy of the figures.

Comptroller A somewhat outdated term that is synonymous with *controller*.

Confirmations Letters sent to a company's customers, investors, lawyers, and others by auditors to obtain independent verification of account balances and other financial information relevant to the financial statements.

Conservatism One of the underlying principles of GAAP, which says that, given a choice of accounting methods, the one that understates net income or book value is preferred.

Consolidation Combining the separate financial statements of subsidiary companies with that of the parent to form a single, combined statement. In a consolidation, transactions between the combined entities are adjusted for by *eliminating entries* (see *Elimination*).

Contra accounts Accounts, such as allowance for bad debt and inventory reserves, that partially offset a related account of the same type. Most commonly found with assets. The balance in the contra accounts is subtracted from the related account to arrive at a net value.

Contribution margin Difference between revenue and the associated variable (direct) costs. An important concept in breakeven analysis and last dollar pricing.

Controller The top accounting and control professional in a company.

COS See *Cost of goods sold (COGS) or cost of sales (COS)*.

Cost accounting An accounting discipline that focuses on unit costs of prducing goods or delivering services. Although some standard techniques exist, cost accounting does not need to conform to external standards and can be adapted to the needs of the individual company. See also *Management accounting*.

Cost center An entity defined for reporting purposes that is measured on costs and has control only over costs. Other reporting entities include revenue and profit centers.

Cost of goods sold (COGS) or cost of sales (COS) Costs directly associated with revenue, such as inventory sold, during a given accounting period. Usually includes all associated production and delivery costs whether direct or overhead.

CPA See *Certified public accountant*.

CPA exam Multiple-part exam, covering topics such as tax, auditing, theory, and business law that those seeking certification as a public accountant must pass.

Creative accounting Derogatory term for accounting methods that, while often permissible, stretch the rules or are used solely to bias the financial statements.

Credit In accounting terminology, the entry made to the right-hand side of a ledger. Increases in liabilities and revenues and decreases in assets all carry credit balances. Does not necessarily conform to nonaccounting uses of the term, such as selling to a customer on open account or reducing a balance owed.

Credit policy Guidelines that spell out how to decide which customers are sold on open account, the payments terms, the limits set on outstanding balances; and how to deal with delinquent accounts.

Current assets Assets that are cash or cash equivalents or convertible to cash within one year, in the normal course of business. Usually includes cash, accounts receivable, inventory, and prepaid expenses.

Current liabilities Obligations due within one year. Usually includes accounts payable, accrued expenses, and the portion of long-term obligations that is due within one year.

Current ratio Current assets divided by current liabilities. Used as a measure of a company's liquidity.

Cut-off The point in time at which a period ends and transactions become included or excluded for reporting purposes. A cut-off statement—perhaps sent to customers to verify a receivables balance—would exclude all transactions beyond a certain date.

Cycle count Periodic test counting of portions of inventory. Cycle counts are frequently done to monitor the accuracy of perpetual inventory systems. They may also substitute for a full-blown physical inventory, provided that all items are counted at some time and controls are strong.

Debit In accounting terminology, the entry made to the left-hand side of a ledger. Increases in assets and expenses and decreases in liabilities all carry debit balances.

Debt-to-equity ratio Used as a measure of leverage and ability to repay obligations, it is equal to total debt divided by equity. There is no consensus, however, on what is included in "debt" or how to treat items such as preferred stock or deferred income taxes.

Deferred revenue A liability that arises when a customer pays for goods or services before delivery is complete. One example would be one-year service contracts billed in advance. Under the accrual accounting method, revenue must be booked when the obligation is fulfilled, not when cash is received.

Depreciation Recognizing part of an asset's cost as an expense during each year of its useful life. Several acceptable depreciation schemes exist, including straight-line and various accelerated methods.

Direct costs Expenditures, such as labor and materials, that vary in direct proportion to units sold or produced.

Double-entry system A characteristic of modern accounting in which each transaction impacts the balances of at least two accounts and total debits equal total credits.

Earnings Used synonymously with *net income*.

Earnings per share (EPS) Total earnings divided by shares of common stock (and equivalents).

EBIT Earnings before interest and taxes. A popular measure for comparing the earnings power of companies, since it eliminates the impact of capital structure and effective tax rates, two nonoperating factors.

EBITDA Earnings before interest, taxes, depreciation, and amortization. Popular as a measure of a business' ability to generate working capital. Like EBIT, excludes nonoperating expenses, but also omits depreciation and amortization, which are noncash expenses.

Economic order quantity (EOQ) The optimum (lowest cost) amount of inventory to order at one time. Determined by considering factors such as quantity discounts, rate of turnover, and handling costs.

Elimination An accounting entry that is used in a consolidation. *Eliminating entries* reverse the impact of transactions between the related companies. For example, a sale by one subsidiary to another will not count as revenue on the income statement of the parent company.

EOQ See *Economic order quantity.*

Equity The sum of capital invested by shareholders, plus accumulated earnings retained by the business. Equal to a firm's *net book value* or *net worth*.

Expenditure Any purchase or spending, whether the resources acquired are consumed immediately or provide future value. Contrast with *expenses*.

Expenses Resources that have been consumed. The time for recognizing an expense in financial accounting is based on when the benefit is received and not when it is acquired or paid for.

Extraordinary item Expense or income that is considered unusual and unlikely to be repeated. To avoid distorting the financial statements, the financial impact is reported separately, on the income statement below such items as operating expenses, interest, and taxes.

Factoring A form of borrowing where receivables are sold to a third party.

Fair market value (FMV) Assessment of what an asset is worth in an arm's-length transaction. FMV is a common accounting method for valuing both assets and liabilities.

FASB Financial Accounting Standards Board. Independent board that issues financial accounting policies. Its rulings, which number more than 100, are referred to by number (such as FAS 33 - Accounting for Changing Price Levels).

FIFO First in, first out. Method of accounting for inventory and cost of sales in which the first items produced or purchased are assumed to be sold first. The advantage is that this method often reflects how companies actually handle stock; the drawback is that cost of sales in a given period may reflect outdated values.

Financial accounting or reporting The branch of accounting most commonly used for preparing financial statements and for reporting to investors. Required of public companies and, basically, the standard for most businesses.

Finished goods Inventory ready for sale.

Fiscal year (FY) 12-month period comprising a single year for financial reporting. Fiscal years that don't coincide with the calendar year are generally referred to by the year in which they end. For example, a fiscal year beginning July 1, 2004 and ending June 30, 2005 would be fiscal year 2005 (FY05). Fiscal months also may differ from calendar months, usually to have month-ends fall on a particular day of the week, such as Saturdays.

Fixed assets Assets assumed to be retained for at least one year. Generally includes equipment, furniture, buildings, and land.

Fixed cost Expense that is assumed not to vary with sales volume, or at least within an expected range of sales volume. An important concept in breakeven analysis and in distinguishing between gross and contribution margins.

Flexible budget A budget where variable expenses are projected as a percentage of sales. This allows a budget to be meaningful over a range of sales figures.

Float Difference between checks you have written and checks that have cleared your bank. Arises because time elapses from when you write a check to when it is received and deposited.

FMV See *Fair market value.*

Footnote Addendum to financial statements that expands on the figures to ensure full disclosure. Footnotes may explain accounting principles used, provide additional detail, or report on significant events that are not recognized for accounting purposes.

Forensic accounting Discipline focused specifically on detecting fraud.

Full disclosure Financial accounting principle that requires that all information meaningful to statement readers be included either in the numbers, in footnotes, or in a parenthetical disclosure.

Funds flow statement Name sometimes used for the *statement of cash flows.*

FY See *Fiscal year.*

FYE Fiscal year-end.

G&A General and administrative.

GAAP See *Generally accepted accounting principles.*

GAAS See *Generally accepted auditing standards.*

General ledger (G/L) The main set of accounts from which financial statements are produced and to which transactions are posted.

Generally accepted accounting principles (GAAP) Standards by which financial statements are prepared. (Pronounced "gap.")

Generally accepted auditing standards (GAAS) Standards by which audits of financial statements are conducted. (Pronounced "gas.")

Going concern assumption Accounting values presume that a firm will remain in business for at least one year from the date statements are prepared.

Goodwill Accounting term for amounts paid for assets over and above fair market value. Usually arises when a company purchases another business and pays a price higher than the value of the assets alone.

Gross margin or gross profit Sales less cost of sales, including both fixed and variable costs. Gross margin is expressed as a percentage of sales; gross profit is the dollar value.

Historic cost What was paid for an asset. The most common way of valuing noncash assets.

IMA See *Institute of Management Accountants*.

Income See *Net income*.

Income statement Also called a *profit-and-loss statement* (P&L). Financial report measuring a company's performance over a period of time. The business's revenue and expenses are netted to arrive at net income.

Indirect costs See *Overhead*.

Institute of Management Accountants (IMA) Association focused on issues of management and cost accounting. Formerly the National Association of Accountants.

Internal audit Audits focusing on internal controls and compliance with policies, often examining operations as well as accounting. Though some internal audits are performed by outside firms, many companies employ internal auditors who function apart from the accounting department. May examine operations as well as accounting.

Internal controls The system of checks and balances that catch and prevent errors from occurring in everyday transaction processing.

Internal rate of return (IRR) Earnings on a project, expressed as an annual compounded percentage return on investment. Related to *net present value*, which equals zero when the discount rate is equal to the IRR.

Inventory Goods purchased or manufactured by a company and held for production or sale. Often subdivided on financial statements into raw materials, work-in-process, and finished goods.

Inventory turn Measurement of rate at which inventory moves through a business, number of times inventory turns over during one year. Generally calculated by dividing annual inventory usage by average (or current) inventory level. See *Turnover ratio*.

IRR See *Internal rate of return*.

JIT See *Just-in-time*.

Job costing Method of tracking costs by project or production run rather than by individual unit of product.

Joint-product costs Costs for a single production process that yields two or more different products. These costs can't be directly traced to a product and must be allocated.

Journal entry Any accounting entry made to the general ledger.

Just-in-time (JIT) Inventory and production control philosophy that emphasizes reducing on-hand inventory and improving quality by "doing it right the first time," making manufacturing "demand-pulled," and reducing setup times.

Kanban Visual system that indicates reorder points for materials or products. Often seen in conjunction with JIT.

Last dollar costing Analytic approach that focuses on incremental costs when evaluating new products or pricing decisions.

Lead time Expected time between when an item is ordered from a supplier or put into production and when it is received or completed.

Learning curve In financial terms, reduced costs as experience in producing a product accumulates. A significant factor in deciding how to price and whether to launch a new product.

Leverage Relationship between debt and equity used to finance a company. A highly leveraged company has relatively high levels of debt compared with equity.

Liability An obligation of a company.

LIFO Last in, first out. Accounting method for inventory and cost of sales in which the last items produced or purchased are assumed to be sold first. Advantage is that cost of sales in a period closely matches current period values; drawback is that this method values inventory at old cost levels.

Liquidity Ability of a company to generate cash in a timely manner to meet its obligations. Often measured by *quick ratio* or *current ratio*.

Lower of cost or market Way of valuing many assets for financial reporting. Applies where assets cannot be written up if market value exceeds cost, but must be written down if the reverse is true.

Management accounting This practice focuses on information needed by internal managers and encompasses the field of cost accounting. Though some standard techniques exist, management accounting does not need to conform to external standards and can be adapted to the needs of the individual company. Unlike financial reporting, management accounting can also include nonmonetary measures such as quality or productivity.

Management letter Report written to management by independent auditors discussing weaknesses in the accounting systems and any operating problems noted in the course of their work.

Marginal cost Incremental cost of producing one additional item.

Marginal revenue Incremental revenue from selling one additional item. In economic theory, a company should continue to expand as long as marginal revenue exceeds marginal cost.

Market value What would be paid for an asset in an arm's-length transaction. A key concept in valuing assets for financial reporting. See also *Lower of cost or market*.

Materiality Measure by which decisions are made on what is disclosed in financial statements and how extensive audit tests must be. The key factor is whether the opinion of a reader of the statements would be affected by the added information.

MRP Materials resource planning. A technique that calculates materials, plant resources, and scheduling needed to meet production targets.

MRP II Manufacturing resource planning. A technique that calculates materials, plant resources, and scheduling needed to meet production targets.

Net book value See *Book value* and *Contra accounts*.

Net income The earnings of a company over a period of time. What is left after subtracting expenses from revenues. Also known as *net profit* or *net loss*.

Net present value (NPV) A measure, in current dollars, of a project's value. Future income and expenses are discounted to adjust for the time value of money and totaled. Theoretically, NPV is the best method for evaluating projects.

Nonoperating income or expense Items not related to the ongoing operations of a company. Interest income and expense, one-time events, and taxes are examples of nonoperating items.

NPV See *Net present value.*

Off-balance sheet financing Debt and similar obligations that don't have to be recorded as liabilities under GAAP. One example is a lease that qualifies for treatment as a rental rather than a capital lease. A means for a company to leverage itself without showing the obligation on its balance sheet, though certain arrangements need to be disclosed in footnotes, thus improving measures of leverage and financial strength.

Operating income Operating income equals revenues, less cost of sales and all expenses of normal operations. Much like EBIT, operating income focuses on the earnings of the core business.

Opportunity costs Earnings that might have resulted if cash or other resources had been employed elsewhere. Theoretically, a better measure of cost than simply cash expended. See also *Sunk costs.*

Overhead Expenses incurred in operating a business that are not directly related to the manufacture of a product or delivery of a service.

Owner's equity See *Equity.*

P&L Profit-and-loss statement. See *Income statement.*

Paid-in capital Amount paid by investors for stock over and above its par value.

Par value Stated value of stock. Usually a minimal value—such as $0.01 (one cent)—with no relation to the market value of the shares.

Payables See *Accounts payable.*

Payback Simplistic method of evaluating projects that calculates the period of time needed to recoup the initial investment.

P/E See *Price-to-earnings ratio.*

Period expenses Expenses recorded in the period they occur. Examples include most administrative and selling expenses. R&D and advertising expenditures are good examples of activities that benefit future periods but must be treated as period expenses according to GAAP.

Periodic inventory Calculation of cost of sales for inventory in aggregate; contrast with *perpetual inventory*. Standard formula is that cost of sales equals beginning inventory, plus purchases, minus ending inventory.

Perpetual inventory Tracking on-hand quantities and costs on a current, item by item basis.

Physical inventory The counting of all inventory on hand.

Posting The process of recording entries in the general ledger, either via journal entries or from subsidiary journals, such as accounts payable and accounts receivable. Often, the input of entries is a separate process from posting, so that their accuracy can be reviewed before permanent changes are made to the general ledger accounts.

PPV See *Purchase price variance*.

Prepaid expenses Services, goods, and intangibles paid for before the period in which they are received or provide benefit. Accounted for as assets until consumed.

Present value See *Net present value*.

Price-to-earnings ratio (P/E) Market value of a company's stock divided by the number of shares (and equivalents) outstanding.

Process costing Tracking production costs by department or procedure and then allocating to units. Used primarily in continuous, high-volume operations.

Profit See *Net income*.

Profit-and-loss statement (P&L) See *Income statement*.

Profit center Department evaluated, for management accounting purposes, by both revenue and expenses generated.

Public companies Companies whose stock is publicly traded. In addition to the difference in ownership structure, financial disclosure requirements are stricter for public companies than for privately owned ones.

Purchase price variance (PPV) Difference between the standard purchase price of an item and the actual price paid.

Qualified opinion A negative audit opinion that expresses the auditor's concern over the fairness of the statements. Reasons might include doubts over the future survival of a company, lack of conformity to GAAP, or uncertainty arising from a major, unresolved lawsuit.

Quick ratio Current assets, excluding inventory and prepaid expenses, divided by current liabilities. Like the *current ratio*, a measure of liquidity.

Ratios Comparisons of financial statement elements, such as *price-to-earnings ratio* and *return on assets*. Often used for financial statement analysis, they are not only very simplistic, but can be severely misleading due to accounting principles and practices.

Raw materials Inventory category for materials that are inputs for manufacturing.

Realization or recognition Recording an income or expense item in a given period. This is independent of when cash is actually exchanged and acknowledges that delivery of goods or services is essentially complete.

Receivables See *Accounts receivable*.

Reconciliation The process of agreeing internal balances to a detailed listing or independent source. The most common example is balancing a checkbook, which agrees the checkbook register to a bank statement.

Register An itemized listing that supports or is posted to a general ledger account. Examples include a listing of all invoices (posted to sales) or checks written (posted to various expense accounts) for a period.

Reserve An estimate of anticipated losses recorded as an expense, even though specific losses have not been identified. Examples include allowances for bad debt or potential inventory write-downs. Usually based on experience, such as the percentage of past due receivables that become uncollectible.

Return on assets (ROA) Net income divided by total assets. Used to measure how efficiently assets are employed.

Return on equity (ROE) or return on investment (ROI) Net income divided by owner's equity. Used as a measure of return on funds invested in the business.

Reversing entry An accrual entry booked in one month and reversed the next. Used, for example, when an expense is incurred in one month, but routine processing of the invoice occurs the following month. The reversal and the routine entry offset each year, leaving the expense recorded in the correct period.

Review An examination of a company's financial statements by independent auditors that is less rigorous and less expensive than an audit. The review results in an opinion stating whether the auditors are aware of any material modifications that should be made.

ROA See *Return on assets.*

ROE See *Return on equity or return on investment.*

ROI See *Return on equity or return on investment.*

Rolling budget or plan Form of planning that continuously updates budgets and projections so that they always look out a uniform length of time. For example, a rolling budget, revised three months into a year, would update the remaining nine months of the existing plan plus an additional three months, so that it remained a year-long plan.

Safety stock Inventory held over and above minimum requirements to guard against unexpected shortages.

Sarbanes-Oxley (SOX) Legislation passed in 2002 in response to accounting excesses. It applies only to public companies. Key provisions include prohibiting auditors from performing certain nonreview activities for their clients, requiring CFOs and CEOs to certify financial statements, and requiring audit committee members to be independent directors.

SEC Securities and Exchange Commission. Body that oversees reporting requirements of all public companies.

Separation of duties An internal control by which responsibility for processing parts of a transaction is assigned to two or more people. This increases the likelihood that errors or fraud will be routinely detected.

Shareholder equity See *Equity.*

Shrinkage Difference between inventory per the accounting records and the value determined by a physical inventory.

Standard cost A target or average cost that may be used to value inventory or as a basis for comparing actual costs.

Statement of cash flows Financial report showing cash provided and used by a company. Required by GAAP, in addition to an income statement and a balance sheet, for published financial statements.

Straight-line method The simplest form of depreciation or amortization, where an equal expense is recorded in each year of an asset's useful life.

Sunk costs Unrecoverable, prior expenditures on a project. These should be ignored when evaluating future decisions.

T-account Basic way of illustrating the impact of a series of accounting entries used in teaching or troubleshooting accounting. The "T" shape allows the name of an account to go above the horizontal line; debit entries go to the left of the vertical line and credits to the right.

Top-down budget Process where top management dictates company-wide spending targets and then asks managers to submit department budgets that are within these targets. See *Bottom-up budget*.

Turn See *Inventory turn*.

Turnover ratio Ratio of annual cost of sales to on-hand inventory. Common rule-of-thumb measurement used to determine inventory management efficiency.

Unqualified opinion A clean audit opinion that states that the financial statements are presented fairly and in conformity with GAAP.

Value added Difference between what a company pays for items and what they are worth after the company has converted or redistributed the goods.

Variable cost or expense An expense, such as direct labor, that changes in proportion to increases or decreases in sales or production volumes.

Variance Difference between actual revenues, expenditures, or productivity and a budgeted or standard target. Usually expressed as favorable or unfavorable.

Work-in-process (WIP) Inventory in a manufacturing process that is in some stage of production. Also known as *work-in-progress*.

Working capital The net of current assets and current liabilities. Net liquid assets of a company.

Write-off An entry reducing the book value of an asset, perhaps for obsolescence or uncollectability.

Index

A

ABC coding, 159
Accelerated closings, 75
Accelerated depreciation, 49, 92
Accountants. *See also* Certified public
  accountants
  certification, 21–22, 25
  examination services, 25–29
  misunderstandings about, 15–16
  overview of role, 4–5
  stereotypes, 116–118
Accounting
  certification programs, 21–22, 25
  controllership vs., 8, 114–118
  double-entry, 41–43
  governing bodies for, 19–21
  importance to small business, 4
  information gap, 5–7
  misunderstandings about, 15–16
  overview of types, 16–19
  recordable entries, 43–46
  staff positions, 4–5
Accounting scandals. *See* Scandals
Accounting software. *See also* Software
  charts of accounts in, 70
  forecasting features, 209
  high-end, 262
  inventory management features, 157
  low-end, 260–261
  organization of, 67
  selection criteria, 264–266
  tracking receivables with, 198
  variety of offerings, 260–263
Account numbers, 69–70, 84–86
Accounts receivable. *See also* Collections
  auditing, 80
  managing, 123, 192–197, 294
  setting terms, 189–192
  tracking in general ledger, 66–67
  as working capital, 176
ACCPAC, 261
Accrual accounting, 17
Accruals, journal entries for, 73–74
Accumulated depreciation account, 49
Acquisitions, accounting manipulations,
  103–104
Activity-based costing, 144–145
Actual cost, 168
Adelphia, 109
Administration, controller's responsibilities,
  124–125
Administrative controls, 158
Adverse audit opinions, 27
Advertising expenses, 47, 55, 97
Allocation of costs. *See also* Overhead costs
  defined, 134
  as management decision, 233
  to profit centers, 232–233
  reevaluating, 296
  simplistic, 138–139, 141–142
American Accounting Association (AAA), 21
American Institute of Certified Public
  Accountants (AICPA), 20
Amortization, 49
Analog Devices, Inc., 207
Analysis
  breakeven, 250–252, 256–258
  common pitfalls, 137–143
  controller's role, 122–123
  of inventory levels, 153–155
  required in project evaluation, 239–240
Annual budgets. *See* Budgeting

Application service providers, 181, 262, 267–268
Asset management, 123–124
Assets
  in double-entry bookkeeping, 42
  presentation on balance sheet, 38
  recognition and valuation, 46–50, 89–90, 91–93
Association of Certified Fraud Examiners, 28
Assumptions
  communicating to line managers, 227–228
  in forecasting models, 209–210, 219
  about inflation, 243
Attainable budgets, 230
Attainable standards, 135, 136
Attorneys, for collection efforts, 197
Audits
  benefits to companies, 26
  conflicts of interest with, 22–23, 24
  elements of, 26–28, 79–83
  as internal controls, 281–282
  of internal controls, 285
  misunderstandings about, 16
  sample opinions, 33–35
Audit trails, 281–282
Authority, delegating for transactions, 279–280
Automated inventory systems, 270
Automatic stays, 195
Automation, impact on cost allocations, 141–142

B
Backups, for computer systems, 284
Bahr, C. Charles, 7
Balanced inventories, 155
Balance sheets
  elements of, 37–38, 46–52
  manipulating, 105–106
  in order of presentation, 12
  projected, 210–211, 221
  samples, 58–59, 221
  shortcomings for management, 89–95
Bankruptcies, 195–196
Banks, 185, 207
Bank statements, reconciling, 277

Bar codes, 270
Baseball analogy, 128–129
BDO Seidman, 23
Ben & Jerry's Homemade, Inc., 204
Benefits (employee), 71–72, 95
"Big bath" write-offs, 102–103
Big Four accounting firms, 22
Bills of materials, 156, 157
Bonuses, 231
Bookkeepers, 4–5
Bookkeeping, double-entry, 41–43
Book value
  defined, 52
  of inventory, 170–171
  market value vs., 92–93
Bottlenecks, 163–164
Bottom-up budgets, 226
Breakeven analysis, 250–252, 256–258
Brodsky, Norm, 132
Budget games, 231
Budgeting. *See also* Planning
  common misperceptions, 223–224
  control functions, 229–233
  controller's role, 121–122
  customizing options, 233–237
  flexible, 145–147, 234
  forecasting vs., 178–179, 208
  planning functions, 224–229, 237
  for software, 265–266
Bula Mines, 244
Business acquisitions, accounting manipulations, 103–104
Business failures, 5–7
Business owners, inadequate financial understanding, 7–9
Business plans
  elements of, 208, 214, 216–218
  failure to follow, 204
Business valuation, 246–247

C
Capacity utilization measures, 131
Capital budgets, 236–237. *See also* Project evaluation
Capital lease payments, 18, 94. *See also* Lease arrangements

Cash-based accounting, 17
Cash flow
  crisis management, 184–186
  forecasting, 122, 178–179, 187, 208
  importance to businesses, 100, 173–174
  maximizing, 180–184, 294
  in net present value calculations, 241–242,
    243–244, 254
  profits vs., 174–178
  short-term measures of, 90
Cash flow statements. *See* Statement of cash
  flows
Cash management strategies
  long-term, 180–181
  short-term, 180, 184–185
CEOs, 7–9. *See also* Top management
Certification, 21–22, 25
Certified public accountants. *See also*
    Accountants
  choosing firms, 22–25
  controllers as, 126
  efforts to manipulate, 100–101
  evaluating, 296–297
  examination services, 25–29
  firms, small, 23–24
  impact of scandals on, 29–30
  negotiating services, 29
  overview of role, 5, 9
  professional requirements, 21
Change, confronting by planning, 205
Channel stuffing, 104
Chapter 7 bankruptcy, 196
Chapter 11 bankruptcy, 196
Chapter 13 bankruptcy, 195–196
Chart of accounts
  defining, 68, 69–71
  relation to general ledger, 66
  samples, 84–86
Checkbooks, internal controls compared to,
  273–275
Checkbook software, 260, 274
Check registers, 67, 273–274
Chief executive officers (CEOs), 7–9. *See*
  also Top management
Chief financial officers (CFOs), 5

Child accounts, 69–70
Clifton Gunderson, 23
Closings, 72–78, 293
Closing schedules, 74–75
Coding expenses, 68–69
Cohen, Ben, 204
Collateral, 183
Collection agencies, 197
Collections. *See also* Accounts receivable
  inadequate efforts, 6
  involving sales force, 190–191
  policies and recordkeeping, 197–200
  strategies, 192–197
Commissions, 190–191
Commitment to inventory management, 158
Communications, benefit of planning for, 207
Companies, valuation of, 246–247
Compensation
  linking to budgets, 224, 231
  modeling, 210
  sales commissions, 190–191
Compilations, 29
Computers. *See also* Software
  errors and, 270–271, 284–285
  evaluating systems, 295
  importance to accounting, 259–260
  system controls, 276, 284–285
Confirmation letters, 80
Conflicts of interest, 22–23, 24
Conservatism in accounting, 44, 117
Consistency, importance to accounting, 43
Consolidated statements, 56–57
Contingent liabilities, 179
Contra accounts, 49
Contribution margin, 134, 250–252, 257
Control, planning versus, 215–216, 224
Controllers
  benefits to companies, 13, 291–292
  budgeting role, 121–122, 227, 228, 235–236
  common shortcomings of, 9–10
  financial accounting role, 10–12
  major job requirements, 118–127, 215
  overview of role, 5, 7–9, 114–118
Control, internal. *See* Internal controls
Control numbers, 278–279

Conversion issues, software, 266–267
Cost accounting. *See* Management accounting
Cost Accounting Standards Board (CASB), 20
Cost allocations. *See* Allocation of costs
Cost control, 123
Cost of sales, 39, 97
Cost-per-unit breakeven analysis, 250–252, 256–257
Covenants with loans, 183
Cox, Jeff, 163
CPAs. *See* Certified public accountants
Creative accounting, 100–101
Credit insurance, 196–197
Credit limits, 191–192
Credit, lines of, 183
Credit policies, 189–192
Credits, in double-entry bookkeeping, 42–43
Crisis management, 184–186, 206
Current assets and liabilities, 38
Current ratio, 90
Current year forecasts, 122, 208, 209–213, 292–293
Customizing budgets, 233–237
Custom software, 262–263
Cutoffs, for closings, 73, 76–77
Cycle counts, 156

D

Daily backups, 284
Data collection software, 270
Data conversion, 266
Data entry timing issues, 76–77
Day-to-day cutoffs, 76–77
Debits, 42–43
Debt, 62, 182, 183–184
Decentralized businesses, controls for, 283
Decision support, 120–121
Delegating authority for transactions, 279–280
Delinquencies. *See* Collections
Deloitte & Touche, 22
Depreciation, 48–49, 92, 237
Direct costs, 133, 170
Direct margin, 134
Discounted payback, 245
Discount rates
  inflation assumptions and, 243–244

selecting, 244–245, 247, 254
Discounts, early payment, 191
Discretionary expense centers, 232
Dividends, 52
Documenting collection efforts, 193–194, 199
Donations and grants, 19
Down time, 140–141
Drucker, Peter, 140
Dun & Bradstreet, 189
Duties, separation of, 275–276

E

Early payment discounts, 191
Earnings before interest and taxes, 39, 98
Earnings before interest, taxes, depreciation, and amortization, 39, 98
Earnings per share, 39, 99
Ease of use vs. features, 265
Economic order quantities, 158–159
Economic value added, 132–133
Economies of scale, 141
Edwards, Emmett D., 16
Efficiency, 131, 272
Employee benefits, 71–72, 95
Employees, sharing financial data with, 78
Encumbrance accounting, 19
Engagement letters, 29
Engineered standards, 135, 136
Enrolled agents, 21, 22
Enron scandal, 94, 108
Entrepreneur Magazine's Creating a Successful Business Plan, 216
Entrepreneurs, inadequate financial understanding, 7–9
Equipment budgeting, 236–237
Equipment valuation, 92
Equity
  in double-entry bookkeeping, 42
  financing cash flow, 182–183
  presentation on balance sheet, 38
  recognition and valuation, 52
Ernst & Young, 22, 29
Errors. *See also* Internal controls
  computer-related, 270–271, 284–285
  in financial statements, 56, 74, 76–77
  fraud vs., 124, 273

inventory variance due to, 156
in projections, 211–212
Estimating expenses, 74
Events, non-accounting, 45
Excess inventory, 164, 171–172
Expense reports, 283
Expenses
  accruals for, 73–74
  coding, 68–69
  matching principle, 43, 97
  modeling for budgets, 228
  recognition and valuation, 55–56
  responsibility for, 230–231
  timing issues, 179
Export sales, 64

F

Factoring companies, 196
Features vs. ease of use, 265
Feedback, as benefit of planning, 206
Fieldwork by auditors, 81–82
Financial accounting. *See also* Generally
  accepted accounting principles (GAAP)
  dominance of, 10–12, 115–116
  elements of, 17–18
  summary of shortcomings, 87–88
Financial Accounting Standards Board
  (FASB), 20
Financial management. *See also* Management
  accounting
  accounting skills vs., 31
  overview of benefits, 290–292
  owners' lack of expertise, 7–9
  ten-step plan, 292–297
Financial Management Association
  International (FMA), 21
Financial statements. *See also* Balance sheets;
  Generally accepted accounting principles
  (GAAP); Income statements; Statement of
  cash flows
  balance sheet elements, 37–38, 46–52
  controller's role in preparing, 119–120
  errors and consolidations, 56–57, 74, 76–77
  income statement elements, 38–39, 53–56
  overview, 17, 37–40
  projected, 209, 219–221

reasons for importance, 11–12
  samples, 58–64, 219–221
  shortcomings, 115–116
  tips for interpreting, 57–58
Financing for cash flow, 182–184
First in, first out (FIFO) method, 91, 95–96,
  167
Fiscal months, 77–78
Fiscal years, 38–39, 77–78
Fixed asset registers, 277
Fixed costs, 250–252, 256–258. *See also*
  Overhead costs
Flash reports, 132, 293
Flexible budgets, 145–147, 234
Footnotes in financial statements, 40, 45,
  62–64
Forecasting. *See* Planning
Forensic accountants, 28, 285
Fraud
  errors vs., 124, 273
  internal controls against, 124
  not addressed in audits, 28, 30, 285
Friedman, Ron, 132
Full cost, 134, 170
Full disclosure, 44
Future deliverables, 54
Future service obligations, 54
Future value, 46. *See also* Assets

G

GAAP. *See* Generally accepted accounting
  principles (GAAP)
Geneen, Harold, 290
General ledger
  audit trails for entries, 282
  elements of, 66–72
  reconciliations, 277–278
Generally accepted accounting principles
  (GAAP)
  advertising and R&D expenses, 47, 55, 97
  balance sheet shortcomings, 89–95
  basic approach to inventories, 48, 49–50, 89
  budget management and, 233
  correcting errors, 56
  income statement shortcomings, 95–100
  for lease arrangements, 18, 51, 93–94

Generally accepted accounting principles
(GAAP) (continued)
limitations for management, 31, 87–88,
107, 137–138
manipulation and, 100–106
rise in importance, 11–12
tax accounting vs., 18
Gimmickry, 101–106
Global Crossing, 108
The Goal: Excellence in Manufacturing,
163–164
Goldratt, Eli, 163
Goodwill, 92–93, 103
Governing bodies, 19–21
Governments, 19, 191–192
Grant Thornton, 23
The Great Game of Business, 78
Great Plains, 261
Greenfield, Jerry, 204
Gross margin, 134
Gross profit, 39

H
Hedging on budgets, 230
Historical cost, 43, 47–48, 89
Historical performance standards, 135, 136
Household budgets, 225
Hurdle rates, 246, 249

I
IBM, 105–106
Incentives
contingent on collections, 190–191
linking to budgets, 224, 231, 235
Income statements
elements of, 38–39
limitations for management, 95–100
in order of presentation, 12
samples, 60, 220
Income taxes
account setup for, 71
reducing reported income for, 101–102
reporting on balance sheets, 95
sample notes about, 63–64
Incremental cash flows, 254
Incremental costs, 135

Indirect costs. See Overhead costs
Industry practices, importance to accounting,
44
Industry-specific software, 262–263
Inflation assumptions, 243–244
Information gap, 5–7
Institute of Certified Management
Accountants (ICMA), 21
Institute of Management Accounting (IMA),
21, 22
Intangibles, 89, 92–93
Internal Control Questionnaire for Cash
Disbursements, 286–288
Internal controls. See also Errors
auditing, 285
basic functions, 272–273
cash disbursements, questionnaire, 286–288
for computer systems, 276, 284–285
controller's role, 124
costs vs. benefits, 286
delegating authority, 279–280
implementing, 294–295
maintaining, 280–283
major concepts, 275–279
Internal rate of return (IRR), 246–247
Internal Revenue Service (IRS), 20, 22
Internet-based accounting services, 267–268
Inventories
account setup for, 71
auditing, 81
as collateral, 183
GAAP shortcomings, 89, 91, 95–96
interpreting reports on, 58
reserves and write-downs, 18, 48, 91
sample notes about, 62
valuation methods, 48, 49–50, 89, 95–96,
166–171
as working capital, 176
Inventory management
analyzing levels, 153–155, 294
assessing, 152–153
controller's role, 124
converting excess inventory, 164
physical controls, 157, 276
shrinkage, 155–157

tools and techniques, 157–164
tracking inventory, 67, 165–166, 270
Investment decisions, 236–237. *See also*
Project evaluation
Investors
additional funding halted by, 185
communicating plans to, 207, 213, 217–218
GAAP directed at, 11, 87, 88
to generate cash, 182–183
maintaining confidence of, 291
Invoice control numbers, 279
Invoicing procedures, 198
IRR (internal rate of return), 246–247
IRS (Internal Revenue Service), 20, 22

J

Job costing, 135
Job descriptions for controllers, 118–127
Johnson, H. Thomas, 130, 139
Joint-product costs, 134
Journal entries, 42–43, 72, 73–74
Just-in-time inventories, 161–162

K

Kanban systems, 163
Kaplan, Robert, 130, 139
Key indicators, 131–133, 136–137, 293
KPMG, 22

L

Labor costs, 141–142, 146–147
Land values, 92
Language barriers, accounting vs. management, 12–13
Last-dollar pricing, 135, 143–144
Last in, first out (LIFO) method, 91, 96, 167
Late payment fees, 192
Laventhol & Horwath, 29
Lawsuits against CPA firms, 29–30
Lawyers, for collection efforts, 197
Lead times, 161
Learning curves, 144
Lease arrangements
accounting difficulties, 51, 93–94
differing accounting treatments, 18
sample notes about, 62–63
Letters, collection, 193, 194

Levitt, Arthur, 101
Liabilities
auditing, 80–81
in double-entry bookkeeping, 42
presentation on balance sheet, 38
recognition and valuation, 50–51, 89, 93–95
year-end examination, 83
Lines of credit, 183
Liquidity measures, 90. *See also* Cash flow
Loans, with covenants, 183
Logs, 278–279, 294–295
Long-term cash management strategies, 180–181
Long-term plans
aligning budgets with, 227–229
functions of, 121–122, 208
using, 213–214
Long-term ventures, recognizing revenues and expenses, 53
Lotus 1-2-3, 259, 268

M

Maintenance, preventive, 162
Maintenance fees, software, 265
Management. *See* Top management
Management accounting
analysis pitfalls, 137–143
baseball analogy, 128–129
certification programs, 21–22
controller's role, 120–121
elements of, 18–19
financial accounting vs., 11, 87–88, 130–133, 137–138
influence on behavior, 147
information needs, 129
traditional methods, 133–137
variable and flexible costs, 143–147
Management letters, 82
Manufacturing resource planning, 160
MAS90, 261
Master schedules, 160
Matching revenues and expenses, 43, 97
Material differences in audits, 28
Materiality of disclosures, 44
Materials resource planning, 159–160, 161
Microsoft Money, 260

Midrange accounting software, 261–262
Min-max targets, 159
Monitoring, controller's role, 122–123
Months, fiscal, 77–78
Morale measures, 131
Moss Adams, 23
Multiple scenarios, 214, 218, 245
M.Y.O.B., 260

N

National Association of Enrolled Agents
    (NAEA), 21
National Society of Accountants (NSA), 21
Navision, 261
Negotiating CPA services, 29
Net income, 39, 175, 177
Net present value, 240–247
Net worth, 52
Newman's Own, Inc., 204
Nominal interest rates, 243–244
Non-accounting events, 45
Nonclassic breakeven analysis, 252, 253
Noncurrent assets and liabilities, 38, 91–93
Nonoperating expenses, 39
Nonoperating income, 39
Nonprofit accounting, 19
Nonrecurring expenses, 98–99
Numbering, for control, 278–279
Numbering accounts, 69–70, 84–86

O

Objectivity, 44
Obsolete plans, 212
Off-balance-sheet financing, 94, 108, 109
Office software, overextending, 263–264
Olsen, Ken, 268–269
Ombudsmen, controllers as, 125
One-time reports, 120
One-year projections, 122, 208, 209–213,
    292–293
On-time delivery targets, 154
Open book management, 78
Operating expenses, 39
Operating income, 39, 98–99
Operating leases, 94
Operating ratios, 136–137

Opportunity cost, 135, 248–249
Optimism in business plans, 218
Oracle, 262
Order entry systems, 6
Orders, formal authorizations for, 279–280
"Out-of-11" settlements, 196
Outsourcing, 141–142, 181
Overhead costs. *See also* Allocation of costs
    activity-based costing and, 145
    allocating, 170, 296
    controlling, 123, 139–140
    covering, 143–144
    defined, 134
    misallocating, 139, 141–142
Overstatements, as audit targets, 28, 80
Owners, inadequate financial understanding,
    7–9
Owners' compensation, 99
Owner's equity, 38, 52. *See also* Equity

P

Parent accounts, 70
Partially funded benefit plans, 95
Par value, 52
Patents, 93
Payables, 80, 180
Payback method, 245–246
Payment terms, setting, 191–192
Payroll modeling, 210
Payroll software, 269
Peachtree, 260, 261
Pension plans, 95
PeopleSoft, 262
Percentage-of-sales breakeven analysis,
    257–258
Performance, linking to budgets, 224,
    230–231, 235
Period expenses, 55
Periodic method of tracking inventory,
    165–166
Perpetual method of tracking inventory, 165
Personal checkbooks, 273–275
Personality traits, 116–117
Peters, Tom, 289
Physical controls, 157, 276, 284

Planning. *See also* Budgeting
    budgeting as, 224–229, 237
    cash flow forecasting, 122, 178–179, 187,
       208
    controller's role, 121–122, 215
    control vs., 215–216
    failure to follow, 203–204
    learning from, 214–215
    products of, 208
    rationale for, 204–207
    twelve-month forecasting models, 122,
       208, 209–213, 292–293
"Pooling" method, 103–104
Posting accounts, 69–70
Precision, overemphasizing, 116–117, 142–143
Present value, 241
Preventive maintenance, 162
PricewaterhouseCoopers, 22, 29
Private companies, reporting practices for, 40
Private Securities Litigation Reform Act of
    1995, 30
Product clutter, 140–141
Productivity measures, 131
Professional organizations, 20–21
Profit-and-loss statements. *See* Income state-
    ments
Profit centers, 232
Profits
    cash flow vs., 174–178
    defining, 232–233
    as imperfect measure, 147
    overemphasizing, 99–100
    presentation on income statement, 39
    relation to sales, 167–168
    setting targets, 295–296
Pro forma earnings, 98–99
Project evaluation
    breakeven analysis, 250–252, 256–258
    implementing, 296
    net present value, 240–247, 254–256
    opportunity cost, 248–249
    overview, 239–240
    payback method and IRR, 245–247
Projections, 12-month, 122, 208, 209–213,
    292–293. *See also* Planning

Project tracking, 208
Public Company Accounting Oversight
    Board, 20
Publicly owned companies, reporting require-
    ments, 40
Purchase orders, 69, 280
Purchases, tracking, 67, 69

Q
Qualifications of accountants, 25
Qualified audit opinions, 27, 34
Quality measures, 131
QuickBooks, 260, 269, 270
QuickBooks Enterprise Solutions, 261
Quicken, 260
Quick ratio, 90
Quotas, 230

R
Radio frequency I.D. sensors, 270
Ratios
    for management accounting, 136–137
    sales, 146
    shortcomings, 90, 99
Raw materials, excess, 164
Receivables. *See* Accounts receivable
Reconciliations, 277–278
Recording entries, 43–46
References, credit, 190
Refinancing to show profit, 105
Remote access software, 270
Rental arrangements, 51, 93–94. *See also*
    Lease arrangements
Reorder points, 158–159
Research and development expenses
    GAAP requirements, 47, 55, 97
    manipulating for acquisitions, 103–104
Reserves
    estimation challenges, 91
    GAAP requirements, 18, 48
    manipulating, 102
    use in inventory management, 168–169
Residual value, 254
Responsibility for expenses, assigning,
    230–231, 279–280
Retained earnings, recording as equity, 52

Return authorizations, 280
Return on assets (ROA), 99
Return on investment (ROI), 99
Revenue centers, 232
Revenues
    matching principle, 43, 97
    recognition and valuation, 53–54, 104, 106
    when recorded, 43, 45
Reversing entries, 73
Reviews, 28–29, 35
Risk, net present value and, 244–245, 254
Roha, Ronaleen, 213
Rolling budgets, 236
Rolling current year forecasts, 122, 208, 209–213, 292–293
Routine controls, 282–283. *See also* Internal controls
Routine expenses, 73–74
RSM McGladrey, 23
Rule of 72, 241

S

Salaries, modeling, 210
Sales
    export, 64
    forecasting, 214, 234
    key ratios, 146
    measures of, 131
    relation to profits, 167–168
Sales force, customer credit information from, 190–191
Sales orders, formal authorizations for, 279
SAP, 262
Sarbanes-Oxley Act, 24
Savings and loan scandals, 29
Scaling controls, 283
Scandals
    conflicts of interest and, 22–23
    Enron, 94, 108
    impact on CPAs, 29–30
    laws in response to, 24
    summary of, 108–109
Schuetze, Walter, 91–92
Scope of audits, 33, 34
Scrap, recording, 156
Seasonal variations, 228

Securities and Exchange Commission (SEC), 19–20, 40
Security measures. *See* Internal controls
Security of spreadsheets, 269
Self-interest concept, 278
Semi-variable costs, 134
Separation of duties, 275–276
Shared financials, 78
Short-term cash management strategies, 180, 184–185
Short-term liquidity measures, 90
Short-term profits, overemphasizing, 99–100
Shrinkage of inventory, 155–157
Sign-off authority, 279–280
Simplistic allocations, 138–139, 141–142
Software
    accounting, 260–262
    charts of accounts in, 70
    choosing accounting programs, 264–266
    conversion issues, 266–267
    costs, 265–266
    for data collection, 270
    errors in, 271, 284
    for forecasting, 209
    internet-based, 267–268
    for inventory management, 157, 159–161, 270
    maintenance fees, 265
    organization of, 67
    for payroll, 269
    spreadsheets, 209, 211, 259, 268–269
    for time tracking, 269–270
    tracking receivables with, 198
    variety of offerings, 260–263
Solomon, 261
Special reports, 120
Spending limits, 279
Spending within budgets, 229
Spreading expenses, 74
Spreadsheets
    checking, 211, 295
    impact on PC popularity, 259
    making projections with, 209
    using properly, 268–269
Springfield Remanufacturing Company, 78

Stack, Jack, 78
Staff positions, 4–5
Standard cost, 133, 168
Standard cost centers, 232
Standards (accounting), 19–21, 135–136. *See also* Generally accepted accounting principles (GAAP)
Statement of Auditing Standard No. 82, 30
Statement of cash flows
elements of, 39–40
importance, 100
samples, 61
Stock options, 96
Stocks, 52. *See also* Investors
Straight-line method, 49, 92
Strategic plans, 208, 213–214, 237
Stratus Computer, 214
Subaccounts, 69–70
Summary accounts, 70
Sunk costs, 138, 243
Synthetic leasing, 105

T
T-accounts, 42
Targets
attainability, 230
implementing, 206
profitability, 295–296
tracking performance vs., 212
Tax accounting. *See also* Income taxes
controller's role, 120
elements of, 18
impact on account setup, 71
sample notes about, 63–64
Ten-step plan for financial management, 292–297
Terminal value of businesses, 247
Timeslips, 269, 270
Time tracking software, 269–270
Time value of money, 240–245
Timing issues
for audits, 81–82
in budgeting, 227–229
in cash flow forecasting, 179, 210
in recording expenses, 74
software conversions, 267

Timing of transactions, manipulating, 104–105
Top-down budgets, 226
Top management
budgeting role, 227–228, 237
inadequate financial understanding, 7–9
planning role, 215
support required for financial staff, 118
Townsend, Robert, 113–114
Transactions
accurate posting, 198–199
control numbers, 278–279
delegating authority for, 279–280
manipulating timing, 104–105
when recorded, 43, 45, 65–66
Troubled accounts, 194–195
Turnover ratio, 153–154
12-month forecasting models, 122, 208, 209–213, 292–293

U
Uncertainty, addressing in long-term plans, 214
Unqualified audit opinions, 27, 33
Unrealized losses on marketable securities, 18
Updating plans, 212–213

V
Valuation methods
when acquiring companies, 103–104
assets, 46–50, 89–90, 91–93
equity, 52
GAAP shortcomings, 89, 90–95
inventory, 48, 49–50, 89, 95–96, 166–171
liabilities, 50–51, 89, 91–93
Value-added costs, 169–170
Value-added resellers, 262
Variable costs, 133, 250–252, 256–258
Variances
from budgets, 235–236
defined, 133
from projections, 212–213
Vertical software, 262–263

W
Wages, modeling, 210
Walk-throughs, 152–153, 294
Warrants, 183–184

Web sites
  accounting functions on, 267–268
  obtaining company information from, 190
  professional organizations, 20–21
Weighted averages, 168, 245
Workarounds, 273, 280–281
WorldCom, 108
Write-offs
  estimating, 48

  manipulating, 102–103
  use in inventory management, 168–169
Writing down assets, 48

X
Xerox, 108

Y
Year-end procedures, 79–83